TURNING POINT

TURNING POINT

Breaking the Shackles of Dependant Thinking

A personal journey in Discovering God and Myself

"God never changes the grace He has bestowed on any people until they first change themselves" (Quran 8:53)

"Say: Each one does according to his rule of conduct, and your Lord is best aware of him whose way is right" (Quran 17:84)

Humera T. Ahsanullah

authorHOUSE®

AuthorHouse™
1663 Liberty Drive
Bloomington, IN 47403
www.authorhouse.com
Phone: 1-800-839-8640

Published by AuthorHouse   01/11/2013

ISBN: 978-1-4772-9185-6 (sc)
ISBN: 978-1-4772-9186-3 (e)

Library of Congress Control Number: 2012921841

With love for my

amma Zainab Toric (Zainab Ahmed Khan)
who is a woman of substance,

phuppy Leila Ahmed
who was in essence my second mother

and

my children Ibrahiem & Zara, & all those who are beginning
their journeys including Shaheen Zafar who ended hers.

Contents

PREFACE

The original inspiration for this text stemmed from a desire to share with others my journey toward knowing Islam, a religion I inherited from my family. As I moved along, my initial approach began losing focus. Whenever I managed to delve deep into the text, I realized as if my own faith was being challenged. This book is in truth my journey, but the final result is a far cry from what at first I thought it would be. It took me almost eight years to study my faith and four years to write this book.

In the beginning, I embarked on this path with only a single thought: Why I have all the best in the world when so many don't. The more I dwelled on this thought, the more I felt that there must be a purpose for me. Perhaps, I thought, I am to receive responsibilities that God knows I can handle. When this dawned on me, I initially felt very honoured but, soon the concept instilled in me a fear of should I fail. At the same time that these worries gripped me, I received severe personal shocks that completely rocked my belief and my faith which I had previously solidly relied on. These shocks made me realize how little I know about my own faith and how little I am. Those shocks led me to a journey of discovering different faiths and eventually made me crawl back to the one I was born with. I have just been lucky! I re-evaluated whether I was to receive a responsibility or it was really I who needed help. I still don't know the answer, but I thought one of the best ways to discover a clearer explanation would be to write this book.

While composing this text, too often I found myself being 'just' and 'fair' with the Quran, (the holy book of Islam). At some point, I realized that there is a verse contained in the Quran which states "stand against yourself" for fairness and justice (4:135 [α]). Considering this, I wondered, "how can I not then pass the very Quran through this test of purity?" I found myself swaying many times towards being biased. I was trying to stretch and justify everything the Quran states, or rather, what we understand to be true. This bias, I realized, was coming into direct conflict with my own reasoning and logic. Eventually I decided that if I cannot be true to myself, then there is no reason for me to write this book—the whole process would lack conviction. If I am unable to justify, I don't need to—simple. In my everyday life, I have to be at peace with my belief and myself: only then the faith will enter and remain. I still don't know whether I have been able to convey my original concept for this book, it is only my readers who can tell. Therefore, I encourage and request your feedback as a means to begin a dialogue.

Having said that, I know that throughout this writing I may sound sometimes apologetic to some, but I am only trying to defend my position for why I chose to remain a Muslim. The

---

[α] Please note that all the verses quoted from the Quran in this book are signified by the surah (chapter) number first and then ayat (verse) number second, such as the verses 4:135 & 39:18 in the 'Preface' means chapter 4 and verse 135, chapter 39 and verse 18. Also note that the chapter numbers are as presented in the Quran from the time of Usman the Caliph and not according to their nuzool or revelation time, which is different. Please see appendix A for detailed list of the 'Time of Revelation Index'.

fact that I did not defend the verses that I can't support myself, yet addressed every issue I could and did not leave them out of the book should speak amply for the credibility of my work.

Some Muslim readers might view the topic headings and think that the text offers nothing new. I offer a different perspective than what many Muslims have been told or brought up to believe. In addition to this perspective and wherever relevant, my critique is imbedded within the text. I want to let my Muslim and non-Muslim readers know that by writing my personal thoughts, I do not intend to be offensive to anyone's belief and hence I seek apology if one feels I have done so.

I have separated this book into seven chapters, each chapter dealing mainly with issues surrounding Islam. My effort has been to consider the Islam that we see today in practice, whose fundamentals are made primarily by men from the Islam that we find in the pages of the Quran. I have also endeavoured to build a connection among the Semitic religions. Islam, as it appears in the Quran, is never referred to as a "religion" *mazhab,* but instead as a "way of life", or *deen* [β]. Although translations refer to "*deen*" as a religion, that is not the correct or literal meaning of the word, it means 'a way of life'.

I have started the first chapter by explaining the concept of God, and discussing what necessitates the existence of God in our lives. Further explored are the types of faith and belief one may hold, the Quranic concept of God, and why I believe in the Quran.

In chapter two, I have covered briefly but concisely why Islam, just as other religions, suffered a downfall. Following this in chapter three, I have dealt with an issue which I feel is one of the major contributing factors toward the downfall of Islam: *hadith,* which literally means "the saying", attributed to

---

[β]   Way of life, habit, governance, law, rules, regulations (Durrani, Zahida. Allama Parvaiz -Lughat-ul-Quran. Tulu-e-Islam Trust. 2007, (daal, yeh, noon) p. 681

Muhammad. What one can't find in the Quran to support their practice can be extrapolated from the *hadith.* Quoting his works but written 200-300 years after the demise of Muhammad, the *hadith* are still controversial, as no one knows whether they are the true sayings or not. What is certain however is that the *hadith* has opened many doors, including those which have lead to the fabrications of sayings in the name of Muhammad.

Chapter four covers several issues that surround both the Muslim and the non-Muslim worlds. One is the concept of God among the non-Muslim world, as the Muslim God is considered different from the non-Muslim God. The concept of *jehad* is looked at from different perspectives; even the concept of Muhammad is discussed from multiple angles. Finally, *halaal* and *haraam* (permitted and forbidden) things and acts that surround the Muslim world are discussed, as well as how this can affect the natural rhythm of one's life.

In chapter five, I have highlighted rituals from the Muslim world with the intention to explain to non-Muslim readers what the rituals *have* been and what they are now. My intention is also to explain to Muslim readers how practices among Muslims have changed from a simple few rituals into highly complicated and burdensome tasks; to the extent that ordinary Muslims are deterred from practicing these rituals at all.

Chapter six is the longest chapter in this book. It deals with issues surrounding women in Islam. As with the other chapters, my attempt here has been to let Muslim and non-Muslim readers know what the Quran actually outlines in contrast to what we see in some contemporary Muslim practices. Many Muslims still do not know what their rights are under the Quran, as the basis for these rules has shifted to the *hadith.* In this chapter, I have also imbedded my own analysis of certain verses. I'm not sure if I have presented convincing arguments, but have at least attempted to understand the reasons and meanings of these verses.

The final chapter deals with the issue of interest in the Islamic financial world. I have explained in detail what 'interest' actually means in Islam, and why it has been totally misunderstood. I have compared two types of banking institutions which lend mortgages: one conventional and the other Islamic, one taking interest and the other not. Finally, I present which one appears to be a better system.

Throughout my book, I have used verses from the Quran extensively to support what I believe to be a better understanding of its message. I have not in any instance used traditions or sayings *hadith* attributed to Muhammad to support my opinions. In some cases I have used verses from the Old Testament to clarify points. I have also quoted where pertinent the views of other authors on common topics. For Quranic translations, I have not relied on one translation but five of them and further analyzing the words of the verses in the light of the *Lughat-ul-Quran* (Quranic language dictionary) which entertains also the polysemic attribute of the Arabic language. All of this has been in an effort to find the "best meaning" of the verses in the Quran, a task which the Quran itself asks us to do (verse 39:18).

This book is related to the belief in a Creator and the path thereof. Those who do not believe in a Creator may find that this book does not have anything to offer them. This book is not an invitation toward any religion but toward examining your beliefs. This book is simply an effort to break oneself from the shackles of dependant thinking and embark on the road of discovery of one's real faith.

I request that whomever wishes to communicate with me must first exercise a great deal of tolerance and respect for every human being regardless of one's opinion, race, colour, language, religion, or sect. I myself have come a long way in realizing this respect.

Thank you for finding the time to read my humble effort.

Humera T. Ahsanullah

September 2012
Coquitlam, BC

ACKNOWLEDGEMENTS

First book and its acknowledgment is always a challenge, and so it is for me: How to thank all those who have taken this journey with me? It is not a solo endeavour but collective. My gratitude therefore, extends to all who have helped me in any way on my quest towards my *deen*, I feel deeply indebted to all of you.

Lindsay Wiens is a growing editor. She is honest and devoted to her passion. Despite occasionally hanging her in between, she remained patient and helped me through every page. And definitely without the help of AuthorHouse team, a member of the Penguin Group, specifically Loraine Goldman and James Raven, I would not have been able to come this far.

Those who have directly or indirectly helped me toward understanding my *deen*, I would like to thank Dr. Abdul Fauq, Dr. Shabbir Ahmed, Muhammad Shafi J. Aga, and countless others. I would like to especially thank Shaheen Zafar who read the first draft of my book and was passionate to see it published. But to my loss, she passed away on March 11, 2010, leaving me with awe.

The books, journals and legitimate websites I consulted while writing Turning Point are resources that were put forth painstakingly through hard work. Those resources have been with me throughout my twelve-year long journey, and have helped me become a better person. I thank all those authors from the depth of my heart.

Among my relatives, I want to thank three people whose continuous support and advice in the writing of this book have surely helped me: First my sister Samina, whose patience is admirable. She made me comfortable discussing any topic with her. Second my brother Asif, who is a dear friend and a shoulder. Third, my sister-in-law Lubna, who is a good friend & a supporter. She helped in some of the research process of this book. In general, my whole family including my dear sister Seema has been supportive throughout this process. I cherish them and thank all of them for their kindness.

Exclusively, I thank my late *bari dadi* (grandma), who passed away long ago but who gave me infinite love when I was growing up. My gratitude goes to my Aunt Leila *Phuppee* who would patiently listen to my never-ending stories and would fulfill my silly demands, only to see the smile on my face. She was in essence my second mother.

My deepest thanks go to my mother Zainab, whom I deem a 'woman of substance'. Her husband passed away when we were young but she never married. She single-handedly took care of her ten children and made sure they were well-educated and settled. She knows very little about her own *deen,* yet never discouraged me from my path; even when she learned that I no longer place the Sunni sect title on myself, she was not upset—she believed that what I had chosen was right. She had been confidant, authoritative, and an independent woman. She is an emblem to me, and from her I have learned many subtle but core meanings of life. She is recently going through difficult times in regards to her health: I pray for her peaceful recovery.

My big sister Tasneem Wafai, throughout the publishing of this book encouraged and supported me. And many thanks to Aijaz Wafai for his editing help while I was writing the back cover of the book.

Finally I would like to thank my immediate family, from whom I have stolen so many hours just for research. Despite this, they all have been patient, supportive, and loving—especially my children Ibrahiem and Zara. They have watched me write page after page, asked questions, accepted my refusal to be with them when I was working, and yet never ceased to love and forgive me when I requested.

My husband Sami: My closest friend, has been a source of reason and analytical thinking through his serious critique of my work. Whenever I found myself lost in a vast jungle, he would show me the way, or sometimes even walk me out safely from every chapter. Although religion is not his interest, he would guide and help me whenever I needed him. He is the one who also thought the title of the book 'Turning Point' simply based on my vision. Thank you Ibrahiem, Zara and Sami for the support you all have provided to me. You have all been the energy from which I have drawn my strength. You have all been the sunshine that brightens up my every single day.

Lastly, my God, who made me so special, gave me much intelligence, courage, and provided me the capability to help others. My whole life is indebted to this God whom I call by the name Allah. I am thankful to the honour that Allah bestowed upon me. I hope, as always, I'll be forgiven for any errors in my work.

CHAPTER ONE

GOD AND THE QURAN ॐ

THE STORY OF GOD

Belief in a God is an abstract notion, because in reality, no one has seen God. It is something to wonder that despite this fact, more than 75 percent of the world's population believes in a God of some form![1]† But why?

When on my quest in search of God, I have gone between phases of belief in a God to no belief at all. Every time I would crawl back to the belief that there is a God. It is because I started to seriously consider the evidence for or against belief, which I hadn't previously considered. I was simply following what I was told or what I heard about my faith without ever independently thinking why I believe what I believe. Or for that matter, what is really written in the Arabic text. And I think this is the same dilemma with many Christians and Jewish people too at this time: We read only the interpretations and never research to discover the rightful meaning of the original text (Arabic and Hebrew). We therefore, tend to feel appalled by what we see in practice and in misinterpreted 'Holy Books' and thus become convinced that this God of the holy books—is horrible. Consequently, we disengage ourselves from practicing the religion altogether—We find it enough to just hold the religious title upon us or in some cases, not even that. And then it becomes much easier for some of us to insult the faith of others. Unless we ourselves start to respect what we believe in, we can never give respect to what others believe in. Therefore it becomes imperative to discover our true faith so that we can believe with reason and have peace within ourselves and with others.

Religion or faith is something that is inherent in all of us. Whether you call yourself an atheist, agnostic, naturalist, and/or a humanist, you are following "some form of orthodoxy"[2] or religion. Whether you call it human, nature, spirit, universe, anything, they all enact a "form" of worship that is relatively equal to the power attributed to God in other religions. We cannot escape from something that is intrinsically present in us.

While on this journey, it is not that I did not question the being of the Creator: I did. Foremost, I found it extremely difficult to explain the very existence of my own being, let alone God. Later, I realized that even if I do not want to believe in a God, I "need" to believe in one in order to have an inner peace. I am too small and insignificant in this vast universe and completely helpless in every second of my life. Nothing is under my control, nothing I can prove or disprove, nothing is there that I can be hundred percent sure of, and all of this is not a belief but an indisputable reality. Considering this, the existence of God to me therefore solidified as an undeniable truth: There has to be a Creator.

Many scientific scholars are seeking a Unified Theory to explain the phenomena of everything. Despite all of the attention given to the subject, these researchers have had difficulty in offering an explanation as to why the universe exist and how can it exist without any ONE force controlling it? Stephen Hawking once said while explaining the origins and the fate of the universe in his book *A Brief History of Time* "It would be very difficult to explain why the universe should have begun in just this way, except as the act of a God who intended to create beings like us".[3]

Personally, I believe that there is much harmony and precision in the universe that the possibility of everything having been created by chance has to be ruled out. Thus, the obvious conclusion is that the need for a Creator is imminent. This need is an inherent part of us—it was there in the past and it will remain in the future. Only its forms will change. Historically, under the matriarchal period this Creator was a Goddess, and now under the patriarchal period, the same Creator is a God.

During pre-civilization pagan times, people worshipped a deity or deities in a fixed form. When societies became more complex and demanded more challenges and changes, new forms of worship emerged. As Karen Armstrong explains in her book *A History of God: the 4000-Year Quest of Judaism, Christianity, and Islam*, when one type of orthodoxy ceases to fulfill the needs of the people, it also ceases to exist.[4] It has ever since been a challenge for a new orthodoxy to work its way into what (by their standards) is a "primitive" society. Similarly, the followers of a new orthodoxy or belief have oft been regarded as atheists by the so-called primitive society[5]; yet, the cycle goes on. This explains why we see so many sects or denominations shooting off from one type of orthodoxy. Islam too was not immune to this predicament.

Once I settled on the existence of God, I came to the question of whether there should be a path that would lead me toward my Creator. I reasoned that to go from one point to another, you do need a path or a map, a road to reach your destination. Even if you deny this, you will be etching your own path. Most certainly the path exists; it just depends on how that path is designed: whether by yourself, a group, an organization, or anything else.

After that, I came to a major dilemma: even if I choose to follow a path, what guarantee there is that this choice will lead me to the Creator? The answer is very subjective and therefore cannot be guaranteed. When it came to choosing a path, I could have etched my own path, but I found that option too risky in terms of defining who God is: Myself or my Creator? Henceforth, I chose an already established path: Islam, which just happens to be a theocratic one, but my choice, was for reasons other than this. I chose the Islam, which in the Quran is called a *deen* (a way of life), and not the Islam that we call *mazhab* (religion). The Islam that can be seen today in practice reflects much that appals me than to lift me to great heights.

I compared the Quranic Islam (not the Islamic religion that we see today) with other religions, and found that Quranic Islam is more appealing than other religions including the Islamic religion in practice today. It speaks to my sense of reason more in its harmony with science and nature, as well its common sense, rationalism, and mathematical interlocking system. Admittedly, a few of the aspects of Quranic Islam are beyond my comprehension. Also, there are a few passages in the Quran with which I do not agree, or, perhaps I do not understand them as they are meant to be understood. Yet, I have chosen this religion because the passages in the Quran that are agreeable to me outweigh the ones that are disagreeable to me. And therefore I believe the Quran will be able to clarify for me those parts of it which I do not yet understand hence seems to disagree. It may also be that it is I who lack the wisdom and the comprehension to fully grasp every single verse of the Quran in its rightful meaning. I cannot rule out that possibility, for if I do, I may halt my growth of learning, of acceptance and of tolerance. I also know now that I could leave out the Quran and stay comforted by settling on simply the existence of God, but then I would open the floodgate of possible paths for myself; and as I stated above I could have etched my own path, but that was too risky in terms of defining who God is: Myself or my Creator. I decided to follow what I believe is the better path at present.

To expand on my thoughts above, I shall deal below in a while with the *Story of the Quran*, including examples of what has made it a far better choice for me and what has given me conviction. I will also deal with the parts that are still questionable to me as they arise throughout the book. In doing so, I will use some comparisons to additional verses, especially from Old and New Testaments, and my intention in doing this is only to justify my choice for Quranic Islam. Despite the fact that other religious books have beautiful and convincing verses just as the Quran, the Quran still embodies a sense of appeal for me that nothing else could. By stating how I feel about Quranic Islam, it is neither my intention to sound apologetic, nor to demean the faith of other people. Quranic Islam perhaps may not be perfect but I find that for me, it is the better path.

In the following paragraphs, I will discuss issues of Islam in an effort to compare what I used to perceive and believe, and share with you how I see and believe now.

† Generally speaking, people believe God to be in their own image and give God anthropomorphic characteristics. In addition, living in a patriarchal society, this God is also often a male God. As such, many "people of the books" (as Quran addresses to Christian and Jewish people) have assigned not only a masculine gender to God, but also human like traits. By comparison, Muslims generally do not attach human like attributes to God, yet the aspect of a masculine gender remains in all discourses and Quranic interpretation, whatever language it may be in. The Quran as the disclosure of God has not classified God in any terms. I have therefore attempted to use non-gender term for God, instead of "He" I have used the term "It" with a capital 'I'. However, I have not altered that in a text when quoting the translation of a verse. Furthermore, because of this patriarchal sense, the translation of some other specific words in the Quran also depicts a similar patriarchal tone. Consequently, I have removed the word "men" from translations of verses quoted in this discussion, most notably because it is not the correct translation of the Arabic word *insaan* or *ins*, which is genderless and literally means "humans".

I have let the term "We" remain which has been used to denote God, although for many non-Muslims the English word "we" implies more than one person (hence many Gods). It has actually been used to denote the authoritative position of God and not plurality. Otherwise, "we" is not the correct translation of the Arabic word *ana* that means 'I' in a literal sense.

FAITH OR BELIEF

I have always asked this question: what does faith or belief in God mean? In our world, faith or belief has resulted in many lives being saved as well as many being destroyed. The problem is how do we find out which type of belief or faith saves and which destroys? As they are so intertwined with each other that it sometimes becomes difficult to separate them. It can also easily change without one knowing that it has. Because of this confusion, one may never become fully aware that his or her belief has completely changed into something they do not stand for.

On a primary level, there are three kinds of belief in God. One is a belief based on reason and logic. The second is a belief based on not just reason and logic, but one that includes an aspect of spiritual thinking. The third kind is a belief that does not require any reason, logic, or proof—in other words, a blind belief. I have found the latter to be very disturbing as it requires no rationality for one's actions, and can freely defy societal norms. With blind belief, there is no moral law. One may kill thousands of innocent people, burn them alive, or do any evil without any remorse. They have the belief that their actions are approved by God and God is pleased with them, and hence they will receive a reward. Whether this is an organized religious group or a small cult, they believe that all of their acts are instructed not only by God but also for God; consequently, they deny accountability of their actions to anyone who might believe otherwise.

I have chosen the middle-ground in defining my faith. Reason and logic alone cannot support unexplained phenomena, which includes the very nature of moral law, or "the law of right behaviour"[6], as stated by Francis Collins in his book *The Language of God.* He is one of the leading geneticists and the head of the Human Genome Project. Collins himself too journeyed through atheism to believing in God. This law of "right behaviour" is intrinsically a part of living creatures, especially homo sapiens. Reason and logic alone cannot explain why humans behave the way they do, especially concerning ethical behaviour, or when or why the principle of right and wrong comes into play.

As we shall see later in the text, I have no objection to Darwin's law of natural selection and the evolution of humans from primates. Despite the fact that it is an often referenced point of disagreement in religious debate, it does not erase God from the picture of creation. Francis said, "the comparison of chimp and human sequences, interesting as it is, does not tell us what it means to be human".[7]

On the other hand, blind faith is born out of insecurity and fear of the unknown. It is also born out of the need for recognition and the incapability of having a desirable position in a society. This belief system therefore feels threatened by independent thinking and judgment, and hence makes every effort to curb those threats. This type of follower sincerely believes that all of their acts are defined by the Highest Authority. Due to this, science and nature cannot be part of blind faith. At a point, science and nature requires independent and rational thinking. God, in a blind faith, does not require any, and thus such a God remains a separate entity.

The incorporation of spiritual thinking into reason and logic helps to define the undefined. It helps to expand the relationship between God, nature, and its sciences. It puts God as the highest authority and the creator of everything, who ultimately knows the answer to everything and can also answer every question we may ask. As a result, this God does not need to defend Itself from anything, as It encompasses everything, and everything is in essence Its creation. This God, is never threatened by our questions but welcomes them. In fact, our questions give "us" the opportunity to better know the Creator. It is this God who has bestowed on us the concept of right and wrong and 'independent thinking'; we are free to use our free will. If God did not want us to have free will and wanted simply to obey It's command, God wouldn't have given us free will in the first place: /*"We verily have created human being with a firm balance:* . . . *Did we not show him the two paths* (of right and wrong to choose from)?*"* (Quran 90:4-10)

It is therefore highly preposterous to think that such an omnipotent God need to defend Itself and is afraid of losing the ground that It would require It's followers to believe in It blindly.

"God of the Gaps" [8]

Sometimes we base our belief on a concept in which we lack knowledge, or a phenomenon that we currently are unable to explain or sciences have not yet reached that far to explain. We then tend to attribute the unexplained phenomenon as the doing of God and try to fill the gaps with what we can comprehend. As Collin describes, this is the "God of the gaps".[8]

Whenever there is something that science has not yet explained, the "God of the gaps" comes to rescue. An example of this is the idea of the earth being flat during Galileo's time, the solar eclipse, or the movement of planets. "This 'God of the gaps' approach has all too often done a disservice to religion . . . . faith that places God in the gaps of current understanding about the natural world may be headed for crises if advances in science subsequently fill those gaps" says Collins.[9]

THE STORY OF THE QURAN

Islam as a religion today is in such an abject and frightening state that had I been a non-Muslim I probably would have never bothered to even glimpse the pages of the Quran. With this in mind, I do not blame those who are not Muslim for their negative views about Islam. Today's Islam is no different from yesterday's Judaism and Christianity, none of them is any better than the other, they are all one and the same. Many Muslims have forsaken the Quran and have taken up other books to (mis)guide them. They have shoved the Quran on their shelves only to be kissed and folded back. Ironically, the Quran itself mentions this in a passage where it states "*The messenger said, "My Lord, my people have deserted this Quran"* (Quran 25:30).

For over 1.2 billion Muslims around the world, the Quran has been the sacred holy book (along with the *Zaboor* (Psalms), the *Torayt* (Torah or Old Testament) and the *Injeel* (Gospel or New Testament). As there have been many holy books in the past, what makes the Quran so unique? What does it have to offer or introduce to us? Looking at the historical data that is available, it seems that Muhammad via the Quran actually did not come to introduce anything new, [10] nor even anything old. The Quran also did not even come to change or abolish anything.[11] It rather came to help improve situations and point humans towards progress. Just as with other holy books, however, the passage of time has seen the Quran succumb to injuries inflicted by readers themselves. I think we humans consider ourselves the best master. Could it be that we are our own worst enemies?

WHY THE ARABIC QURAN?

One thing that amazes me about the Arabic language is its polysemic attribute. This quality of the Arabic language helps to make the Quran dynamic instead of static, particularly when it comes to interpreting its verses over different times and eras.

As the Quran states (39:18), to find the "best meaning"*(husan)* of its verses, it becomes our job to interpret the verses that stand out as the best and most suited for our time. People ask, "Since Muslims in general assert that the message of the Quran is universal, then why does it have to be in the language of Arabic"? But obviously, this is inconsequential in the sense that it had to have been written in a single language.

> *And of His signs is the creation of the skies and the earth, and the difference of your languages and colours. Lo! herein indeed are portents for men of knowledge.* (Quran 30:22)

THE ARABIC ISLAM

Politically speaking, the fact that the Quran is in the Arabic language made some Arabs of the peninsula feel quite superior, just as members of other religions throughout history have felt. It is the weakness in human nature to desire for power and to have greed. It is ironic though to note that the very same Arabic Quran directly states: /*"The Arabs of the desert are the worst in unbelief and hypocrisy, and most fitted to be in ignorance of the command which Allah hath sent down to His Messenger . . ."* (Quran 9:97)

Despite this clear verse, Muslims throughout the world are under the influence of Arabs. Many feel that when they speak Arabic language or emulate Arabic culture (in every sphere of life including changing their names to Arabic names), only then are they truly Muslims. They have essentially created an "Arabic Islam" religion in parallel to the *deen* of the Quranic Islam. For this reason, Arabic language itself has become very sacred, but as Amina Wadud contends, "it is unfathomable that the Lord of all the Worlds [as mentioned many times in the Quran] is not potentially multi-lingual"[12] (bracket is mine). Quranic Islam, on the other hand, provides no warrant for any such claims. Since "Arabic Islam" limits the Quranic boundary only to the Arabs, this "arabization" has done much more to harm than to benefit the universal message of the Quran. Wadud further states,

10

"The Quran must be flexible enough to accommodate innumerable cultural situations because of its claims to be universally beneficial to those who believe. Therefore to force it to have a single cultural perspective—even the cultural perspective of the original community of the Prophet—severely limits its application and contradicts the stated universal purpose of the Book itself".[13]

Moreover, when the Quran has already stated that the best among us is the one who is best in conduct, there remains no need to distinguish oneself with any other factor than "conduct". *"O humans! Lo! We have created you male and female, and have made you nations and tribes that ye may know one another.* **Lo! the noblest of you, in the sight of Allah, is the best in conduct.** *Lo! Allah is Knower, Aware"* (Quran 49:13).

I still remember how since childhood, I had been told to read the Quran in Arabic because it has more reward and credits *sawaab* than if it were read in other languages. I learned then that it is irrelevant as to whether we understand it or not. But isn't the Quran there to understand and follow?

THE WORLD OF THE ARABIAN PENINSULA

We have often heard about the 'Glory Days' of Islam, and how Muslims have been the purveyors of arts, culture, knowledge, and scientific breakthroughs in the world. What astonishes me is the fact that Islam did not have any 'Glory Days' as long as it was within the Arabian peninsula, but only when it moved out. The majority of Muslims that were at the forefront of a refined civilization were not the nomadic Arabs of the peninsula, but rather other individuals who later became Muslims.

What I find curious is why there is nothing of heritage or of historical significance with regards to culture and knowledge within the birth place of Islam. No renowned schools such as the Al-Azhar University of Egypt, no well-known past scientists of nomadic Arabian origin, nor any famous arts or culture associated with those Arabs. What history tells us

11

about the part that Muslims played in the civilization of the world does not involve the nomadic Arabian Muslims, but rather Muslims from other countries that conceived Islam and helped themselves break away from the shackles of dependent thinking. This included individuals from many nomadic tribes such as the Tartar in central Asia, as well the Mongols. History is full of their achievements which embraced the good in culture, arts, and science from many religions, including Islam, and they became the supporters and purveyors of it.

The Quran emphasizes the importance of learning and growing. Even the first verse that was revealed to Muhammad stated to *"read in the name of God who created human from a clinging substance .... and taught by the pen"* (Quran 96:1-4). Its overall teachings in essence free the human mind and allow it to engage in independent thinking without constraints. It has instilled the concept of 'wonder' and 'question' and built the relationship between human and God on a direct and personal level with no intermediary to assist or supersede. It therefore had appealed to people in many countries, and had made it easy for them to embrace the Islamic concept and message, further polishing their already established independent way of thinking.

An example of this occurred in a region of Spain when the Moors-Berber Muslims of Morocco brought their cultural heritage to a city named Cordoba. Cordoba was considered one of the most advanced cities in the world at this time. The famous libraries of Al Andalus in Spain during the Moors reign were a hub for learning. All of the scientific and cultural breakthroughs associated with this assisted in the renaissance of the Europe.

At this time, the Babylonian and Persian civilizations were already advanced. On top of this, the Syrians, Egyptians and Indians already had their own legacies of culture and heritage. When Islam reached these places, it integrated itself into the culture because it allowed people to think freely, and led them towards advancement which complemented their own already advanced civilization and their own desire for the acquisition of knowledge and growth. When some of them advanced into other countries, they took their knowledge as well as this newly found religion with them, thus helping to stamp Muslims as the purveyors of culture and science.

If Islam has been shoved down people's throats and spread through the 'tip of the sword', that is another issue. History is full of many different empires and dynasties that spread their culture in this manner. Even one of the most peaceful religions, Buddhism, at one time conquered India under Asoka by force. I do not mean to defend Islam in this context, but my agenda in addressing this issue is to put into context the history of Islam and the history of other religions. In these cases and others, the desire to grow and spread was primarily political—though religion did go hand-in-hand with politics. When smaller countries grew in population and needed more space and food, they relied on the method of force to procure their needs. This behaviour resulted in the creation of empires and dynasties, including for example the vast Roman Empire. Though Islam was initially spread in this same forceful manner, many people chose not to disown it when they later had the option.

Coming back to our topic, many Arabs of the desert have never accepted the concept and the message of Islam as some other civilizations have. Perhaps there is some truth to this verse: *"The Arabs of the desert are the worst in unbelief and hypocrisy, and most fitted to be in ignorance of the command which Allah hath sent down to His Messenger . . . ."* (Quran 9:97). Islam found its solace only when it moved out of what I would consider the utterly uncivilized and barbaric nomadic regions of the Arabic peninsula.

Much of the troubles I am outlining live within the monarchism in the Arabian world, which the Quran has never advocated (Quranic principles are mainly egalitarian based). Despite this, the Arabs adapted a monarch system and became a full-fledged kingdom relatively recently (1932).

The state of Saudi Arabia was originally a development of the British Empire, through the aid of Thomas Edward Lawrence (popularly known as Lawrence of Arabia). He helped Arabs break away from the Turks and the rule of the Ottoman Empire, enabling them to create their own sultanate state with its own enforcement based on a kind of Islamic sect called Wahabism (which is an offshoot of the Sunni sect). This is a sect within Islam that mainly bases its doctrine on the teachings of *hadith*, (a topic discussed in Chapter three 'Hadith').

Wahabism was started by Muhammad Ibne Abdul Wahab in the 18th century. He later received support from Muhammad ibn-e-Saud, developing family ties to reinforce the teachings of Wahabism. This was also an effort to unify the various provinces of the Arabian Peninsula which in turn formed what is now called the modern day Saudi Arabian Kingdom. Through the funding of mosques in different countries, this Kingdom implements and spreads "Wahabism" and calls it the teachings of Islam. As with any sects, Wahabism is also not exclusively Quranic Islam. Through these teachings, leaders of Wahabism justified massacres such as that of Karbala in 1802 (a city in Iraq). A large Wahabi invasion took place to "cleanse" Islam from the innovations of the Shiite's belief, which were not considered Islamic to the Wahabism doctrine. This invasion lead to the displacement of many Shiites from Karbala who eventually settled into Najaf (Iraq), making it the capitol of their religion. *

Saudi Kingdom feels that they themselves are the guardians and the rulers of this religion. It is the belief of the Saudi Kingdom that only they can teach those non-Saudis who they call the *miskeens* (poor, un-enriched) the faith of Muhammad. These poor *miskeens* remain nothing but a pawn in this whole scenario.

All of this hard-lined behaviour has nothing to do with religion, but instead facilitates and maintains monarchism.

---

*   http://en.wikipedia.org/wiki/Wahhabi

This monarchism in turn helps to fulfill the goals of Western Imperialism; religion in this situation is simply a cover under which it becomes much easier to achieve one's motives. This monarchism helps the Arabs supply oil and energy to the West, and therefore the West for their own best interests leaves the situation as it is. True Islamic teaching cannot favour either side, so neither party would want to acknowledge or promote such an Islam.

I simply shake my head to think that the American "war against terrorism" wanted to root out extremists, many of whom are and were fervently Wahabist, while literally ignoring the financing and the support of the expansion of *the same* Wahabi ideology as practiced by the Saudi Royal family.

At this point, it should be noted that there are inevitably many sincere and humble people living within the Saudi Arabian Kingdom who are not a part in what their government does, and who do not follow what their state religion dictates. However, the dominancy of the Saudi Arabian Kingdom has created a serious problem in all Muslim worlds, because many follow the "Arabic Islam" believing that it is the truth. Consequently, other Muslim countries have yielded to the doctrine of the Saudi Monarchy believing that it is their true Guardian.

They have essentially made Saudi Arabia the Vatican of Islam. But the question remains: will Muslims be able to realize their situation and break away from this chain, or is it too late?

THE QURAN AND ITS HERMENEUTIC ISSUES

*"Those who listen to the Word, and follow the **best (meaning)** [*] husan in it: those are the ones whom Allah has guided, and those are the ones endued with understanding (the translation)"* (Quran 39:18).

---

[*]   Since 'meaning' can be subjective, a myriad of 'meanings' can be attributed to the Quran, ranging from the best to the worst scenario.

15

I have been quoting translations of the Quran that were completed between 50 and 100 years ago, these dated translations are commonly referred to in modern-day Islam. It is essential to note that inevitably, the interpretation of verses in different translations reflects the time and era of when they were written. An example of this is a translated verse that allows the beating of a rebellious wife, (verse 4:34). This verse more recently translated has a very different meaning, as I will further discuss in chapter six. Another example of dated translation is about the verses related to science: because of the scientific progress that commenced at the end of the Quranic revelation, the Muslim exegetes from the time of Rashidun (the time of the four Caliphs after Muhammad) and onwards lacked specific scientific knowledge—knowledge that is imperative for translating verses specifically related to science. As a result, these verses could only be translated reflecting the development of the time and the comprehension of their interpreters. There have recently been many attempts to produce fresh translations of the Quran. However, regardless of the time or age in which we may translate the verses, they will always reflect our limited comprehension based in a specific period. On a positive note, this situation illustrates that the adaptable Quran is applicable in different ways at all times.

In very recent history, ineffective efforts have also been made to confine the meanings of the Quran to the uncivilized 6th century Arabian culture of the Peninsula. Because of this error, the Quran (which is meant to be dynamic), became static and started to take on the appearance of being rigid and savage. If we assert that the Quran has a universal message that is flexible enough to accommodate every time period, then we have to pull it out from the pits of the 6th century and make it dynamic once more. To do this, we need to study the etymology of the Arabic lexicon in order to grasp the best meaning of the Quran for ourselves, one that is well suited to our time.

Another issue with regards to Quranic hermeneutics is the out of context and un-thematic interpretations. As Asma Barlas had said in her book *Believing Women in Islam* that Quranic verses have been taken in isolation for interpretation, and as a result the "thematic and structural *nazm* (coherence)" has been lost.[14] There are many examples of hermeneutics that I will cite in accordance with the topics of given chapters. I would like to cite just two here to give an idea that how a lack of proper hermeneutics can result in completely wrong interpretation of the verses:

Examples:

This is the story of Solomon (*Sulemaan*), who was the son of David and had unusual powers. According to the Quran (Chapter 38: 31-33), one day he got preoccupied with special breed of horses till the night fell and the horses were gone. He realized that the whole day passed without him ever thinking or talking about God and Gods commands, he felt remorse. He asked for the horses again and began lightly massaging their legs and necks (perhaps to think of God this time). This part of a verse where he began lightly massaging or rubbing the legs and the neck of the horses has been translated as *"he began slashing (with his sword) their legs and necks"(38:33)*. The word used is *"muss-han"* from *muss-ha* the literal meaning of which is to rub, cleanse or lightly massage/heal * hence the word '*musseeha*' connoted to Jesus as healer/cleanser. Such rendition as 'slashing' with the sword is (a) not written in the verse, (b) it is the understanding of the exegist according to his time and (c) does not fit with the whole thematic structure of the story. Where in the Quran Solomon's high qualities and steadfastness is highlighted, there suddenly he is brutally slashing the poor horses with his sword does not make sense or congeals with the *nazm* of the verses. The horses are not at all at fault on their own and have nothing to do with his preoccupation.

---

*   Durrani, Zahida. Allama Parvaiz -Lughat-ul-Quran. Tulu-e-Islam Trust. 2007, (meem, seen, hay), pp.1539-1540.

What I see in the above example is the lack of thematic structure, and the "extra textual"[15] meaning that has been integrated by past Muslim exegetes as manifest from the psyche of their time. What they failed to conceptualize is the very epistemology of the Quran; It has a definite theme and concurrent knowledge, and every chapter is somehow related to the others. If parts are taken in isolation and/or out of context, a singled out verse may not cohere with its skeletal body. This lack of science in hermeneutics results in variant readings of the Quran, which are non-coherent with the theme of the writing as a whole.

In the next example the rendition had its limitation due to the lack of scientific advancement during the time of revelation. Consequently, the exegists were handicapped in comprehending the right meaning and so translated as they deemed proper according to their time:

*"Read: In the name of thy Lord Who createth, createth human from **a blood clot** (alaq)"* (96:1-2). 'Clot' for the word *alaq* is the wrong translation. According to the Lughat-ul-Quran (Quranic lexicon) it means something that clings, that hangs *. The exegist could not therefore understand what it really means to 'hang' so decided perhaps to translate as 'blood clot' which is more comprehensible to be as part of our creation. (Please refer below point number 3 under 'human reproduction' for detail explanation of this verse)

THE QURAN AND SCIENCE

"Ignorance more frequently begets confidence than do knowledge: it is those who know little, and not those who know much, who so positively assert that this or that problem will never be solved by science."

—Charles Darwin, *The Descent of Man*[16]

---

* Durrani, Zahida. Allama Parvaiz-Lughat-ul-Quran. Tulu-e-Islam Trust. 2007, (ayin, laam, qaaf), p.1184.

We have witnessed in Judeo-Christian traditions and now in manmade Islamic traditions ones how scientific development can be taken as anti-God, and has sometimes been considered threatening to God's existence. It is especially astonishing to see this in Islam, because the Quran itself encourages the study of science and nature. Previously, it was mainly Muslims who were credited with major scientific discoveries, but now, today's Islam disowns any affiliation with science and nature. Collins says "a believer need not fear that this [scientific] investigation will dethrone the divine; if God is truly almighty, He will hardly be threatened by our puny efforts to understand the workings of His natural world"[17] (bracket is mine). And why should God be threatened by our efforts to understand Its creation, when it is God Itself who has provided us the intellectual and reasoning capabilities to do so? Otherwise, what would the need be for God to endow us with these abilities? I therefore believe that science can never contradict or annihilate God, but will only help to make sense of God's world and exalt the Creator.

I shall now focus on what is written in the Quran to support science, a major aspect of what has led me to my conviction. The majority of all considerable scientific discoveries have happened during the 20th century. It is therefore unexplainable as to how those discoveries are mentioned (in harmony with the knowledge available today) in a book which was revealed 1400 years ago! As I shall unfold some of the scientific information provided in the text of the Quran, it is obviously beyond comprehension as to how this book contains scientific data that was never unearthed at the time of its revelation.

One may though wonder why scientific data needs to be included in a book that is purely of religious nature, and what the purpose this might serve. The most obvious purpose is to bestow conviction and to ponder the beneficence of God. One must remember that all of these arguments become valid only when one has a belief in a God, a Creator, or a High Power.

Although there are innumerable verses that deal with contemporary scientific discoveries, I shall discuss below only the specific verses that have led me to believe that the Quran is perhaps miraculous and original, which explains my choice to subscribe to Quranic Islam. I have considered the book *The Bible, The Quran, and Science*[18] written by Maurice Bucaille, who was a French Surgeon, and who made an effort to learn Arabic in order to study the Quran. I have also referred to the book "Before We Are Born: Essentials of Embryology and Birth Defects" by Keith L. Moore and T.V.N. Persaud. Moore is the professor emeritus (human anatomy) at the University of Toronto in Ontario, Canada and Persaud is also the professor emeritus (clinical embryology, history of anatomy and medical education) at the University of Manitoba in Manitoba Canada. I have also included examples from books written by Stephen W. Hawking[19] who holds the Isaac Newton Chair at Cambridge University as a Lucasian Professor of Mathematics and is a multiple Nobel Prize winner.

The Human Reproductive System

During the middle ages, people were surrounded by myths and conjectures about human development within the body. They did not have any knowledge of human anatomy or physiology. Partially due to the fact that the microscope had not yet been invented which, took place at the end of the 16th century [α]. It is therefore quite fascinating to see that almost ten centuries before the invention of the microscope; the Quran stated with complete accuracy the microscopic and detailed mechanism of the human reproductive system, which is not observable through the naked eyes. Only recently and with the help of state-of-the-art equipment have we been able to observe such minute microscopic details within the human body.

Although the reproductive process is mentioned in great detail in the Quran (Bucaille has explained intricately), I have

---

[α] http://en.wikipedia.org/wiki/Microscope

chosen select parts that have profoundly affected my decision to follow Quranic Islam. This is to summarize how consistent the Quran is with contemporary science.

1. Reproduction in the human body is a process that happens in stages / *"He is the One who created you in stages"* (Quran 71:14).

2. Fertilization takes place within only a small quantity of liquid / *"He has created humankind from a sperm (mani)-**drop** (nutfa $^\beta$)"* (Quran 16:04).

3. Once the egg is formed, it implants itself into the female uterus where the egg "clings" and grows into a fetus while acquiring all of its nourishment for a certain predetermined period / *"We cause what We will to remain in the wombs for an **appointed term**"* (Quran 22:05), *"Read: In the name of thy Lord Who createth, createth man from **a clinging substance** (alaq)"* (Quran 96:1-2). Science learnt about *"alaq'* only in the 20th century. In the meaning of *alaq,* Bucaille explains how the English language lacks a specific word to translate the Arabic word *alaq*: he describes that *alaq* in precise terms means "something which clings" and not "blood clot" as the old translations state[21]. Dr. Keith Moore has described the egg in this state as something that clings like a leech, or something of a leech-like form. [22] Bucaille reasons that it is imperative to have the scientific knowledge in order to translate precisely, this being an example of that need. The lack of scientific knowledge has been one of the fundamental reasons why even the well-versed Arabic translators have made mistakes in translating specific words within the field of science. In this case they lacked the knowledge of embryology.[23]

$^\beta$ means to dribble or to trickle (semen)[20]

4. The embryo initially looks like chewed flesh, then passes through stages of forming bones, *mesenchyma*, muscles, etc. / *"We fashioned the thing which clings into **a chewed lump of flesh** (madga) and We fashioned the chewed flesh **into bones** (izzaama) and we clothed the bones with **intact flesh** (lahm)"* (Quran 23:14).

5. As Baucaille explains, "[there are] three anatomical layers that protect the infant during gestation: [1] the abdominal wall, [2] the uterus itself and [3] the surroundings of the fetus (placenta, embryotic membranes, amniotic fluid)"[24] / *"He makes you, in the wombs of your mothers, in stages, one after another, in three veils of darkness"* (Quran 39:6).

6. Until 20th century, it was believed that the mother's body is responsible for determining the sex of the baby. Science now confirms that it is the male sperm which carries the X and Y chromosomes and hence responsible for determining the sex of the baby. Whereas, Quran confirmed this fact 1400 years back when it stated / *"And He created the pairs, the **male** and the **female** from the **sperm** emitted"* (Quran 53:45-46)

Unified Theory (Theory of Everything)

As aforementioned, science is looking for a Unified Theory to explain everything. At the moment, we have partial theories that may eventually result in the "unification of [the] laws of physics",[25] described by Stephen Hawking. From vast and lengthy observation to mathematical calculations, science has come a long way in understanding the history of the universe. Hence, many classical theories have been developed which govern the laws of this universe and thereupon claim to aid in discovering the origins and the fate of the universe. An example of one such theory: the universe could have started from a singularity—a big bang—and thereafter spread out, constantly expanding but perhaps only to re-collapse into a singularity—big crunch.[26] It is intriguing to note that scientific observations and discoveries have revealed the precision and the harmony with which the whole universe is being governed.

> *"If there had been in them any gods except Allah, they would both have certainly been in a state of disorder; therefore glory be to Allah, the Lord of the dominion, above what they attribute (to Him)"* (Quran 21:22).

> *"No son did Allah beget, nor is there any god along with Him: (if there were many gods), behold, each god would have taken away what he had created, and some would have lorded it over others! Glory to Allah! (He is free) from the (sort of) things they attribute to Him!"* (Quran 23:91).

The Big Bang Theory and Other Interstellar Discoveries

1. The popular theory of the origin of the universe generally states that it began with a massive explosion from a single speck of matter at a very high density and temperature. This is strengthened by the observation that since galaxies are receding from each other (refer to point 4), they must have been much closer together in the past. /*"Do the unbelievers not realize that **the skies and the earth used to be one solid mass (ratqa) that we exploded (fataq) into existence?**"* (Quran 21:30).

2. The theory of the creation of the earth states that the planet initially started as a gaseous mass[27] / *"Then He turned to the sky, when it was still gas (dukaan)"* (Quran 41:11).

3. Hawking in one of his lectures describes that stars, including our sun, will eventually lose their light. This will result from the burning of fuel in the form of hydrogen and other nuclear matter (this burning is what we observe as the light of a star). As the star burns out and contracts, its gravitational field becomes stronger, making the light cones bend inwards. As a result, the light is unable to escape and

thus to a distant observer the light appears dimmer and redder. He further states that since the theory of general relativity indicates that nothing can travel faster than light, and that light cannot escape this gravitational pull, neither can anything else escape it. Thus, to a distant observer, this phenomenon appears as a "black hole".[28] Could the Quran be describing the same phenomenon? /*"So when the stars are extinguished* ... *That is the appointed day"* (Quran 77:8-12).

4. One of the major breakthroughs in the field of science was the discovery that the universe is expanding. This resulted in the establishment of the Big Bang Theory (as mentioned above). The Big Bang Theory states that the universe is expanding, and will collapse once it reaches its critical rate (usually referred to as big crunch). In 1929, Edwin Hubble demonstrated through observation and calculations on the light spectrum of stars that there is more than one galaxy, and that all the galaxies are moving outwards. This meant that the universe was not static as previously believed, but is instead expanding.[29] Could the Quran be describing the same phenomenon? /*"We constructed the sky (sama-a—sky, surrounding or space all around) with our hands, and we **will continue to expand** (musi-oona) it"* (Quran 51:47) / Big crunch—/ *"The day that We roll up the sky like a scroll rolled up for books"* (Quran 21:104) / *"... and He holdeth back the sky from falling on the earth **unless by His leave"*** (Quran 22:65). Also, regarding planets: *"So verily I call to witness the planets—**that recede"*** (Quran 81:15).

5. A picture of the Cat's Eye Nebula below taken through the Hubble telescope on October 31, 1991 [30], shows the dying star 3000 light-years away resembling a red rose (see image below). Scientists have only been able to confirm this discovery during the 20th

century. It is fascinating to note that 1400 years ago, the Quran already mentioned it exactly the way we have observed it today: /*"And when the sky splitteth asunder and becometh **rosy like red hide**"* (Quran 55:37).

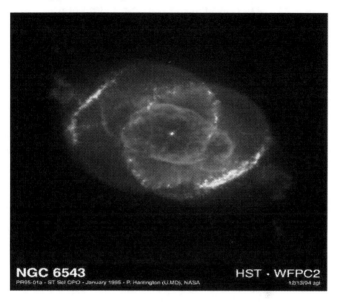

NGC 6543
PR95-01a · ST Scl CPO · January 1995 · P. Harrington (U.MD), NASA
HST · WFPC2
12/13/94 zgt

6. Only 400 years ago, it was commonly believed that the moon has its own light. Today we know that the sun is a blazing star, a ball of fire, and that the moon has no light of its own but borrows it from the sun. /*"And hath made **the moon a light** (Noor) therein, and made **the sun a lamp** (siraaj means torch)?"* (Quran 71:16) / *"Blessed is He Who made constellations in the skies, and placed therein a lamp and a moon giving light"* (Quran 25:61) / *". . . and placed a blazing (wahaaj) lamp"* (Quran 78:13). What stumps me is how the Quran could 1400 years ago describe very accurately using separate terms (such as light and lamp) what we have just recently discovered?

7. During the time of the revelation, it was believed that the earth was the center of the galaxy and remained static, and that the sun revolved around the earth, (revolving but remaining still on its own axis). Only recently have we come to know that the sun is the center of our solar system and that all of the planets within (including earth) revolve around it, that the planets revolve on their own axis, that the moon orbits around the earth, and that the sun itself orbits around the center of the galaxy:/"*And He it is Who created the night and the day, and the sun and the moon. Each floats in its own orbit*" (Quran 21:33).

8. Gravitational force keeps the sun, planets and moons apart and in their own orbits:/ "*It is not for the sun to overtake the moon, nor doth the night outstrip the day. They float each in an orbit*" (Quran 36:40).

9. The sun rises and sets at two different points in the East (orient) and West (occident) depending on the season:/ "*Lord of the two Easts, and Lord of the two Wests!*" (Quran 55:17).

10. Modern data establishes that the sun is moving toward a destined place which has been given the name "solar apex". Also, it has been established that the sun (our star) like other stars will eventually die:/ "*And the sun runs its course for a period determined for it…*" (Quran 36:38) / "*… He committed the sun and the moon, each running (in its orbit) for a predetermined period*" (Quran 13:2).

11. Within only the last fifty years, we were able to discover galaxies apart from our own. Due to these and other calculative observations, it is believed by modern science that there may be more than one universe, as well other habitable places within the universe. The Quran states: /"*GOD created seven universes and the same number of earths*" (Quran 65:12). Could the Quran be correct in this stance as

well? Further bolstering this hypothesis, many verses in the Quran see God referring to Itself as the Lord of the **worlds**, (not singular but plural).

12. Today we believe that one day humans will be able to penetrate much of space, or what we would call a "conquest of space". Could the Quran be mentioning the same idea?/ *"O company of jinn and humans, if ye have power **to penetrate** (tanfuzoo-nafaaza) (all) regions of the skies and the earth, then penetrate (them)! Ye will never penetrate them save with (Our) sanction"* (Quran 55:33).

13. Could this verse be talking about extraterrestrial beings (!) as some believe it is?/ *"And among His Signs is the creation of the skies and the earth, **and the living creatures that He has scattered through them** (meaning on earth and outside) and He has power to gather them together when He wills"* (Quran 42:29).

14. The earth has a protective layer of atmosphere which is responsible for supporting life on earth. Our atmosphere absorbs the ultraviolet light of the sun and the extremes of temperature that may be harmful to our sustenance (see image below). [31] Perhaps this verse is speaking of the same:/ *"And we rendered the **sky as protected ceiling** (saqfam[roof]-mahfooz[protect]). Yet, they are totally oblivious to all the portents therein"* (Quran 21:32).

Water Cycle, Hydrology, and Electricity

Up until 1600, many people including Plato and Aristotle believed that water on earth came from a deep abyss called "Tartarus" that underground lakes were formed by the condensed water from soil on mountains, and that spring water came from these lakes. It is therefore amazing to see that during the years around 600 and 700 AD, the Quran states a detailed and accurate description of hydrology and electricity in the atmosphere (when only during and after the 1700's we have been able to figure this out):

"Seest thou not that Allah makes the clouds move gently, then joins them together, then makes them into a heap?—then wilt thou see rain issue forth from their midst. And He sends down from the sky mountain masses (of clouds) wherein is hail: He strikes therewith whom He pleases and He turns it away from whom He pleases, the vivid flash of His lightning well-nigh blinds the sight" (Quran 24:43).

"It is Allah Who sends the winds, and they raise the clouds: then does He spread them in the sky as He wills, and break them into fragments, until thou seest rain-drops issue from the midst thereof..." (Quran 30:48).

"It is He Who sendeth the winds like heralds of glad tidings, going before His mercy: when they have carried the heavy-laden clouds, We

drive them to a land that is dead, make rain to descend thereon, and produce every kind of harvest therewith: thus shall We raise up the dead: perchance ye may remember" (Quran 7:57).

"He is the One who shows you the lightning as a source of fear, as well as hope, and He initiates the loaded clouds. The thunder praises His glory . . . He sends the lightning bolts . . ." (Quran 13:12-13).

"He sends down water from the sky, causing the valleys (rivers) to overflow, then the rapids produce abundant foam . . ." (Quran 13:17).

"Seest thou not that Allah sends down rain from the sky, and leads it through springs in the earth? . . . Truly, in this, is a message of remembrance to men of understanding" (Quran 39:21).

*"We send down from the sky water, in exact measure, then **We store it in the ground**. Certainly, **we can let it escape**"* (Quran 23:18).

*"A sign for them is the earth that is dead: We do give it life, and produce grain there from, of which ye do eat. And We produce therein orchard with date-palms and vines, and **We cause springs to gush forth therein**: That they may enjoy the fruits of this (artistry): It was not their hands that made this: will they not then give thanks?"* (Quran 36:33-35).

The Earth's Crust and the Mountains

Compared to the size of the entire planet, the earth's crust is very thin (about 4 to 25 miles in thickness). Resting beneath this crust is a hot molten fluid, a part of our ecosystem which is a necessary aspect of supporting life. Hence, we rely on this thin shell upon which we live (see image below).[32] Over this, mountains on the surface of the earth work as weights or pegs to help keep the earth and the earth's crust stable. The Quran's mention of the crust as a carpet and mountains as stakes is quite captivating as well as in harmony with modern data:

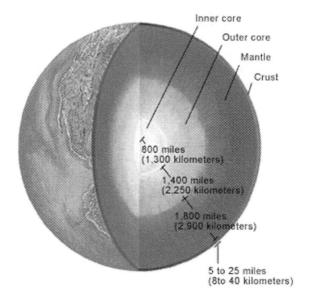

"And Allah has made the earth for you as a carpet (spread out), That ye may go about therein, in spacious roads" (Quran 71:19-20).

"And the earth We have spread out (like a carpet); set thereon mountains firm and immovable; and produced therein all kinds of things in due balance" (Quran 15:19).

"Have We not made the earth as a wide expanse, And the mountains as pegs (autaad or pl. watad—**anchor)?"** (Quran 78:6-7).

"He created the skies without pillars that you can see. He established on earth **stabilizers (mountains) lest it tumbles with you**" (Quran 31:10).

"When you look at the mountains, you think that they are standing still. But they are moving, like the clouds . . ." (Quran 27:88). Could this verse be referring to the tectonic plates?

About The Depth of the Ocean

With the help of modern equipment, scientists in recent years have been able to confirm that in regular circumstances, humans cannot go beyond 20 or 30 feet below sea level. They will not be able to survive due to the pressure exerted by the high density of water. In addition, light rays cannot pass deep into the ocean as certain and then all colours are eventually absorbed at greater depths (hence the deep ocean is pitch black). The deep sea (between 1000m to 11000m) is broken into 3 zones: bathypelagic, abyssopelagic and hadopelagic. It has also been confirmed that the ocean has layers of waves that separate the surface waves from the internal waves of other layers of the ocean.

"Or as darkness on a vast, abysmal sea. There covereth him a wave, above which is a wave, above which is a cloud. Layer upon layer of darkness. When he holdeth out his hand he scarce can see it. And he for whom Allah hath not appointed light, for him there is no light" (Quran 24:40).

Altitudes

We now know that due to the lack of oxygen and the low pressure in space, astronauts will experience constricting pain in their chests.

*"Those whom Allah (in His plan) willeth to guide,—He openeth their breast to Islam; those whom He willeth to leave straying,—**He maketh their breast close and constricted, as if they had to climb up to the skies**..."* (Quran 6:125).

Source of Life

As we now know, water makes up the majority of all living cells. Life therefore is of aquatic origin; even our own bodies contain water as a major component, about 70 percent. It is therefore again very amazing to observe the Quran being so precise in this matter:

*"**And Allah has created** (khalq) **from water** (maa-in) **every moving creature** (da-ab-batin) . . ."* (Quran 24:45).

*"And He it is Who **hath created** (khalq) **living being** (bashar) **from water**"* (Quran 25:54).

Constituent of Mammalian Milk

It wouldn't be difficult for a physiologist to accept the accuracy of scientific observation with regards to the formation of mammalian milk as mentioned in the Quran: / *"Verily in cattle there is a lesson for you. We give you to drink of what is inside their bellies (batn-butoonay-he), coming from a conjunction between ((baini) the contents of the intestine and the blood, a milk pure and pleasant for those who drink"* (Quran 16:66).

Animal Communities

During the last decade, extensive research has been conducted into animal behaviour. This has proven that there actually exist communities of animals just as that of humans:/ *"There is not an animal (that lives) on the earth, nor a being that flies on its wings, but are communities like you"* (Quran 6:38).

CREATION OF HUMAN BEINGS AND DARWIN'S THEORY OF EVOLUTION

Most of the major religions put humans as the highest and the greatest creation of God, and claim that the world (and the universe!) was created for humans, thus placing every other life form beneath us. What baffles me the most about this is two main points: first, there are only 20,000 to 25,000 genes that make up proteins for the whole human genome*. Second, this number of genes is astonishingly similar to insects like worms or flies * (which are very simple organisms compared to humans). So, what's so special about us? Perhaps it would

---

* Collins, Francis S. The Language of God. Toronto: A Division of Simon and Schuster, Inc., 2006, pp. 124-125

be apt to take a second glance into this verse:/ *"Assuredly the creation of the skies and the earth is greater than the creation of humankind; but most of mankind know not"* (Quran 40:57).

The story of Adam and Eve is known in every household of the three Semitic faiths with only slight variations. With regards to the creation of humans, I do not see the story contradicting the scientific discovery of the source of life, water. It could be that Adam and Eve came along, long after the living beings (not human) had already started to roam the earth. The Quran has not stated a time-line for the creation (It only states that all living beings are created from water [24:45, 25:54]), and "living beings" include humans and non humans both.

In addition, the particular verses that states the creation of the human beings, specifically says that human beings were created from foul smelling, sticky, rotted, and gooey muck (15:26, see below). This description rather gives the impression of the primordial soup present early in the history of the earth. This is consistent with Darwin's theory of evolution. Because of their observations and mathematical calculations, scientists claim that life began some 6.5 billion years ago in a primordial soup. This was something of a black muck, appearing as a gooey and well-chewed bubble gum, and had a foul rotten egg smell as can be observed in Yellow Stone National Park (USA), which is considered to be presently closest to the primordial earth environment.[33] It was Stanley Miller (who is known as the "father of pre-biotic chemistry") that first successfully completed the Miller-Urey experiment and created amino acids, building block of proteins, further confirming the primordial soup where life initially emerged—[34] /*"Verily We created man of potter's clay of black mud altered"* (Quran 15:26).

Please note the above translation of 15:26 of the Quran does not do justice to the literal meaning of its Arabic words, explained in detail here:

potter's clay: (*salsaalay* or *tayn*: "sticky mud")[35]

black mud: (*hama*: "gooey, foul smelling muck")[36]

altered: (*masnoon*: "rotted")[37]

Arabic: "*Laqad khalq* (created) *nal-insaana* (humans)—*min salsaalay-immin-hama-im-masnoon*" (15:26)

When we plug-in the literal meanings into verse 15:26, we get *"Verily We created human beings of sticky mud which was gooey, foul smelling, rotted muck"*. As mentioned above, this is precisely what scientists have recently discovered.

Now that we have established what the Quran says compared with science today with regards to when and how the creation of living beings took place, let us explore Darwin's Evolutionary theory. The question that has been raised by the Semitic faiths is about the Darwin's theory of natural selection for the origin of species. His theory proposes that all humans gradually evolved from a 'common ancestor'. It explains that random variations of the species occur with long lapse of time depending on the species adaptability with its environment. This 'common ancestor' has been firmly established by the scientific community as 'primates', chimps has also evolved from primates. This observation of the scientific community is abominable for the orthodox groups in all three faiths, or sometimes, they even consider this an insult to the entire human race. When we humans are placed on such a high level by the edicts of our religions, how can we be debased on such a low level? "The chimp that has no sense, no intellect, nothing at all can evolve into a human being is very shocking, how can it be!?" This paradox to their belief is the reason why some religious types deny the theory and make all efforts to disprove it.

My effort here is to explain why I have no objection to this theory, and how I see it neatly fitting into the schematic plan of the Designer. Recent human genome studies have revealed that there is almost a 98 percent similarity between humans and primates, especially chimpanzees—so much so that there are current considerations to revise the genus Homo and have it enlarged.[38] As an example of how similar humans and chimpanzees are, take the gene caspase-12. It is present in the "identical relative location in both humans and chimps".[39], but it is a functioning gene in chimps only and not in humans, so why is it there in humans to begin with? Francis Collin says that "if humans arose as a consequence of a supernatural act of special creation, why would God have gone to the trouble of inserting such a non-functional gene in this precise location?" [40] It is indeed something to think about. Another important gene called FOXP2, which is also present in both humans and other mammal, is found to be remarkably stable in all mammals except humans. It has two major changes in the coding region of the gene in humans, as a result of which, this gene is responsible for the development of language in human beings.[41]

These are two simple examples I have cited in order to establish that the evolution did take place and is still going on. Today we see humans so different from primates is because the evolution took place over a long lapse of time. This long lapse sometimes blurs comprehension, and it is difficult to understand how we may have gradually evolved. As Darwin says in his book *The Origin of Species*, "We see nothing of these slow changes in progress, until the hands of time has marked the long lapses of ages, and then so imperfect is our view into long past geological ages, that we only see that the forms of life are now different from what they formerly were".[42] Take an example of the Chinese population, who have grown in their average heights by two to three inches with a lapse of approximately a hundred years, imagine then what changes many millions of years could bring?

One orthodox Christian woman argued with me that if we have evolved from chimps than why we still see chimps alive, they should be extinct? The problem is many religious groups have never read the book of Darwin "Origin of Species" but are ever so ready to discredit it. They do not know that it is not only the extinction that makes changes but also branching out—other original species may survive if they are fit to survive. As the saying goes "you can't judge a book by its cover", we must do our own due diligence to know the truth rather than to rely on feeds.

At least we all agree on the fact that we were created from water, so, if we can originate in water, why not accept the notion of evolving and branching out from primates to humans?

As I stated Quran did not give a time line for human creation. While there can be many meanings, there is no other way I fit this verse into my comprehension other than that the Quran is speaking of the same: *"He is the One who created you in stages"* (71:14 Quran). 71:41 Implies, apart from other meanings, that it is not necessary for Adam and Eve to have arrived on earth so suddenly, but that they were instead created in stages through long lapses in time: from simple to complex organisms, then to animals, and finally to homo sapiens with the birth of Adam and Eve themselves.

I can only believe that our pretentious nature deters us from accepting our "lowly" origin.

"We must, however, acknowledge, as it seems to me, that man with all his noble qualities, with sympathy which feels for the most debased, with benevolence which extends not only to other men but to the humblest living creature, with his god-like intellect which has penetrated into the movements and constitution of the solar system—with all these exalted powers—Man still bears in his bodily frame the indelible stamp of his lowly origin".[43]

(Charles Darwin)

*"Doth not man remember that We created him before, **when he was nothing**?"* (Quran 19:67).

*"Such is the Knower of the invisible and the visible, the Mighty, the Merciful, who made all things good which He created, and He began the creation of man from sticky mud; Then He made his seed from a draught of **'despised' fluid**"* (Quran 32:6-8).

THE QURAN AND THE MATHEMATICAL
INTERLOCKING SYSTEM

This amazing aspect of the Quran has also been a contributing reason for my choice to follow Islam. When reading the Quran, you come across certain letters at the beginning of each chapter. What the meanings are of those letters is still not understood and remains a mystry. However, some have been able to find other interesting facts leading to the interlocking mathematical system of the Quran, especially with regards to the number 19. The credit of this discovery goes mainly to Rashad Khalifa, an Egyptian born American biochemist. He had extensively and painstakingly worked through the letters in the Quran to discover the interlocking system. I do not agree with all of his views neither am I belonging to his group or any other groups, but I do credit him for this discovery.

In Mathematics, the number 19 is the highest prime number. It can also be related to the binary code digit system: 19 = 1+9 = 10. In the Quran, for example, the second chapter starts with the letters A L M (many chapters begin with certain letters, and no one has yet discovered what those letters mean). But, within the second chapter, According to Khalifa's calculations, if one counts all the 'A's, 'L's and 'M's, one will find a correlation: The number of letter As will always be greater than Ls, and subsequently the number of Ls greater than Ms. Also, the total number of each letter is divisible by 19.

Why would there need to be within the Quran such an intricate mathematical interlocking system? Could it be to attest that the Quran is holy, miraculous and is a divine book? Or to prove that no human could possibly have written this book? These are questions that are beyond the scope of this particular book to address.

In the beginning of this topic, I wrote that this mathematical miracle is *part* of the reason for my choice of Islam, because I don't believe the number 19 phenomenon is THE phenomenon. Some schools of thought believe this number 19 miracle to be the greatest of all miracles of God. I agree that perhaps this phenomenon is "one of" the greatest miracles of God but "the" greatest would be putting God on a very lower level. Quran itself states too: *"Lo!* **this is one of the greatest** *(portents)"* (70:35); please note "one of the". So, if the number 19 phenomenon is the greatest miracle of the Quran, then the Quran is not divine to me. The God who created everything but whose greatest miracle halts at number 19, that God to me has limitations and that God to me is very small.

The Quran on the other hand, in order to sustain belief in the beneficence of God, has put more emphasis on so many phenomena other than the number 19 such as science, nature, common sense, culture, and ethics, to name but a few. It has repeatedly stressed us to ponder, to understand, to learn, to consider and have sense and intellect about these phenomena that number 19 miracles tend to exist only on the side.

THE QURAN AND NORMS, NATURE, AND COMMON SENSE

These parts of the Quran that have more to do with the beauty of the Quran itself are not necessarily the criteria for my choice; however, they have put a lot of credence into my decision. It is beyond the extent of this book to write every single verse dealing with this subject. I have chosen only two examples to mention as they have acted as inspiration for me, especially the consideration of human interaction:

> *"O ye who believe! Shun much suspicion; for lo! some suspicion is a crime. And spy not, neither backbite one another. Would one of you love to eat the flesh of his dead brother? Ye abhor that (so abhor the other)! And keep your duty (to Allah). Lo! Allah is Relenting, Merciful. O humankind (un-naas)! Lo! We have created you male and female, and have made you nations and tribes that ye may know one another.* **Lo! the noblest of you, in the sight of Allah, is the best in conduct.** *Lo! Allah is Knower, Aware"* (Quran 49:12-13).

We see people from all walks of life and religions (including Muslims) designating themselves as superior, or as the "chosen ones". But, as per the Quran, God only favours the ones who are **best in conduct**, regardless of what *deen* (way of life) they may follow. The use of the word humankind (*naas*) in the above-mentioned verse is sufficient to indicate that this verse is not solely addressed to Muslims, but to everyone at large. Moreover, this verse should be enough to rule out any possibility that Muslims (or for that matter Arabs), are superior.

And, how natural I find these couple of verses below that deal with issues of fairness and justice:

"O ye who believe! stand out firmly for Allah, as witnesses to fair dealing, and let not the hatred of others to you make you swerve to wrong and depart from justice. Be just: that is next to piety: and fear Allah. For Allah is well-acquainted with all that ye do" (Quran 5:08).

*"O ye who believe! stand out firmly for justice, as witnesses to Allah, **even as against yourselves,** or your parents, or your kin, and whether it be (against) rich or poor: for Allah can best protect both. Follow not the lusts (of your hearts), lest ye swerve, and if ye distort (justice) or decline to do justice, verily Allah is well-acquainted with all that ye do"* (Quran 4:135).

Apart from what I have written above, there are innumerable verses in the Quran that deal with ethics, principles, education and rights and wrongs. When the Quran explains the phenomena of nature, it continuously states that "those who have knowledge", "those who learn", "those who have sense" or "those who reflect" are the ones endued with intellect and are to succeed. Even the Quran puts itself at par when it explains in a verse not to accept any information or knowledge unless one may verify it:

"O you who believe, if a wicked person brings any news to you, you shall first investigate, lest you commit injustice towards some people, out of ignorance, then become sorry and remorseful for what you have done" (Quran 49:06).

SOME QURANIC VERSES THAT ARE INCOMPREHENSIBLE

On this topic, there are some examples of Quranic verses I find difficult to understand. It is quite disturbing to observe that the Quran, whose overall theme is peace *salaam*, (and every now and then emphasizes the importance of justice), can in some of its verses appear to be unreasonable. Could it be that we have not been able to fully grasp the meaning of certain verses and perhaps have wrongly interpreted them? As Asma Barlas says in her book *Believing Women in Islam*, "if God never does *Zulm* (harm) to anyone, then God's Speech (the Quran) also cannot teach *Zulm* against anyone".[44]

When it comes to justice, God is unrelenting. But, the same God is also most Merciful, Beneficent and never commits injustices. How can the words of that very God be so oppressive and unjust in some verses? It doesn't square very well. An example of this: *"As for those of your women who are guilty of lewdness, call to witness four of you against them. And if they testify (to the truth of the allegation) then confine them to the houses until death take them or (until) Allah appoint for them a way (through new legislation)"* (Quran 4:15).

When this verse speaks only about women, one is left to wonder, what about men? Is there a gap in comprehension? After all, men can be equally guilty of lewdness.

The verse continues to 4:16, stating *"if two (men) among you are guilty of lewdness, punish them both. If they repent and amend, leave them alone; for Allah is Oft-returning, most Merciful"*.

It seems it is either in favour of women or against: In verse 4:16, although the Quran commands to straightaway punish lewd men, it does not put any condition for carrying out the punishment (such as, to have four witness or any proof, whereas in the case of women it does ask for proof). This can be interpreted as favouring women. However, in women's cases the punishment is mentioned:/ *"confine them to the houses until death take them or (until) Allah appoint for them a way (through new legislation)"*. This is a very harsh punishment and does not appear to be in favour of women. In the case of men, the Quran does not detail the type or the kind of punishment to be given. It is therefore open to any interpretation whatsoever, and could theoretically range from lenient to harsh.

In another incidence, the Quran states:

"Recall that your Lord inspired the angels: "I am with you; so support those who believed. I will throw terror into the hearts of those who disbelieved. You may strike them above the necks, and you may strike even every finger. This is what they have justly incurred by opposing GOD and His messenger. For those who oppose GOD and His messenger, GOD's retribution is severe" (Quran 8:12-13).

Islam essentially advises peace and suggests fighting only for defence (please read more about the issue of *Jehad* in chapter four). These above verses are therefore talking about those who fight and not those who are at peace. However, to fight so mercilessly even in defence does not fit right with the most "Merciful" God. Unless, I interpret this in terms of human nature: when your own survival is threatened, you may kill for self-preservation. This type of self-defence killing is justified even today.

These are but a couple examples I have cited. There are further verses specifically related to wars and which condone merciless fighting. However, all of them are addressed specifically towards those who oppress and attack first.

I could only find a few verses with which I am discomforted but the major bulk of the verses comfort me that is why I choose to remain a Muslim. Compared to such questionable verses that are a few in number, the whole Quran has innumerable verses that address love and mercy, forgiveness and compassion. It has many verses on as humble a topic as decent mannerism, such as: *"When a (courteous) greeting is offered to you, meet it with a greeting still more courteous, or (at least) of equal courtesy. Allah takes careful account of all things"* (Quran 4:86).

As we shall see in chapter six, despite the terrible fate of a woman in verse 4:15, there are countless verses with favourable words for women.

NOTES:

1.   Bauer, Gabrielle. "God and Other Mysteries". Reader's Digest, November 2003, p. 53

2.   Irshad, Manji. *The Trouble With Islam: A Wake Up Call For Honesty and Change.* Toronto: Random House Canada, 2003

3.   Hawking, Stephen. *A Brief History of Time.* Bantam Press, Ealing: Transworld Publishers Limited, 1988, p. 134

4.   Armstrong, Karen. *A History of God: the 4000-Year Quest of Judaism, Christianity, and Islam.* New York: Alfred A Knopf Inc., 1993, p. xx-xxi

5.   Ibid., p. xxi

6.   Collins, Francis S. *The Language of God.* Toronto: A Division of Simon and Schuster, Inc., 2006, p. 22

7.   Ibid., p. 140

8.   Ibid., p. 93

9.   Ibid.

10. Armstrong, Karen. *Islam, A Short History.* London: The Orion Publishing Group, 2000, p. 4

     Armstrong, Karen. *Muhammad, A Biography of the Prophet.* New York: Harper Collins Publishers Inc., 1992, p. 86-87

11. Ibid.

12. Wadud, Amina. *Qur'an and Women, Rereading the Sacred Text from a Woman's Perspective*. Oxford: Oxford University Press, 1999, p. xii

13. Ibid., p. 6

14. Barlas, Asma. *Believing Women in Islam: Unreading Patriarchal Interpretations of the Qur'an*. Austin: University of Texas Press, 2002, p.8

15. Ibid., p. 33

16. Darwin, Charles. *The Descent of Man*, 1871. London: John Murray, Albemarle Street. Bank of Wisdom eBook edition, p. 18. Accessed June 17, 2010. http://www.gutenberg.org/cache/epub/2300/pg2300.epub

17. Collins, Francis S. *The Language of God*. Toronto: A Division of Simon and Schuster, Inc., 2006, p. 88

18. Bucaille, Maurice. *The Bible, The Quran, and Science: The Holy Scriptures Examined in the Light of Modern Knowledge.* New York: Tahrike Tarsile Quran, Inc., 2003

19. Hawking, Stephen W. *The Theory of Everything: The Origin and Fate of the Universe.* New Millennium Press, 2003

    Hawking, Stephen W. *A Brief History of Time.* Bantam Press, Ealing: Transworld Publishers Limited, 1988.

20. Baucaille, Maurice. *The Bible, The Quran, and Science: The Holy Scriptures Examined in the Light of Modern Knowledge.* New York: Tahrike Tarsile Quran, Inc., 2003, pp. 176-179

21. Ibid., pp. 181-182

22. "Dr. Keith Moore Confirms Embryology in Quran". Date Accessed: February 02, 2010 http://www.quranandscience.com/human/135-dr-keith-moore-confirms-embryology-in-quran.html.

    Keith L. Moore, T.V.N. Persaud. *Before We Are Born (Human Development): Essentials of Embryology and Birth Defects.*

Saunders, an imprint of Elsvier Inc. Philadelphia, 7th edition, 2008, pp. 49-61, 4-7, 243-245

23. Baucaille, Maurice. *The Bible, The Quran, and Science: The Holy Scriptures Examined in the Light of Modern Knowledge.* New York: Tahrike Tarsile Quran, Inc., 2003, pp. 176-179

24 Ibid., p. 182

25. Hawking, Stephen W. *A Brief History of Time.* Bantam Press, Ealing: Transworld Publishers Limited, 1988, p. 163

26. Ibid., pp. 48-49, 121, 160

27. Baucaille, Maurice. *The Bible, The Quran, and Science: The Holy Scriptures Examined in the Light of Modern Knowledge.* New York: Tahrike Tarsile Quran, Inc., 2003, p. 129

28. Hawking, Stephen W. *A Brief History of Time.* Bantam Press, Ealing: Transworld Publishers Limited, 1988, p. 90

29. Ibid., p. 9

30. Robert Nemiroff, Jerry Bonnell. "Astronomy Picture of The Day". Accessed July 26, 2010 http://apod.nasa.gov/apod/ap991031. html

31. "Earth Observatory". NASA Goddard Space flight Center, last updated Tue, 26 Jan 2010. Posted: February 2, 2007. Accessed July 26, 2010.

    http://earthobservatory.nasa.gov/IOTD/view.php?id=7373

32. Brian Dunbar. "World book at NASA" : Earth's Interior. Last updated on November 29,2007. Accessed July 27,2010. http://www.nasa.gov/worldbook/earth_worldbook.html

33. Monastersky, Richard and Mozzatenta, O. Louis. "What kind of place was Primordial Earth; Earth—History, Evolution". *The National Geographic Journal*, Vol 193, No. 3 (1998): pp. 58-79

34. Ibid.

35. Zahida, Durrani. *Parvaiz, Allama: Lughat-ul-Quran.* Toronto: Tolu-e-Islam Trust, 2007, (swad, laam,swad, laam), pp. 1033-1034

36. Ibid., (hay, meem, alif), p. 548

37. Ibid., (seen, noon, noon), p. 908

38. Wildman, Uddin, et. al. "Implications of Natural Selection in Shaping 99.4% Nonsynonymous DNA Identity between Humans and Chimpanzees: Enlarging Genus Homo". Contributed by Morris Goodman. *National Academy of Sciences of the United States of America (PNAS).* April 14, 2003. Date accessed: January 29, 2010. http://www.pnas.org/content/100/12/7181.abstract

    Lovgren, Stefan. "Chimps, Humans 96 Percent the Same, Gene Study Finds". *National Geographic News*, August 31 2005. Date accessed: January 29 2010. http://news.nationalgeographic.com/news/2005/08/0831_050831_chimp_genes.html

    http://news.nationalgeographic.com/news/2005/08/0831_050831_chimp_genes_2.html

39. Collins, Francis S. *The Language of God.* Toronto: A Division of Simon and Schuster, Inc., 2006, p. 139

40. Ibid.

41. Ibid., pp. 139-140

42. Darwin, Charles. *The Origin of Species.* New York: Random House Value Publishing Inc., 1979, p. 133

43. Darwin, Charles. *The Descent of Man*, 1871. The Project Gutenberg Etext. Etext prepared by Sue Asscher. Project Gutenberg, P.O Box 2782, Chamaign, IL 61825, USA. August 2000 Etext #2300, FB Reader, p. 811. Accessed June 17, 2010. http://www.gutenberg.org/etext/2300

44. Barlas, Asma. *Believing Women in Islam: Unreading Patriarchal Interpretations of the Qur'an.* Austin: University of Texas Press, 2002, p. 14

CHAPTER TWO

DOWNFALL OF ISLAM ᪣

WHY THE DOWNFALL OF ISLAM? A BRIEF TOUCH

This topic is an oft debated subject. It is sad indeed to see how history repeats itself—the downfall of Judaism, then Christianity, and now Islam. The signs of the downfall of Islam began promptly after the death of Muhammad. Arguments started as to who would be the next leader or caliph. Some preferred Ali because he was the Prophet's cousin; however, he was very young at that time. Finally, Abu Buker, a long-time companion of the Prophet and well matured in terms of age, was chosen to lead.[1]

THE SECT OR SCHISM

Those who wished to have Ali as leader were eventually called the *Shias* (Shiites—*Shia-e-Ali*—sect of Ali), and those who wished to have Abu Buker as leader, were later called the *Sunnis*. Both groups emerged solely due to political reasons,[2] but later became the major religious sects in Islam. Since then, there have been many offshoots of these two sects. *Shias* believe only relatives of the Prophet have the right to lead and to follow the practices, while Sunnis believe that anyone can follow the Prophet's *Sunnas* or practices. I see nothing more here than the egg fight of Gulliver's Travels between the Belfuscu and Liliputs.

Both I consider to be inordinately wrong. I was born into a Sunni family, but have disowned all sect titles and call myself simply a Muslim, or one who wishes to abide by the laws of the Creator or nature. I believe the Shiite sect to be wrong because when Muhammad (or for that matter when the Quran itself) did not ordain the system of "royal" family lineation, who are we to introduce it? In the case of Sunni sect, what can possibly make them so sure of what the practices of Muhammad really are? The *hadith* (sayings attributed to the Prophet)? I am appalled to mention it, but there is a lot of controversy on this major contributing factor to the downfall of Islam.

On another note, the whole schism issue has no base and is completely refuted when we consider the following verses:

*"Lo! As for **those who divide (farraqu) their religion and become into sects (shia),** no concern at all hast thou with them. Their case will go to Allah, who then will tell them what they used to do"* (Quran 6:159).

*". . . .—**Lo! the evil-doers are in open schism**" (Quran 22:52-53).*

COLLUSION IN ISLAM

Major collusion in Islam began in the middle of the 7th century CE and continued to increase until its final downfall. It started with the Dynasty of Ummayads, increased during that of the Abbasid's, and continued on into the Ottoman Empire until completely fell apart. Monarchism, indulgence, deception, and negative innovations such as the *Shariah* laws (discussed in chapter three) are but a few of the evils of the medieval, rather mid-evils! These have now shattered the pure egalitarian principles of Islam.[3]

But hasn't Allah said in the Quran that/ "*Ye are the best community that hath been raised up for humankind*", and why? Because "*. . . Ye enjoin right conduct and forbid indecency*" (Quran 3:110). Did we uphold that principle? God also states that if a community does not follow God's laws in the right manner, it is not difficult for God to introduce a substitute,/ "*We verily are able to replace them by (others) better than them. And we are not to be outrun*" (Quran 70:40-41).

Judaism and Christianity went through the same evil practices and suffer the resulting predicament, being reduced to the confines of the four walls of synagogues and churches. Due to the variant readings of the Bible, we witnessed the Crusades, the French and British colonization, along with the Spanish inquisition. We witnessed many other such disasters, along with the recent downfall of Iraq (the very Iraq that was once called "the Cradle of Civilization"). Still to date, Jewish and Muslims are fighting for a piece of land under the guise of their religions, when the matter is purely political. Both feel that the other is oppressing them. For this situation, I recall a verse saying to leave the land where you are being oppressed, because Allah's land is spacious enough:

"Lo! as for those whom the angels take (in death) while they wrong themselves, (the angels) will ask: In what were ye engaged? They will say: We were oppressed in the land. (The angels) will say: Was not Allah's earth spacious that ye could have migrated therein? As for such, their habitation will be hell, an evil journey's end". (Quran 4:97)

When we look around in the world, we find that the most abject states are those of Muslims. These places rank higher in the corruption index, as well human rights (including women's and children's rights) are completely vanquished in all of the Muslim states. We are the most poverty stricken and illiterate in the world. All the negatives are associated with us.[4]

The ironic part of this is that Muslims were once responsible for the renaissance of the Dark Ages. Muslims have been the fathers of many scientific breakthroughs. Eminent scholars from all around Europe used to go to Cordoba, Spain, where the major Muslim library containing more than 400,000 volumes resided. Indeed! These are very disturbing facts for a sincere Muslim. We console our hearts with how we were, but close our eyes to what we have reduced ourselves to now: an "Arabic Islam" full of rituals: essentially a return to the Dark Ages.

When we believe in God and It's book, we also believe that there will be accountability in the court of God. We also know that the Quran states/ *"Allah is swift at reckoning . . ."* (3:19). And alas to our loss, we also know that the Quran states we are not the "chosen ones" or "superior", instead only those who are righteous and best in conduct (3:142, 18:107, 49:13, and many others).

Further to that, Muhammad introduced the Quran to actually rid the people of the social malaise and evil *Jahiliah* (ignorance) state which they were in.[5] He came with the Quran to implement a decent and just society where the poor and vulnerable were safe.[6] Many Muslims may remember the long speech of Jaffir Ibne Abi Talib in front of the Egyptian Christian king Najashi (Negus) in Abyssinia (modern day Ethiopia) when they escaped there to seek refuge from the oppression of the Arabs. The speech clearly stated the conditions at which the Arab world was during that time. Those stated conditions contradicted the teachings of the Quran that Muhammad brought: Quran exhorts to educate people and move them forward to become a better part of the progressing world.[7] This is because the Quran states/ *"Ye are the best community that hath been raised up for humankind. (and it is only when) Ye enjoin right conduct and forbid indecency; and ye believe in Allah"* (Quran 3:110). Bracket is mine.

Do we see any iota of that Islam fulfilled today? If we did, the overall picture would be much different from what it is today. Hence, I believe that we are being substituted.

THE FUTURE OF ISLAM

In the past we have seen religions at their heights (mainly Judaism and Christianity) but eventually they declined, exactly the same as we see Islam today. There is no difference. What simply happened is that they failed to uphold the natural values and laws and consequently suffered the loss. They were all reduced to lumps contained within churches and synagogues. Could it be possible that Islam will bear the same fate in the future?

I personally believe that as long as any country, community, or group keeps claiming Islam, there will be no true justice in the core values of Islam, and subsequently it will be reduced to simply nothing. As long as Islam will be claimed, it will be exploited and abused.

NOTES:

1. Armstrong, Karen. *Islam, A Short History*. London: The Orion Publishing Group, 2000, p. 25

2. Ibid., pp. 23-37, 63

3. Ibid., pp. 41-65

    Rahim, Sir Abdur. *Principles of Mohammadan Jurisprudence*. Karachi Pakistan: Mansoor Book House, 1911, pp. 14-28

4. Afkhami, Mahnaz (et al). *Faith and Freedom*. Syracuse, NY: Syracuse University Press, 1995, pp. 1-50

5. Armstrong, Karen. *Islam, A Short History*. London: The Orion Publishing Group, 2000, p. 8

Armstrong, Karen. *Muhammad, A Biography of the Prophet.* New York: Harper Collins Publishers Inc., 1992, pp. 72-90

6. Armstrong, Karen. *Islam, A Short History.* London: The Orion Publishing Group, 2000, pp. 30, 70

7. Muhammad, Fakhanda Noor. *Islamiat for Students*, Rawalpindi, Karachi, Pakistan: Ferozsons td. Lahore, 1992, p. 6

CHAPTER THREE

AHADITH ﷺ
(SAYINGS OR STATEMENTS ATTRIBUTED TO MUHAMMAD)

GOD has revealed herein the best hadith; a book that is consistent, and points out both ways. (Quran 39:23)

My attempt in this topic is not to go into elaborate details about *ahadith* (plural of *hadith*) except to briefly explain what it is and what issues surround *ahadith*.

WHAT IS *HADITH*?

Hadith is the sayings other than the Quran that are attributed to Muhammad. Many scholars agree that *hadith* is synonymous with the Bible: It was officially written down two to three centuries (almost 8 to 12 generations) after the demise of the Prophet. It has been passed down through oral tradition by a chain of narrators called *asnaad*.[1]

After the demise of the Prophet and during the time of the first four caliphs, *ahadith* literature was never encouraged to be written down or to be transmitted; even the reporting of *ahadith* was prohibited during the time of Umar the second Caliph. It was the Quran alone that was authorized by the state to be written down and compiled. It was finalized by the time of Uthman, the third caliph.[2] The sayings and decisions of the Prophet (as attributed to him), on the other hand, were not collected by the authority of the state but remained with private enterprises, explains Abdur Rahim in his 1911 edition *Principles of Muhammadan Jurisprudence*.[3] This book of Abdur Rahim's is used as one of the academic books for law students in Pakistan.

After this, all sorts of *ahadith* some fake and some true came into circulation, even including those that were inconsistent with the Quranic injunctions. This phenomenon was one of the reasons for the birth of various schools of thought, primarily two: the *Sunni* school and the *Shia* school. From the *Sunni* school emerged four main schools: *Hanafi, Shafi, Maliki* and *Hanbali* (*Wahabism* is an offshoot that emerged from the *Hanbali* sect), and from the *Shia* school emerged the twelve *Shiite Imams* and their schools of thought. These different schools in Islam later endorsed and compiled many of those circulated *ahadith*. This process was carried out by many scholars and *ulemas* of the past: prominently, the *Sunni's* six authentic collection by Bukhari, Muslim, Abu Dawud, Ibne Majah and Nisa'i.[4] Besides this, there were also other collections of traditions such as that of Malik's Al-Muwatta, Musnadu'l Imam Hanbal and Usul and principles of Ash-Shafi'i.

Abu Hanifa, one of the earliest in the lineage of the *ulemas* and through whom the *Hanafi* sect emerged, applied a very stringent test in sifting the authentic traditions. He only accepted 18 *ahadith* out of the vast heap of traditions—only this amount he considered reliable.[*] Every sect would accept

---

[*] Rahim, Sir Abdur. Principles of Mohammadan Jurisprudence. Karachi Pakistan: Mansoor Book House, 1911, p. 19.

and reject *hadith* based on what may benefit and support their faction. *Hadith*, as is mentioned earlier, played a major role in the downfall of Islam. It was utilized by the Ummyad and mostly Abbasid dynasty to meet their means. Later, the Safavid, the Moghul, and the Otoman Empires utilized in a similar fashion. Consequently major collusion and corruption ensued [5]

With many *ahadith* already in circulation (including fabricated ones), how can one be sure what truly are the words of the Prophet? Each sect states that its compilation is true, without giving much of a compelling argument to support this claim. An example of one collection which is considered most authoritative for the Sunni school is the *Sahih-Al-Bukhari*. In *The Principles of Muhammadan Jurisprudence* by Abdur Rahim, we find that Bukhari collected 600,000 *ahadith* out of which 7000 traditions were selected as authentic.[6] This 7000 adds up to less than 1.2 percent considered as authentic! Yet, even if in that miniscule percentage we find discrepancies then what credibility we can attach to it as a whole? (I shall later provide examples below).

It is no wonder why God says in the Quran: /"*. . . then in what hadith other than Allah and His verses will they believe*" (Quran 45:6)

Having said that, I do not mean to assert that we should reject all *ahadith* completely, we can use them as historical data. But as a guide, Quran, common sense, reasoning, and nature should be sufficient.

ISSUES OF *HADITH*

"Or do you think that most of them do hear or use their reasoning? They are nothing but as cattle; nay, they are straying farther off from the path" (Quran 25:44).

From 1100 to 1600, many arguments started due to the doors of *Ijtehad* (independent thinking) being wide open.[7]

Sadly, the end of this period marked the beginning of the Dark Ages for Islam. There arose at this time many sects based on these arguments, but two were quite prominent: the "Quran only", and "*hadith* Only". [8] Both were in error and lacked grounding. "*hadith* Only" were putting the Quran second to *hadith*. Daniel Brown in his dissertation *Rethinking Tradition in Modern Islamic Thoughts*, writes: "In theory Prophetic sunna was ascendant, even over the Quran. Hence the Maxims 'The sunna rules on the Quran, but the Quran does not rule on the sunna' and 'The Quran has greater need of the sunna than the sunna of the Quran'".[9] It is absurd to do this because the very basis of the existence of Islam is the Quran, and not *hadith/ Sunnah*. On the other hand, the "Quran Only" were rejecting all *ahadith*, consequently making it hard to ground the historical background of the Quran, which is the basis of the whole existence of this issue.

PROPONENTS OF *HADITH*

Judaism and Christianity have gone through the same dilemma as Muslims are facing now. There are two reasons to explain this predicament:

First, it is human nature to intervene between the Divine Speech and the Divine. This could be to make a symbolic connection between what we cannot explain and what we can. When we put a bit of human touch into the divine, we tend to make a conceptual idea more believable to ourselves.

Second, the addition of human *hadith* into the Divine *hadith* helps us to remain in authority; however much less perfect the human *ahadith* may be, is irrelevant. It could be that the proponents of *hadith* felt that they would lose the "guardianship" of the words of the Prophet if they lost the *hadith* attributed to the Prophet, says Brown.[10] Those guardian *ulemas* are the voice of Muhammad, the very Prophet who explained the Quran. Consequently, those *ulemas* become the controlling figures. This is exactly what Priests and the Rabbis have done in the past, except that they went a bit further by denying the ordinary people the right to have access to the Bible! Brown further writes that the proponents of *hadith* went to the length of giving *hadith* more authority than the Quran on the pretext that the Quran depends on the *hadith* to be explained whereas the *hadith* is independent.[11]

Yet, the Quran states that it is self sufficient: /*"Shall I seek other than Allah for judge, when He it is who hath revealed unto you (this) Scripture, **fully explained**?"* (Quran 6:114). The Quran in 50:45 further instructs Muhammad to *". . . admonish **with** the Quran"* (and not any other book). Quran remains astonished and asks the readers: *"In what hadith, after this, will you believe?"* (77:50).

Thus, we see the introduction of *Shariah* in Islam. *Shariah* is a combination of Divine disclosure and human disclosure. Jewish people produced a similar discourse named *Mishna* and *Gemara,* together called the *Talmud*—a book of law that explains the *Torah*. We must ask ourselves the question of whether these introductions of extra textual books have helped us towards betterment, if indeed that was the reason for their introduction. I will give two glimpses of what chaos *Shariah* has created in the Muslim world:

1. Stoning To Death

In very recent history, we learned that a Nigerian woman was sentenced to death by stoning because she became pregnant out of wedlock.[12] The man involved, on the other hand, was free of any blame or consequences. This type of stoning to death is never mentioned in the Quran, but in a *hadith* narrations attributed to the Prophet. The *hadith* says to stone to death the adulterer and adulteress (however, in practice, it is carried out only on the woman).[13] The way it is carried out is by partially covering the women under ground near her father's house, then stoning her to death! This *hadith* is therefore in direct violation of the Quranic injunction. When in essence the Prophet was to explain or dictate the Quran, this *hadith* puts the Prophet in a position where he can clearly be accused of defying the very Quran he was meant to uphold! Despite the inherent contradiction, this *hadith* (which has no bearing with verses of the Quran) is incorporated into the *Shariah*.

Narrated by Abu Huraira and Zaid bin Khalid:

*While we were with the, a man stood up and said (to the Prophet), "I beseech you by Allah, that you should **judge us according to Allah's Laws*.**" Then the man's opponent who was wiser than him, got up saying (to Allah's Apostle) "Judge us according to Allah's Law and kindly allow me (to speak)." The Prophet said, "'Speak." He said, "My son was a laborer working for this man and he committed an illegal sexual intercourse with his wife, and I gave one-hundred sheep and a slave as a ransom for my son's sin. Then I asked a learned man about this case and he informed me that my son should receive one hundred lashes and be exiled for one year, and the man's wife should be stoned to death." The Prophet said, "**By Him in Whose Hand my soul is, I will judge you according to the Laws of Allah**. Your one-hundred sheep and the slave are to be returned to you, and your son has to receive one-hundred lashes and be exiled for one year. O **Unais! Go to the wife of this man, and if she confesses, then stone her to death**. Unais went to her and she confessed. He then stoned her to death.*[13]

It would be shocking to know that such an injunction as above is present not in the Quran but in the Bible (Old Testament):

"But if this thing be true, and the tokens of virginity be not found for the damsel, then they shall bring out the damsel to the door of her father's house, and the men of her city shall stone her with stones that she die: because she hath wrought folly in Israel, to play the whore in her father's house: so shalt thou put evil away from among you." (Deuteronomy 22:20-21 King James Version). [14]

I am perplexed by this discovery. Is this supposed to be the saying of the Prophet, or is it the transcription of the Bible into Islam? When scholars were faced with this dilemma and were asked to provide proof that this information belongs in Islam

---

*   Note that it asks to judge according to Allah's law that is Quran, yet it is not being judged as such.

with respect to the Quran, some scholars stated that there were certain verses that were abrogated from the Quran, and certain ones that were "eaten up by the goat"(!?). Stoning to death was one of these. I don't think any person in his or her sane mind would accept such an outrageous apology.

2. Apostasy

The Quran talks extensively about apostasy, but never in a single verse does it mention the death penalty which the edicts of *Shariah* stipulate. Although there are many, I will quote one verse that addresses those who are repeated renegades yet it is void of any capital punishment:

"Lo! those who believe, then disbelieve and then (again) believe, then disbelieve, and then increase in disbelief, **Allah will never pardon them, nor will He guide them unto a way***"* (Quran 4:137).

Since the Quran could not support the apostasy punishment as dictated by the *Shariah*, it had to come from some other source: *hadith* narrations. It was incorporated into *Shariah* through the *ahadith* attributed to the Prophet. Two examples of this are as follows (please also note that the same *hadith* orders the death penalty for adulterers, which is also nowhere to be found within the Quran): [15]

Narrated by Abdullah:

"Allah's Apostle said, "The blood of a Muslim who confesses that none has the right to be worshipped but Allah and that I am His Apostle, cannot be shed except in three cases: In Qisas for murder, a married person who commits illegal sexual intercourse and the **one who reverts from Islam (apostate) and leaves the Muslims."** [15]

Narrated by 'Ikrima:

"Some Zanadiqa (atheists) were brought to 'Ali and he burnt them. The news of this event, reached Ibn 'Abbas who said, "If I had been in his place, I would not have burnt them, as Allah's Apostle forbade it, saying, 'Do not punish anybody with Allah's punishment (fire).' I would have

*killed them according to the statement of Allah's Apostle, **'whoever changes his Islamic religion, then kill him'.*"* [15]

I am baffled to see that the Prophet, who was to uphold the Quran and its teaching, would rather choose to have his own say or cite Biblical commands to be enforced. To me, it is utterly preposterous and unacceptable to append such *ahadith* to the high esteem of Muhammad; it cannot be Muhammad's statements. Quran instead lifts the persona of Muhammad and says: *"You are blessed with a great moral character."* (68:4)

Moreover, when the Quran explicitly states (2:256) *"There is no compulsion in religion . . .",* and even questions in astonishment:/ *And if your Lord had willed, all those who are on the earth all of them would have believed. Then, will you compel mankind till they become believers?* (10:99), the above *sahih hadith* (canonical *hadith*) is in direct contradiction to the Quran when it orders to kill the apostate. No wonder why today's Islam has become so intolerant.

OPPONENTS OF *HADITH*

There have been schools in the past and now in the present that reject *hadith* completely. But, to me this is equally self-destructing. There were revivalists who stood somewhere in between,[16] and there are some who are busy in scrutinizing every single word of the Quran to interpret it with the present time. But whether they really find the "***best meaning***" *husan* (39:18) is still in question.

Why I call the deniers of *hadith* equally self-destructing and evil is because if the *hadithists* feel that they are the guardians of the law, the deniers would become the same. The difference is nothing, one just replaces the other. We require the religious-historical background for the acknowledgment of the Quran, and hence the acknowledgment of the Divine. Denying the *hadith* and *Sunnah* completely leaves us with no historical data to ground the Quran on (no matter how fabricated the data may be). The deniers of *hadith* with time would become as extreme as the advocators of *hadith* where they then become the "interpreters" and thus—"the guardians".

The key to this quandary lies in judging the *hadith* in the light of the Quranic verses. *Hadith* must depend upon the Quran, and the Quran should remain independent. Even if Muhammad have had made some decisions on subject matters for which till then no Quranic injunctions had come to pass, he would himself alter them when Quranic ruling would come in place.

In both groups, there are scholars past and present who have been and are genuine in their efforts. They would not think that they are doing anything detrimental to the *deen*. Despite their sincere efforts, the *deen* has been abused in the past and will be now. It is human nature to crave power and authority, thus a little dust of such license is irrepressible and eventually becomes detrimental to our own well-being.

CRITERIA IMPLEMENTED FOR THE AUTHENTICITY OF *AHADITH*

Since there were already many fabricated *ahadith* in circulation before there arose a need to set measures and sift through to determine the fake from the true, the task, for many reasons, became complicated.

It was agreed upon that the transmitter of a *hadith* must be of sound character, reliable, and of excellent memory. Yet we see canonical *ahadith* transmitted by people who are unreliable and possess questionable characters. Nevertheless, once this measure was established, there came the criterion to ascertain the continuity of the chain of narrators (called *asnaad*), who should also be reliable and their chain unbroken. It was also considered that the closer the *asnaad* is to the time of the Prophet (especially those who lived in Muhammad's time or were among his companions), the more authentic the tradition is. However, the Quran directly states that there were among the companions of the Prophet those who were also hypocrites (9:101, 59:11, 63:1). How can we reconcile this fact with the criteria chosen as a litmus test for the authenticity of the *ahadith*? Nonetheless, based roughly on these criteria, each *hadith* was given a general approval for reliability: *sahih* (the most reliable, canonical), *hasan* (fair), *zaif* (weak), *mouzu* (fabricated).[17]

Even though the above measures were set and approved by scholars, the dilemma with this is that the *ahadith* were never transmitted verbatim from the Prophet but the "sense", says Brown.[18] Obviously, a tradition could be quite unreliable if just the *meaning* is transmitted. The disciples and later scholars are all humans and therefore prone to error. People can only comprehend according to their limited intellectual capacity, as well the time that they live in. Moreover, there is no sure guarantee that if the *asnaad* is reliable or unbroken that the *hadith* is legitimate. We have heard about "Chinese whisper", where the chain of *asnaad* is very well established, yet the meaning of a sentence completely changes once the message has traveled back to its originator.

Based on the aforementioned, the canonical compilation of *ahadith* was initiated. Hence, the most reliable and canonical is the *Sunni's Sahih Al-Bukhari* and *Sahih Muslim*. These compilations did not look into the 'substance' called *matn* of the *hadith*.[19] Much of the efforts were genuinely painstaking, but the very disregard for the substance of a *hadith* resulted in an outright disregard for the *sahih ahadith*, even though it is stamped extremely reliable. When the content of a *sahih hadith* is completely unacceptable and objectionable, what credibility (if any) can we then affix to the *sahih*, let alone the *hasn*, *zaif* and *mouzu*? An example, the *sahih* traditions in Bukhari that specify deplorable sexual details attributed to the Prophet's life, or the *sahih* tradition "*when the devil hears the call for prayer, he flees, farting*",[20] both make a jest of Islam rather than doing it any good.

Now that I have severely criticized the Bukhari collection, to be fair, I must add here that even though it severely lacks in the integrity of its *ahadith*, it contains *ahadith* that are quite beautiful too. There may be contradictions within its collection, or these might as well be fabricated. Such examples of beautiful parts in this collection is the *ahadih* relating to the Prophet's sincere, simple and loving character, and those *ahadith* that are very rational and true in their meaning.

ULEMAS OF THE PAST AND THEIR CREDIBILITY

We have seen by now from the above discussion how the arguments amongst past scholars have sometimes been bizarre or even perhaps overshadowed by ulterior motives. But we cannot rule out the possibility that there may have been scholars in the past who were wholly sincere in their efforts. They did intend to reform or bring the Muslim community *ummah* together, but whether they upheld the true values and egalitarian principles of Islam or whether their efforts produced a different result is another story.

One thing I question is why there is a lack of female past *ulemas*. Is it true that there were no female *ulemas* in the past, or have none ever come to light? The Quran states that *"God chooses messengers from among angels as well as humans (naas—includes both men and women) . . ."* (22:75—bracket is mine), it did not say *rijaal* (men). This is something to think about. Annemarie Shimmel in her book *My Soul is a Woman* has mentioned that there were women scholars as early as the 8th century CE such as Rabia Basri, who was a mystic scholar. Additionally, there were women theologians as early as 1600 CE, and poetesses such as Fadwa Tuqan, Moghul princess Zebunnisa, and Fakhri Harawi, to name but a few.[21] Schimmel further identifies Muslim women as teachers and professors from whom men acquired education. Also, there were female politicians in the arena of religion, and this includes the caliph's wives and mothers. She even mentioned that there were many women calligraphers whose works has been well preserved.[22]

If there were women *ulemas* who were writers and educators, why do we not see any of their works?

ABOUT ABU HURAYRA

Since Abu Hurayra had transmitted major bulk of the canonical *ahadith*, I found it imperative to briefly outline who he was. Abu Hurayra's real name was Abdu-Shams, but because of his love of cats, he was generally known as Abu-Hurayra (father of kittens). He was a convert from Judaism, and remained the companion of the Prophet for only the last three years of Muhammad's life.[23] Despite this short companionship, he has narrated the highest number of the *ahadith* in the *sahih* collection compared to the number transmitted by Aisha (the Prophet's wife), or Abu bukar, who spent a life time with the Prophet. Abu Hurayra was said to be the most prolific transmitter of *ahadith*,[24] but on the other hand, Umar Abdul Aziz, one of the first four caliphs, accused him of being a liar. Umar reprimanded him, and even discharged him from his post. Not only that, he was also severely criticized by Aisha for transmitting fabricated *ahadith*. As Brown says: "biographical literature provides ample material for criticism of Abu Hurayra's character, [and] this literature has been utilized to severely criticize the *sahih* collection which states most of the single *ahadith* narrated by Abu Hurayra".[25] When biographical literature portrays Abu Hurayra as being of detestable character and lacking honesty, it is questionable how he managed to pass through the rigorous criteria implemented to sift through the *ahadith*, where one of the important and deciding factors of authenticity were the narrator's character and credibility.

HADITH VS. SUNNAH
(Practices of Muhammad called *sunatul nabi*)

Some deniers of *hadith* accept the general practices of Muhammad, such as the five daily ritualistic prayers called *salaat* which are followed as the *sunnat-ul-nabi*. The Quran talks about the ritualistic *salaat*, but does not provide in detail what to say, or how to do it, except for the timings, the numbers and to stand, bow, and prostrate (*salaat* details are included in chapter five). This has been used by proponents of *hadith* to endorse the *ahadith* and declare that it is needed and is incumbent upon us to follow it, otherwise how can we know what to say and how to say the *salaat*. They assert that Allah says to follow Muhammad's example *sunnah*, and the only way of this is through the *hadith*. But the Quran also addresses Muhammad and says to follow the *sunnah* of Abraham "*And afterward We inspired thee (Muhammad, saying): Follow the millat* (ways, written law) *of Abraham, as one by nature upright. He was not of the idolaters*" (Quran 16:123). Shouldn't we then be following the *sunah/hadith* of Abraham?

As far as *salaat* goes, it has existed from the time of Abraham. The Quran states that "*Abraham was not a Jew, nor yet a Christian; but he was an upright man who was a Muslim, and he was not of the idolaters*" (3:67), and thus, *salaat* has nothing to do with the *sunnah* of Muhammad.

Furthermore, where the Quran states that "*Verily in the messenger of Allah ye have a good example*" (33:21), It also states the same for Abraham: "*There is for you an excellent example (to follow) in Abraham and those with him.*" (60:4). Even the Quran mentions Abraham's companions in a positive light: "*There was indeed in them an excellent example for you to follow*" (60:6).

To pluck out words from the Quran to suit our purpose disrupts the whole thematic structure of it. Not only does it make the Quran senseless, but it also puts our words into the mouth of God.

On the other hand, when it comes to obedience, the Quran never stated that the '*hadith*' of the Prophet is to be obeyed. It says to "*obey Allah and the messenger*" (Quran 3:32) but it does not say to obey the messenger's hadith that goes against the Quran. This verse has been greatly abused and taken out of context to mean that the Quran itself endorses the following of the *hadith* of the Prophet. Quran stated in strong words that had the Prophet uttered words apart from the Quran God would have severed his life: /*"It is a revelation from the Lord of the Worlds. And if he had invented false sayings concerning Us, We assuredly had taken him by the right hand, and then severed his life-artery, and not one of you could have held Us off from him. Lo! it is a warrant unto those who ward off (evil)."* (Quran 69:43-48). When we are already not sure whether the a*hadith* attributed to the Prophet were his actual words or not, what further merit can we attach to them and the relevancy with this verse?

Moreover, the verses 16:44 below have also been exploited to approve the *hadith* collections attributed to Muhammad:

"*With clear proofs and writings; and We have revealed unto thee* **the Remembrance** *that* **thou mayst (explain, clear, proclaim) to mankind that which hath been revealed for them**, *and that haply they may reflect"* (Quran 16:44).

The *hadithists* claim that God Itself asks Muhammad to explain Its book, and the only way Muhammad could explain the Quran was through his *hadith*. Hence, one must obey the *ahadith* and apply it in their daily lives. Under the thematic "*nazm*" (coherence)[26] of the Quran, the only possible way to cohere this verse is to look into the whole verse itself. The complete verse is speaking about the message of "remembrance". It can therefore be concluded that it is the application of the message of the Quran, and nothing outside It's realm that the Prophet was to administer. Further, what shall we make of the verse 77:50 where the Quran strikes a questions that *"In what hadith* (statement), *after this* (i.e Quran), *will they believe?"*

Hadithists also claim that the only way to obtain the biography of the Prophet is through the *hadith* literature. For me it is very astounding to accept the biography from a source that both elevates and praises the Prophet, while at the same time attaches abominable vulgarities of character to his sanctity. As William Muir in his book *Life of Mohamet* contends that, "the Quran alone represents a reliable source for Muhammad's biography".[27] Do we still need other sources when the biography is more superbly and respectfully represented by the very Quran for which the messenger Muhammad came?

All of the above arguments become pointless when we consider only one question: How can we prove that the *ahadith* are Muhammad's actual spoken words and not words put in his mouth?

With much resentment and a heavy heart, I would like to quote a few very disturbing *sahih ahadith*, which are considered canonical and reliable. They are from the canonical Bukhari collection but are entirely against the spirit and direct command of the Quran. All of these *ahadith* are attributed to the Prophet but they are unsubstantiated by the Quran. They are nonsensical, they are degrading to women, disregarding to animals, undignified, and sexually vulgar and repugnant. I believe the following *ahadith* are a deep blotch on the sanctified character of Prophet Muhammad. Quran speaks volumes of Prophet's reputable, respectful character and personality, verse 68:4 of the Quran states *"You are blessed with a great moral character"*, yet the *ahadith* instead do otherwise. Such *ahadith* actually portrays the Prophet as nothing but as a concupiscent person. Going in favour of these *ahadith* would go in direct opposition to the Quran. Yet, there are many who blindly defend every single *ahadith* attributed to the Prophet, and that the denial of even one *hadith* may instantly label one a *kafir* (unbeliever).

SOME DETESTABLE CANONICAL *AHADITH* FROM THE SAHIH-AL-BUKHARI

NARRATIONS WITH EXPLICIT SEXUAL DETAILS:

1. *"The Prophet said, "When a man sits in between the four parts of a woman and did the sexual intercourse with her, bath becomes compulsory."* [28] (narrated by Abu Hurayra)

2. *"The Prophet used to visit all his wives in a round, during the day and night and they were eleven in number." I asked Anas, "Had the Prophet the strength for it?" Anas replied, "We used to say that the Prophet was given the strength of thirty (men)."* [29] (narrated by Qatada: Anas bin Malik narration)

3. *". . . 'Aisha said: "I scented Allah's Apostle and he went round (had sexual intercourse with) all his wives, and in the morning he was Muhrim."* [30] (narrated by Muhammad bin Al-Muntathir)

4. *"The Prophet used to visit all his wives in one night and he had nine wives at that time."* [31] (narrated by Anas bin Malik)

5. *"I asked Allah's Apostle about a man who engages in sexual intercourse with his wife but does not discharge. He replied, "He should wash the parts which comes in contact with the private parts of the woman, perform ablution and then pray."* [32] (narrated by Ubai bin Ka'b)

6. *"My father and I went to 'Aisha and she said, "I testify that Allah's Apostle at times used to get up in the morning in a state of Janaba from sexual intercourse, not from a wet dream and then he would fast that day."* (without bathing?!) *Then he went to Um Salama and she also narrated a similar thing."* [33] (bracket is mine) (narrated by Abu Bakr bin 'Abdur-Rahman)

The Prophet which the Quran claims has a great moral character had nothing better to do but have sex all night and talk in explicit details about it?! Also, when the Quran clearly commands to bathe after intercourse (verse 4:43), how can the last couple *ahadith* command otherwise?

NARRATION THAT DENIGRATE OTHER PROPHETS:

Many *ahadith* such as the one below, do not hesitate from putting a blemish on the past Prophets, reducing them to those having nothing better to do than be sexually inclined. Whereas, according to the Quranic portrayal, they all were of a high moral character and integrity. Here I would like to add that Bible interpretations have also disgraced the Prophet such as one of the high esteemed Prophets Lot has been portrayed to have had intercourse with his own daughters[*]

"Allah's Apostle said, "Once Solomon, son of David said, '(By Allah) Tonight I will have sexual intercourse with one hundred (or ninety-nine) women each of whom will give birth to a knight who will fight in Allah's Cause.' On that (i.e. if Allah wills) but he did not say, 'Allah willing.' Therefore only one of those women conceived and gave birth to a half-man. By Him in Whose Hands Muhammad's life is, if he had said, "Allah willing', (he would have begotten sons) all of whom

---

[*]   And the firstborn said unto the younger, Our father is old, and there is not a man in the earth to come in unto us after the manner of all the earth: Come, let us make our father drink wine, and we will lie with him, that we may preserve seed of our father. And they made their father drink wine that night: and the firstborn went in, and lay with her father; and he perceived not when she lay down, nor when she arose. And it came to pass on the morrow, that the firstborn said unto the younger, Behold, I lay yester night with my father: let us make him drink wine this night also; and go thou in, and lie with him, that we may preserve seed of our Father. And they made their father drink wine that night also: and the younger arose, and lay with him; and he perceived not when she lay down, nor when she arose. Thus were both the daughters of Lot with child by their father (Genesis 19:31-36)[α]

would have been knights striving in Allah's cause." [34] (narrated Abu Hurayra)

NARRATIONS THAT ARE PREPOSTEROUS AND NONSENSICAL:

Notice the irrationality and ludicrousness of the following two narrations. This is from a *sahih hadith* which has passed through the rigorous measurement of sifting the *ahadith* (as previously discussed), and incorporated into the canonical collection!

1. *"During the pre-Islamic period of ignorance I saw a she-monkey surrounded by a number of monkeys. They were all stoning it, because it had committed illegal sexual intercourse. I too, stoned it along with them."* [35] (narrated by 'Amr bin Maimun)

2. *"Jews used to say: If one has sexual intercourse with his wife from the back, then she will deliver a squint-eyed child." So this verse was revealed:—"Your wives are a tilth unto you; so go to your tilth when or how you will." (Quran 2.223)."* [36] (narrated by Jabir). It is contemptible how they have interpreted the verse.

4. *"Allah's Apostle said, "When the adhan is pronounced satan takes to his heels and passes wind with noise (farting) during his flight."*[37] (narrated Abu Huraira). And this is a canonical *hadith?!*

NARRATIONS THAT ARE MISOGYNISTIC:

I have written below only two, but the Bukhari collection is filled with misogynistic *ahadith* ascribed to the Prophet, such as: women are evil temptresses, bad omen (these passages though from the Bible); all such negations are associated with women. In contrast, the Quran has upheld women's personas to a level that no religion or tradition has previously matched it (Please see chapter six).

1. *"Once Allah's Apostle went out to the Musalla (to offer the prayer) of 'Id-al-Adha or Al-Fitr prayer. Then he passed by the women and said, "O women! Give alms, as I have seen that the majority of the dwellers of Hell-fire were you (women)." They asked, "Why is it so, O Allah's Apostle?" He replied, "You curse frequently and are ungrateful to your husbands. I have not seen anyone more deficient in intelligence and religion than you. A cautious sensible man could be led astray by some of you." The women asked, "O Allah's Apostle! What is deficient in our intelligence and religion?" He said, "Is not the evidence of two women equal to the witness of one man?" They replied in the affirmative. He said, "This is the deficiency in her intelligence. Isn't it true that a woman can neither pray nor fast during her menses?" The women replied in the affirmative. He said, "This is the deficiency in her religion."* [38] (narrated Abu Said Al-Khudri)

2. *"The Prophet said: "I was shown the hell-fire and that the majority of its dwellers were women who were ungrateful." It was asked, "Do they disbelieve in Allah?" (or are they ungrateful to Allah?) He replied, "They are ungrateful to their husbands and are ungrateful for the favors and the good (charitable deeds) done to them. If you have always been good (benevolent) to one of them and then she sees something in you (not of her liking), she will say, 'I have never received any good from you."* [39] (narrated by Ibn 'Abbas)

NARRATIONS THAT FOULED AND DISGRACED THE ANIMALS:

The following two narrations are against the very verses of the Quran. The Quran never stated in its verses any animal being of any disadvantage to humans, or for religious matter forbidden in any way. Dogs are one of the great blessings to humankind—they guard ones home, and are protective and loyal to their master. Dogs are the very eyes of the blind, yet we Muslims have attributed foulness to dogs and call them *Haram* (forbidden). Contrary to this view, there is even a verse in the Quran that states to eat the food which the trained dog catches (Quran 5:4). This is further discussed in Chapter 4 under "Haram and Halal Issues" (please see 'Dogs' section for details in chapter 4).

Please note, on the other hand, I do not mean to state that the dogs or any animal are so purified or clean as to be sleeping with you, but they must be treated as all other animals: with love, care and dignity. When God speaks with dignity about Its animals, who are we to speak about them or treat them otherwise?

"Allah's Apostle said, "Whoever keeps a dog, one qirat of the reward of his good deeds is deducted daily, unless the dog is used for guarding a farm or cattle." [40] (narrated by Abu Hurayra)

Could it be that since Abu Hurayra hated dogs and loved cats, he incorporated such *ahadith* that would make dogs *haram* and cats *halaal*? Jewish community also to-date hate dogs and Abu Hurayra was once a Jewish. Since childhood, I have heard how cats were loved by Muhammad that if a cat slept on his prayer rug, he wouldn't disturb it, but instead cut a portion of the rug to say his prayers on. And so, we were encouraged to love and care for cats.

The Prophet said, "Angels do not enter a house which has either a dog or a picture in it. [41] (narrated Abu Talha)

This above hadith appears very irrational and contradictory to what Quran reveals in verse 18:18, referring to the story of cave people "*. . . and We caused them to turn over to the right and the left, and their dog stretching out his paws on the threshold.*" When there appears to be the Divine presence Itself despite the presence of dog in the cave, it is absurd to consider angels not entering ones house.

NARRATION THAT IS REPUGNANT:

"Some people of 'Ukl or 'Uraina tribe came to Medina and its climate did not suit them. So the Prophet ordered them to go to the herd of (Milch) camels and to drink their milk and urine (as a medicine) . . ." [42] (narrated by Abu Qilaba)

When the very thought of drinking urine is so nauseating and abominable to a common person, the notion that a man with the stature and repute of Muhammad would go to the length of suggesting such, is highly unthinkable.

NARRATION THAT IS CALLOUS, SAVAGE AND UNJUST:

Finally, notice the callous and torturous approach in the following *hadith* from the Book of Abu-Dawud. Below is the whole *hadith*. This and many such *ahadith* are perhaps the precedent for the crude *Shariah* laws, despite the fact that the Quran never advocated or endorsed any such rulings. It is unimaginable for an ordinary person to do or accept such horrendous acts. Should we still assign this to the high stature of Muhammad?

"A blind man had a slave-mother who used to abuse the Prophet (peace_be_upon_him) and disparage him. He forbade her but she did not stop. He rebuked her but she did not give up her habit. One night she began to slander the Prophet (peace_be_upon_him) and abuse him. So he took a dagger, placed it on her belly, pressed it, and killed her. A child who came between her legs was smeared with the blood that was there. When the morning came, the Prophet (peace_be_upon_him) was informed about it.

He assembled the people and said: I adjure by Allah the man who has done this action and I adjure him by my right to him that he should stand up. Jumping over the necks of the people and trembling the man stood up.

He sat before the Prophet (peace_be_upon_him) and said: Apostle of Allah! I am her master; she used to abuse you and disparage you. I forbade her, but she did not stop, and I rebuked her, but she did not abandon her habit. I have two sons like pearls from her, and she was my companion. Last night she began to abuse and disparaged you. So I took a dagger, put it on her belly and pressed it till I killed her". [and the baby?!] *Thereupon the Prophet (peace_be_upon_him) said:* **Oh be witness, no retaliation is payable for her blood."** [43] (Narrated by Abdullah Ibn Abbas) (Square bracket is mine)

With much dismay, I leave this chapter for my readers to ponder.

[α]   University of Michigan Digital Library. *Holy Bible, King James Version,* Deuteronomy 22:20-21. Date accessed: November6, 2012. http://quod. lib.umich.edu/k/kjv/browse.html

NOTES:

1.   Rahim, Sir Abdur. *Principles of Mohammadan Jurisprudence.* Karachi Pakistan: Mansoor Book House, 1911, p. 16

2.   Ibid., pp.15-16

3.   Ibid., p. 15

4.   Ibid., p. 24

5.   Armstrong, Karen. *Islam, A Short History.* London: The Orion Publishing Group, 2000, pp. 41-77, 120, 133, 134

      Brown, Daniel. *Rethinking Tradition in Modern Islamic Thought.* Cambridge Middle East Study (For Students). Cambridge: Cambridge University Press, 1996, p. 96

6.   Rahim, Sir Abdur. *Principles of Mohammadan Jurisprudence.* Karachi Pakistan: Mansoor Book House, 1911, p. 24

7.   Brown, Daniel. *Rethinking Tradition in Modern Islamic Thought.* Cambridge Middle East Study (For Students). Cambridge: Cambridge University Press, 1996, pp. 6-80

In his book *Rethinking Tradition In Modern Islamic Thought,* Daniel Brown discusses in detail the classical concepts of prophetic authority and its modern challenges, and how *ijtihad* and many other factors have played roles in the shaping of the traditional Islam that we see today.

8. Ibid., pp. 27-42

9. Ibid., p. 18

10. Ibid., pp. 133, 165

11. Ibid., 18

12. Staff Writer. "Amina Laval's Death Sentence Quashed at Last". *Afrol News*, September 25th 2003. Date accessed: February 8, 2010. http://www.afrol.com/articles/10527

13. Khan, M. Muhsin (translation). "Translation of Sahih-Al-Bukhari". Los Angeles: Center for Muslim Jewish Engagement, University of Southern California. Volume 8, Book 78 and 82, Number 629 and 815; Volume 8, Book 82, Number 806; see also number 804, 816-17. Date accessed: February 8, 2010 http://www.usc.edu/dept/MSA/fundamentals/hadithsunnah/bukhari

    Date Accessed: October 20, 2012. http://www.usc.edu/org/cmje/religious-texts/hadith/bukhari/

    Volume 8, Book 78 and 82, Number 629 and 815: Narrated Abu Huraira and Zaid bin Khalid:

    Two men had a dispute in the presence of Allah's Apostle. One of them said, "O Allah's Apostle! Judge between us according to Allah's Laws." The other who was wiser, said, "Yes, O Allah's Apostle! Judge between us according to Allah's Laws and allow me to speak. The Prophet said, "Speak." He said, "My son was a laborer serving this (person) and he committed illegal sexual intercourse with his wife, The people said that my son is to be stoned to death, but I ransomed him with one-hundred sheep and a slave girl. Then I asked the learned people, who informed me that my son should receive one hundred lashes and will be exiled for one year, and stoning will be the lot for the man's wife." Allah's Apostle said, "Indeed, by Him in Whose Hand my soul is, I will judge between you according to Allah's Laws: As for your sheep and slave girl, they are to be returned to you." Then he scourged his son one hundred lashes and exiled him for one year. Then Unais Al-Aslami was ordered to go to the wife of the second man, and if she confessed (the crime), then stone her to death. She did confess, so he stoned her to death.

Volume 8, Book 82, Number 806: Narrated Abu Huraira:

A man came to Allah's Apostle while he was in the mosque, and he called him, saying, "O Allah's Apostle! I have committed illegal sexual intercourse.'" The Prophet turned his face to the other side, but that man repeated his statement four times, and after he bore witness against himself four times, the Prophet called him, saying, "Are you mad?" The man said, "No." The Prophet said, "Are you married?" The man said, "Yes." Then the Prophet said, 'Take him away and stone him to death." Jabir bin 'Abdullah said: I was among the ones who participated in stoning him and we stoned him at the Musalla. When the stones troubled him, he fled, but we over took him at Al-Harra and stoned him to death.

14. University of Michigan Digital Library. *Holy Bible, King James Version,* Deuteronomy 22:20-21. Date accessed: October 3, 2010. http://quod.lib.umich.edu/k/kjv/browse.html

15. Khan, M. Muhsin (translation). "Translation of Sahih-Al-Bukhari". Los Angeles: Center for Muslim Jewish Engagement, University of Southern California. Volume 9, Book 83 and 84, Number 17 and 57. Date Accessed: July 31, 2010. http://www.usc.edu/dept/MSA/fundamentals/hadithsunnah/bukhari

    Date Accessed: October 20, 2012. http://www.usc.edu/org/cmje/religious-texts/hadith/bukhari/

16. Brown, Daniel. *Rethinking Tradition in Modern Islamic Thought.* Cambridge Middle East Study (For Students). Cambridge: Cambridge University Press, 1996, pp. 108-110

17. Ibid., pp. 81-83, 110

18. Ibid., pp. 87-8, 96, 112-116

19. Ibid., pp. 96, 112-116

20. Ibid., p. 95

21. Schimmel, Annemarie. *My Soul is a Woman: The Feminine Islam*. New York: The Continuum Publishing Company, 1999, pp. 19-37

22. Ibid., pp. 10-13

23. Brown, Daniel. *Rethinking Tradition in Modern Islamic Thought*. Cambridge Middle East Study (For Students). Cambridge: Cambridge University Press, 1996, p. 86

24. Ibid., p. 95

25. Ibid., p. 86

26. I borrowed the word "*nazm*" from:

    Barlas, Asma. *Believing Women in Islam: Unreading Patriarchal Interpretations of the Qur'an*. Austin: University of Texas Press, 2002, p. 8

27. Brown, Daniel. *Rethinking Tradition in Modern Islamic Thought*. Cambridge: Cambridge Middle East Study (for Students). Cambridge University Press, 1996, p. 35

28. Khan, M. Muhsin (translation). "Translation of Sahih-Al-Bukhari". Los Angeles: Center for Muslim Jewish Engagement, University of Southern California. Book 5 (Bathing), Volume 1, Number 290. Date accessed: February 13, 2010. http://www.usc.edu/dept/MSA/fundamentals/hadithsunnah/bukhari

    Date Accessed: October 20, 2012. http://www.usc.edu/org/cmje/religious-texts/hadith/bukhari/

29. Ibid., Number 268

30. Ibid., Number 270

31. Ibid., Number 282

32. Ibid., Number 292

33. Ibid., Book 31 (Fasting), volume 3, Number 153

34. Ibid., Book 52 (Jehad), Volume 4, Number 74i

35. Ibid., Book 58 (Merits of the Helper in Medinah—Ansaar), Volume 5, Number 188

36. Ibid., Book 60 (Prophetic Commentary on the Quran—Tafseer of the Prophet), Volume 6, Number 51

37. Ibid., Book 11 (Call to Prayers "Adhaan"), Volume 1, Number 582

38. Ibid., Book 6 (Menstrual Periods), Volume 1, Number 301

39. Ibid., Book 2 (Belief), Volume 1, Number 28

40. Ibid., Book 39 (Agriculture), Volume 3, Number 515

41. Ibid., Book 54 (Beginning of Creation), Volume 4, Number 448

42. Ibid., Book 4 (Ablution "Wudu"), Volume 1, Number 234

43. Hasan, Professor Ahmed (translation). "Introduction to Partial Translation of Sunan Abu-Dawud". Los Angeles: Center for Muslim Jewish Engagement. University of Southern California. Book 38 (Prescribed Punishments "Kitab-al-Hudud"), number 4348. Date accessed: February 15, 2010. http://www.usc.edu/schools/college/crcc/engagement/resources/texts/muslim/hadith/abudawud/

    Date Accessed: October 20, 2012. http://www.usc.edu/org/cmje/religious-texts/hadith/abudawud/

CHAPTER FOUR

ISLAM AND ITS ISSUES ﻦ

Before I touch on the issues of Islam, I would like to offer an explanation for those readers who may not know what the words "Islam" and "Muslim" mean. The term "Islam" means "submission to the will of God", and is referred to in the Quran as the faith of Prophet Abraham. The term "Muslim" means "the one who submits or abides by the law of God", and it was also the name given by the Prophet Abraham as per the Quran. Both of these terms are mentioned in the Quran, and were not coined by followers of a religion.

*"This day have I perfected your religion for you, completed My favour upon you, and **have chosen for you Islam as your religion**"* (Quran 5:3).

*"And strive for Allah with the endeavour which is His right. He hath chosen you and hath not laid upon you in religion any hardship; **the faith of your father Abraham** (is yours). **He hath named you Muslims of old time and in this** (Scripture), that the messenger may be a witness against you, and that ye may be witnesses against*

mankind. So establish worship, pay the poor-due, and hold fast to Allah. He is your Protecting friend. A blessed Patron and a blessed Helper!" (Quran 22:78).

As per Quran, Islam is not the religion of Muhammad although many claim that it is. It was there from the beginning, just as were Christianity and Judaism—all are but offshoots of one religion:

"And afterward We inspired thee (Muhammad, saying): **Follow the religion of Abraham**, *as one by nature upright. He was not of the idolaters" (Quran 16:123).*

"He hath ordained for you that religion which He commended unto Noah, and that which We inspire in thee (Muhammad), and that which We commended unto Abraham and Moses and Jesus, saying: Establish the religion, and be not divided therein." (Quran 42:13).

ISSUE OF ALLAH AS GOD

Few "People of the Book" (as the Quran addresses mainly Jewish people and Christians—*ehlal-kitaab*) have made it a big issue that Allah is not the same God as the God of Ibrahiem (Abraham). They say Allah was a pagan deity whom the pagans used to worship; this is a failed attempt to discredit Islam and prove that Muhammad was an impostor. They don't see the fact that by doing this they are discrediting themselves too, each one striving to be superior to the other and to be the upholder of the truth. Following this, all of the hegemony may lead to nothing but the very death of God!

This trivial issue and many such others remind me again of the childhood story *Gulliver's Travels*. In this story, there are two countries, Liliput and Blefuscu, which were for many years constantly waging war on each other. The reason for the war was "whether to break the egg from the narrow side or the wide". One believed the first and the other the latter, a beautiful satire that fits into every era.

So, perhaps Allah was a Pagan deity. When we look into the meaning of *Al-lah* we see that it means "The God" or as the pagans perceived it "The High God". [1] It could be that Muhammad wanted to bring all of the communities together to worship only one God who does not have any shape, form, or gender. When the nucleus of the concept is to believe and worship only one God, what difference does the name we call this ONE God make? This High God can be Allah, Bhagwaan, God, Buddha, or whatever name we give, it does not change *the* Creator when we all believe in only one!

On the other hand, history tells us that the Arabs had forgotten Abraham and his religion, but believed that there is a high God.[2] We see the name of Allah pronounced in many different ways in both Judaism and Christianity, such as "Eloha" or "Yahweh" (in Arabic: *El-hoa*—the one who is. *Ya-hoa—oh who is*). This to me seems to reminiscently echo the same God as that of Abraham. As a comparison, I call "butter" in my language "*makhan*". Does this change of name in any way change the form of butter into something else?

JEHAD ISSUE

Jehad is the most distorted word associated with Islam. When we try to rule out God's disclosure in favour of our own, we ultimately witness our own cataclysm. There must be God's wisdom as always to choose a term such as *jehad* best suited for the purpose. I cannot say much better than what Karen Armstrong has written in her book *Muhammad*: [3]

> The Quran began to urge the Muslims of Madina to participate in a Jihad. This would involve fighting and bloodshed, but the root JHD implies more than a 'holy war'. It signifies a physical, moral, spiritual and intellectual effort. There are plenty of Arabic words denoting armed combat, such as harb (war), sira'a (combat), ma'araka (battle) or qital (killing), which the Quran could easily have used if war had been the Muslims' principle way of engaging in this effort. Instead it chooses a vaguer, richer word with a wide range of connotations. The jihad is not one of the five pillars of Islam. It is not the central prop

of the religion, despite the common Western view. But it was and remains a duty for Muslims to commit themselves to a struggle on all fronts—moral, spiritual and political—to create a just and decent society, where the poor and vulnerable are not exploited, in the way that God had intended man to live. Fighting and warfare might sometimes be necessary, but it is only a minor part of the whole jihad or struggle. A well-known tradition (hadith) has Muhammad say on returning from a battle, 'We return from the little jihad to the greater jihad,' the more difficult and crucial effort to conquer the forces of evil in oneself and in one's own society in all the details of daily life.

Yet Muslims are constantly waging wars against the supposed infidels, and killing the innocent. Some cults are training young minds as "God Soldiers" and suicide bombers, who then believe that the innocent victims of their suicide attack, will directly go to paradise, and thus they are not doing wrong to anyone. These cults are also indoctrinating people to lead them to believe that they are the sacrosanct, and as such there awaits for them in heaven voluptuous female *hoors* (discussed further in chapter six). Ironically, As Irshad Manji mentioned in her book *The Trouble with Islam*, there was once a time when there were 70,000 libraries in Cordova; now it is the parallelism of 70,000 *hoors* in the paradise. [4]

To wage war in a literal sense is only mentioned in the Quran specifically to fight in defence or oppression (Quran 4:75). Even in that case, if the opposing party offers peace, Muslims are not allowed to continue the fight against them. If non-Muslims were to be killed regardless of this, there wouldn't have been the following verses:

Allah forbiddeth you not those who warred not against you on account of religion and drove you not out from your homes, that ye should show them kindness and deal justly with them. Lo! Allah loveth the just dealers. Allah forbiddeth you only those who warred against you on account of religion and have driven you out from your homes and helped to drive you out, that ye make friends of them. Whosoever maketh friends of them—(All) such are wrong-doers (Quran 60:8-9)

81

So, if they hold aloof from you and wage not war against you and offer you peace, Allah alloweth you no way against them". (Quran 4:90)

These Muslim cults have also devised various killing methods including suicide attacks, many of these orchestrated by training children to become the perpetrators. Just one example of this is a suicide-bomb attack in October 2009 in Pakistan where a 13 year-old boy flung himself at a military convoy in the Sawat Valley, killing himself and 41 people.[5] Events like this occur, despite the emphasis in the Quran on the preservation of life: /*"whoever killeth a human being for other than manslaughter or corruption in the earth, it shall be as if he had killed all humankind, and whoso saveth the life of one, it shall be as if he had saved the life of all humankind"* (Quran 5:32). Yet, suicide attacks have become rampant.

If war, battles, killing, blood shedding vengeance, etc were the main crux of jehad and pillar of Islam then we must also find life of Mohammad filled with bloodshed and war and as "*the*" emphasis of his life, but it is otherwise: He only spent less than two months altogether in wars in all his 25 long years in Islam. (See appendix B for detail dates and duration of the battles)

ISSUE OF SHAHADAH (witness)

Is the *shahadah* "There is no God but Allah", or is it "There is no God but Allah and Muhammad is God's messenger"?

I was born and raised with the recitation of the latter statement above. Now, one may see varied schools of thought: some may prefer the first and some the latter.

Those who prefer the first, present the argument that the Quran itself states only the first *shahadah* and not the latter. They say that by adding Muhammad's name we are making distinction among the messengers of Allah. To support their claim, they quote these verses:

*But those who believe in Allah and His messengers **and make no distinction between any of them**, unto them Allah will give their wages; and Allah was ever Forgiving, Merciful* (Quran 4:152),

*The messenger believeth in that which hath been revealed unto him from his Lord and (so do) believers. Each one believeth in Allah and His angels and His scriptures and His messengers—**We make no distinction between any of His messengers**—and they say: We hear, and we obey. (Grant us) Thy forgiveness, our Lord. Unto Thee is the journeying.* (Quran 2:285).

Though I agree with them, I do not find myself accepting this view completely. I will give two reasons:

Firstly, the Quran in one of its verses states that *"**Muhammad is the messenger of Allah**"* (48:29). When Allah has Itself mentioned "Muhammad is the messenger of God", I don't see any harm in adding that to the first *shahadah*. But by doing so, are we making a distinction here? I don't think so, unless we start elevating him over other Prophets and make him an infallible miraculous man.

Secondly, I have written in the first chapter that "belief in a God is an abstract thought". We live in a world of matter; we are a part of matter. When Muhammad preached about one God, just as the previous messengers had done, he was grounding the religio-historical background for the Quran, just as the previous Prophets have. When we erase the name of Muhammad completely from this history and make him serve as a postman whose only job was to deliver the message, we are jeopardizing the very existence of God's future. This to me is evil. Generations later, people may forget Muhammad, and they may look at the Quran and ask "why do we need to follow this book for guidance?" "Where did it come from?" Thus, they may say that "we know how to live our lives, we don't need this Quran, we are our own God" This is as Karen Armstrong foresees "The death of God".[6]

I therefore believe that we need to acknowledge Muhammad in order to be able to acknowledge the Quran and ground it within human history.

MUHAMMAD

STATUS OF MUHAMMAD

Having discussed the *shahadah*, we come to the next issue where we have to ask what we mean by acknowledging Muhammad.

Some people regard acknowledging Muhammad the same as considering him as one of the greatest Prophets. Yet, most of these people take a leap forward and believe that acknowledging Muhammad means regarding him as being on the level of God, or as a partner of God. It may sound very bizarre to a Muslim to think that any Muslim in his or her right mind would ever consider Muhammad as such.

The truth of the matter is that, we do. We are no better than any "people of the book"*. The difference is that the Christians publicly deify Jesus as Lord or God and come to worship Jesus, and ask only Jesus for help rather than God, while Muslims do it unobtrusively. In truth, we are worse than Christians in this respect, for not only do we deify Muhammad but also the priest and the companions of the Prophet. Otherwise, we wouldn't see priests, *pirs* (saints) or *wali's Dargahs* (monuments) and shrines. We wouldn't have been performing pilgrimages toward their monuments. We wouldn't have had songs in praise of Muhammad and others when God strongly states many times in the Quran that: "***All remembrance and praise is for Allah alone!'*** (22:64, 64:01 and many others).

It may still be argued that it is mere homage that we pay to Muhammad and the others, and nothing more. I wish it was that simple to identify. The question is, if Muhammad is not to

---

*   Christians and the Jewish people as per Quran because they are considered to have received the holy books too with the same message, hence the meaning of Quran—a Reminder (of the previous).

be worshipped, how did we come to worship him and others? There are two explanations:

One—During the time of Muhammad and following him, Islam had a magical influence on people because of its simplicity, fairness, rationalism, and also its harmony with science. People from every walk of life and religion were welcome to become a part of it. They found that in Islam, they could have direct contact with God. There was no concept of priesthood in Islam. They learned that they did not need a Priest or a Rabbi to connect them or to communicate between them and God. [7]

This influence was huge, and when Islam was at its peak during the 6th to the 10th centuries CE spreading far and wide, the converts were increasing. But, the problem was that people were not only accepting Islam as their path, they were also bringing along baggage of past practices which they had been used to engaging in before. Thus, those who worshipped many idols or those who had been performing many rituals or even those who humanized God were eventually finding Islam to be too boring and simple. Therefore, they gradually tried to accommodate their past practices into Islam one way or the other. This phenomenon is one of the reasons that we see so many innovative rituals and the worshipping of Muhammad and others. Islam therefore became reduced to nothing but a man-made Islam.

Two-There were also hypocrites in the Muslim community whose sole mission was politically oriented. There was the birth of *mullahism* (priesthood) and *pirs* (saints), many of whom were placed in their positions for political reasons only and were provided handsome salaries. So if Muhammad is elevated to the level of God, it becomes much easier to form words and put them in his mouth—and make it sacrosanct—hence the birth of *hadith. Pirs* and *mullahs* simply were the tools to achieve this end. Muhammad needed to be worshipped if not religiously then politically. This was done so they could dictate what "they" wanted and to have control over the masses, the same way as the Ummayad and the Abbasid dynasties did—a tradition that even continues today.[8] There were no religious influences in this whatsoever. All they were doing was playing with the psyche and emotions of easily influenced and poor people, whose weakest and most vulnerable point is religion. Religion often provides this class the hope they need in order to carry on with their lives when in despair. Carl Marx said, "religion is the opiate for the masses", it very well may be defined as such. The intoxication that religion bestows on the masses is such that helps one forget the uncertainties and hopelessness of life. This reminds me of the thoughts of the former member of the parliament of England, Tony Benn, who in an interview for Michael Moore's documentary movie *Sickos* gave reasons why people are so hopeless and pessimistic:

> Choice depends on the freedom to choose and if you are shackled in debt, you don't have a freedom to choose . . . When people are in debt they become hopeless and hopeless people don't vote . . . There are two ways in which people are controlled: first of all, frighten people and secondly demoralize them. An educated, healthy and confidant nation is hard to govern. And I think there is this element in the thinking of some people. We don't want people to be educated, healthy and confidant, because, they would get out of control. The top one percent of the world population owns eighty percent of the world's wealth. It is incredible how people put up with it—but they are poor, they are demoralized, they are frightened and therefore, they think perhaps the safest thing to do is to take orders and hope for the best.

Perhaps this is the reason why priests did not allow the public access to the Bible. Likewise the *Mullahs* and the *Pirs* eventually became themselves the guardians of the Quran. If a common Muslim wishes to read the Quran, he or she must only read the Arabic, and there is no need for understanding it. The guardians are there to explain the understanding. They put words into the mouth of God through Muhammad and dictate. Who can then dare to defy them?

Thus, Islam became a *mazhab* from a *deen* (i.e. a 'religion' from a 'way of life'). And just like other religions had been exploited and shrank to a religion of terror and oppression, so did Islam. Considering this, it is no wonder why the Muslim countries throughout the world are the least educated and among the highest in the corruption index.[9]

IS MUHAMMAD TO BE PRAISED AND SALUTED?

Since childhood, we were stressed the importance of praising Muhammad: sending greetings to him and saluting him including in the five daily prayers. It was forbidden to take Muhammad's name with an impure mouth or if one was "not clean" (what that means is still unclear to me). From an early age, I questioned why I could take the name of God anywhere, anytime even in a bathroom and in whatever clean or unclean state of hygiene I am but I cannot take Muhammad or other saints' name? Even then, my tiny mind could not logically fit anyone into being equal to the Creator or apparently supersede the Creator.

Below, I have made effort to illustrate how language has been appropriated to suit the needs of those who believe that Muhammad is to be praised. (But before we venture into that we must find the correct meaning of 'praise' as mentioned many times in the Quran. For this please read *tasbih/ibaadat* under *salaat* in chapter 5):

Muslims in general believe that the Quran states to praise Muhammad, that is, to send *darood* blessings to him and greetings or salutation to him. This has been accomplished by not only parroting specific words, but also by its incorporation into the basic five daily prayers. This assertion to praise Muhammad comes from a specific verse: /*"Lo! Allah and His angels shower blessings (u-salloona)* **on the Prophet.** *O ye who believe! Ask blessings (sallu) on him and salute (sallaymoo) him with a worthy salutation (tasleema)"* (Quran 33:56). But then God also mentions the same for everyone: *"He it is who sends blessings (u-sallee) on you, as do His angels"* (Quran 33:43).

I therefore don't see any need to praise or salute Muhammad in particular, when the same is encouraged for any ordinary person. Besides, translation of verse 33:56 as above tends to elevate the Prophet over other Prophets, and therefore it comes in direct violation of the verse where the Quran states to "make no distinction" among God's Prophets (4:152, 2:136, 3:84, 2:285). Even more so, it comes into the direct breach of the basic fact of *tawhid* oneness of God. When we praise and salute Muhammad, it equates to him being on the same level as God. The Quran, on the other hand, clearly states that all praise is only due for God:

> "*Unto Him belongeth all that is in the skies and all that is in the earth. Lo! Allah, He verily is the **Absolute, the Owner** of Praise*" (Quran 22:64).

> "*Whatever is in the skies and whatever is in the earth declares the glory of Allah; to Him belongs the kingdom, and **to Him is due (all) praise**, and He has power over all things*" (Quran 64:01).

Another issue that makes the *darood* reading questionable or out of place is its inclusion in the five daily prayers—s*alaat*. Readings in the Quran reiterate that the ritualistic *salaat* prayer is only for God to be worshipped. Hence, inclusion of *darood* in the basic prayers to praise Muhammad would indicate that he is a partner in the realm of God.

Moreover, all of the Arabic as highlighted above in brackets which it is believed to suggest praise and salute for Muhammad is also mentioned in the following verses but translated very differently:

> "*But no, by the Lord, they can have no (real) Faith, until they make thee judge in all disputes between them, and find in their souls no resistance against Thy decisions, but **accept** (sallaymoo) them with the **fullest conviction** (tasleema)*" (Quran 4:65).

> "*And it only added to their faith and their zeal **in obedience** (tasleema)*" (Quran 33:22).

> "*and **pray** (sallee-alayh) on their behalf. Verily thy **prayers** (salawaat) are a source of security for them*" (Quran 9:103).

The literal meaning of *sallee-alayh* or *sallaymoo* which is derived from *salawaat* has several basic meanings: to respect, to pray, to encourage and support, to nurture or to follow, and to preserve, from the root *salaama*.[10] *Tasleema* means to follow, to help, to support[11] and also to salute or bend, as is evident in the verses 4:65 and 33:22.

The question is, why were these verses translated so differently to mean "to praise" or "salute", when the same Arabic is translated in other verses as "obedience" or "conviction"? With such varied meanings available and the language to dictate this is flexible, these words could have easily been translated to imply that we should respect and honour Muhammad and regard or accept him as the Prophet.

I wonder if it is because Jesus is praised and equated with God, so on some level Muhammad needs to be equally praised and elevated too. Since the Quran stresses the concept of *tawhid* "oneness" so strongly, the only way to legitimize Muhammad's elevation is by incorporating such meanings as in verse 33:56. Due to the varied meanings taken, when God Itself praises Muhammad and asks us to do the same, who are we then not to elevate him? Who can then dare contest such a claim, and choose any action but to submit?

The issues of praising Muhammad remind me of the occasion in Pakistan named "*meelad-un-nabi*", where we hymn the praise of Muhammad to commemorate his birth. It is interesting to note in this context that the date of birth and date of death of Muhammad is the same, the 12th *Rabi-ul-awwal* (third month in the Islamic calendar). Could it mean that it should neither be celebrated nor be mourned? I myself had participated with full conviction on many such gatherings and had been very vocal. Even I have sung such hymns where I am not only praising Muhammad but also asking him to help me and grant me my prayers, instead of asking God, exactly the way Christians do toward Jesus:

"Moojh dukhya ki dheer bandhaana, peyarae Muhammad chor na jaana.Matlab ki hay dunya saaree, kon soonae faryaad hamaaree, her ek bibta may kaam aana peyarae Muhammad chor na jaana".

(Oh please Muhammad support and help my poor self, oh my beloved Muhammad do not leave me alone. The world is full of meanness, there is no one to listen to my prayers, please help me in each and every problems of mine, oh my beloved Muhammad do not leave me alone.)

Does not all this amounts to *shirk?**

DID MUHAMMAD KNOW THE FUTURE?

We have a huge number of books suggesting that since Muhammad was a Prophet, he knew the future. Let us see what the main Criterion says about this assertion:

Say (O Muhammad, unto the disbelievers): **I know not whether that which ye are promised is nigh, or if my Lord hath set a distant term for it** (Quran 72:25).

*Say: I am no new thing among the messengers (of Allah***), nor know I what will be done with me or with you.*** I do but follow that which is inspired in me, and I am but a plain warner* (Quran 46:09).

Say: For myself I have no power to benefit, nor power to hurt, save that which Allah willeth. **Had I knowledge of the Unseen (future), I should have abundance of wealth, and adversity would not touch me***. I am but a warner, and a bearer of good tidings unto folk who believe* (Quran 7:188).

Say (O Muhammad, to the disbelievers): I say not unto you (that) I possess the treasures of Allah, **nor that I have knowledge of the Unseen (future); and I say not unto you: Lo! I am an angel.** *I follow only that which is inspired in me. Say: Are the blind man and the seer equal? Will ye not then take thought?* (Quran 6:50)

---

* Shirk means to set partner or equal to God. Polytheism was always there, the crux of the teaching of all Semitic religions was to instil the concept of one God and the worshipping of one God. Shirk therefore, is the only unforgivable sin in the Quran.

MIRACLES OF MUHAMMAD

Just as Muhammad didn't know the future, according to the Quran, he couldn't perform any miracles either: /*"They say: Why hath no portent (miracles) been sent down upon him from his Lord?* Say: Lo! Allah is Able to send down a portent (miracle). But most of them know not"* (Quran 6:37).

Despite this, we see in the *hadith* books and many other books, elaborate writings about the many miracles that Muhammad performed.

When Quran never supports the miracles attributed to Muhammad, then how did we come to believe that they occurred? I think one of the reasons is the fact that during the advent of Islam, Judaism and Christianity had already taken root. As many sources cite (including the Quran), the Prophets Moses and Jesus could perform many miracles. By comparison, here is Muhammad, claiming to be a Prophet in the same chain, but not able to perform any such miracles as the previous Prophets could. Some might then believe that he must be an impostor who wrote down the Quran himself by borrowing the stories from the Bible and started to call it a "Holy Book", thus creating the religion "Islam". This is how he is still labelled by some "people of the book". He was labelled the same during his time also, and the non-believers at that time used to make mockery of it:

"Hath Allah sent a mortal as (His) messenger?!" (Quran 17:94),

Also:

"And they say: What aileth this messenger (of Allah) that he eateth food and walketh in the markets? Why is not an angel sent down unto him, to be a warner with him. Or (why is not) treasure thrown down unto him, or why hath he not a paradise from whence to eat?" (Quran 25:7-8).

Or:

"And they say: We will not put faith in thee till thou cause a spring to gush forth from the earth for us; Or thou have a garden of date-palms and grapes, and cause rivers to gush forth therein abundantly; Or thou cause the sky to fall upon us piecemeal, as thou hast pretended, or bring Allah and the angels as a warrant; My Lord be Glorified! Am I aught save a mortal messenger?" (Quran 17:90-93).

And Muhammad is advised:

"Say: I am only a mortal like you" (Quran 18:110).

Later, after the demise of Muhammad, news started to spread that he was nothing but a fake prophet. I believe therefore, to give credibility to his Prophet-hood, there arose a need to associate miracles with Muhammad to make him infallible.[12] Consequently, it elevated him to a stature equal to God, just like Jesus. This is regardless of the fact that the Quran states how other messengers have been denied even though they could perform miracles:

*"And if they deny thee, even so did they deny messengers who were before thee, **who came with miracles** and with the Psalms and with the Scripture giving light"* (Quran 3:184).

It is not difficult for God to perform miracles. "Miraculous" is a very weak attribute to be used to approve Prophets as God's messengers. In fact, the most significant and ultimate miracle of Muhammad was the Quran. Muslims in general have overlooked this book completely, in spite of the fact that this is also supported by Quran itself: / *"They said, "If only miracles could come down to him from his Lord!" **Is it not enough of a miracle that we sent down to you this book**, being recited to them?"* (Quran 29:50-51).

But why is it that Muhammad couldn't perform miracles when other Prophets could? It is of course quite understandable to see non-Muslims finding it hard to believe that Muhammad was a Prophet when he couldn't see the future or perform miracles. But, is it necessary for a Prophet to do these things to endorse his or her Prophet-hood?

Could it also be that these Prophets were recognized in accordance to the psyche and comprehension level of people during their time? An example of this is that during the time of Moses and Jesus, communities were small and simple. Because of their relatively sheltered lifestyles, it was more an era of belief in magic and miracles. As a reflection of this, their Prophets could perform magic and miracles. By the time of Muhammad, communities and societies were becoming more and more complex and the age of reasoning and technology had already taken root. Magic and miracles would not provide the kind of conviction as they had before, and those that could were the type to be proved by science and reason. It was now reason itself that could make people believe in God.

Muhammad was therefore just a mortal like any other. The era we are in at the moment, the only certain way for conviction is through reason and logic. Those are the only tools available in our time that can help us define the abstract realm of the Creator.

MUHAMMAD AND THE OTHER PROPHETS

"Muhammad is but a messenger, messengers (the like of whom) have passed away before him" (Quran 3:144).

We have already elevated Muhammad to the level of God and are ever on a quest to make him far better and superior than other Prophets. This clearly violates the direct command of God:

*"But those who believe in Allah and His messengers and **make no distinction between any of them**, unto them Allah will give their wages; and Allah was ever Forgiving, Merciful"* (Quran 4:152).

*"Say (O Muslims): We believe in Allah and that which is revealed unto us and that which was revealed unto Abraham, and Ishmael, and Isaac, and Jacob, and the tribes, and that which Moses and Jesus received, and that which the prophets received from their Lord. **We make no distinction between any of them**, and unto Him we have surrendered"* (Quran 2:136 and see 3:84).

*"The messenger believeth in that which hath been revealed unto him from his Lord and (so do) believers. Each one believeth in Allah and His angels and His scriptures and His messengers—**We make no distinction between any of His messengers**—and they say: We hear, and we obey. (Grant us) Thy forgiveness, our Lord. Unto Thee is the journeying"* (Quran 2:285).

All Prophets were sent down from God to deliver the same message of one God; hence any distinction between them is not needed.

MUHAMMAD'S LITERACY ISSUE

Non-believers and the People of the Book used to deride Muhammad and say that the Quran is not a holy book, and that he himself wrote it down on a whim. Because of this, Muhammad needed to be for the believers an illiterate who could not read or write. This way, the Quran can become miraculous and holy. In the Muslim world, it is therefore generally believed that Muhammad was illiterate and could neither read nor write. This belief has been supported by the *hadith* traditions, and by wrong interpretations of the verses in the Quran:

*"Those who follow the messenger, the Prophet who can **neither read nor write (ummi)**, whom they will find described in the Torah and the Gospel (which are) with them. He will enjoin on them that which is right and forbid them that which is wrong"* (Quran 7:15).

I shall revisit this verse in a moment to explain its wrong interpretation.

It is absurd to consider Muhammad an illiterate, especially when he is preaching a book that itself stresses the importance of education. The overall theme of the Quran is to gain literacy so that one can have much deeper belief and appreciation of God. Even the first revelation received by Muhammad emphasized the importance of pen and book: *"**Read**: In the name of thy Lord Who createth, . . . **Read**, and your Lord, most Exalted, **teaches by means of the pen**"* (Quran 96:1-4).

On the whole, the Quran stresses sciences and the phenomena of nature, and says that those who have studied these fields will be in a better position to value the true gift from God. As Bucaille says: "The description of Divine omnipotence are what principally incites man to reflect on the works of creation",[13] once we educate ourselves, we won't be able to help but believe that there is a God. So, if Muhammad himself was not educated despite the Quranic emphasis on education, some could say that he is a hypocrite for not following what he is being instructed to preach.

The *hadith* books also state that since Muhammad couldn't read or write, as soon as he received the Quranic revelation, his companions penned it down as dictated verbatim by him. But, historically speaking, Muhammad belonged to a very esteemed and well-off clan of Mecca called Qureysh. It is therefore unfathomable to believe that despite belonging to such a high status clan and having friends and family all well-educated; Muhammad would choose to remain illiterate! Moreover, how can we reconcile his illiteracy with his business aptitude? It is known traditionally that he had a successful trading business, yet he couldn't read or write?! It is also historically proven that Arab traders used to follow strict guidelines of business by documenting everything. They even had a rudimentary banking system. How then could a well-known Arabic person like Muhammad not have been able to read or write?

This emphasis on his supposed illiteracy gradually resulted in a critical problem for the whole Muslim world: it drifted from being the cradle of civilization toward the cradle of another Dark Ages. If Muhammad was himself illiterate, why should other Muslims be literate? It was therefore understood or rather those were "made to understand" that the only literacy a person should acquire is the literacy of the Quran, which pertained to only the rote memorization and recitation of the Arabic. It is irrelevant whether one can make sense of the Quranic verses or not, but that the words are themselves holy and should remain beyond human comprehension. So, the conclusion drawn was that these sacred words are not to be understood but recited. With much dismay, it is no surprise to see the overall literacy rate in Muslim countries to be of no significance.

There is a well-known canonical *hadith* where Muhammad says to "*acquire education even if for that, one has to travel to China*". If it is only the Quranic verses that need to be learned, then why did he emphasize going to China? Did the Chinese know the Quran? of course not. It was because during the time that Muhammad was in Arabia, Chinese had advanced towards the acquisition of technology. So, in order to have the Muslims march toward progress and to move forward with the world, it was necessary to acquire the same knowledge of advancement in technology. For example, paper was already introduced by the Chinese at that time, and in 712 CE, Muslims (long after the demise of Muhammad) learned the art of paper making from them.[14]

Early Muslims were therefore hungry for knowledge, and would find any means or ways to acquire it. They translated works and many teachings of the past scholars into Arabic, such as Aristotle, Plato and Socrates. Today, we will not find those works written in Arabic but in Latin. This is because those translations were destroyed by the church during the Spanish inquisition. The Jewish people of that time who knew Arabic were slain after they had finished translations of works into Latin.

Coming back to the wrong interpretation of the verse 7:157, the word *ummi* or *ummi-yin* actually means "the one who does not know", or is "unaware"[15] of the holy book, or "the one who is ignorant not in education but with regards to God". As translated in the verse 3:75:/ "*they say, "there is no call on us (to keep faith) with these **ignorant (ummi-yin) (Pagans)**" or in verse 62:2:/ "He is the One who sent to the gentiles **((ummi-yin)** a messenger from among them . . .*". It has therefore but only `wrongly translated and emphasized in verse 7:157 to mean 'neither read nor write'.

If *ummi* meant illiterate, then why should we invent the term *jaah-e-loon*? *Jaah-e-loon* is the word that mainly means illiterate, or describes one who cannot read or write and is completely ignorant not only in formal education but even in common sense in the sphere of everyday life.[16] Colloquially, it means one who is totally uncivilized. On the other hand, *ummi* was used for people who did not have the Holy Book, the primary text to teach them about God and how to live their lives. This is the reason why in the Quran, Jewish people and Christians have oft been referred to as "the People of the Book", and those who did not yet have the Holy Book were described as *ummi* or gentile.[17] This is also evident in the following verse where it compares 'People of the Book' and those without a book—gentiles: *"say to the People of the Book and to those who are **unlearned** (ummi-yin)"* (Quran 3:20).

In summary, verse 7:157 could very well mean to state that the Prophet (who although is formally educated), was not aware of Allah (God and Its Book). We cannot rule out the possibility of such meaning. Additionally, this verse 7:157 never even remotely suggested that it is talking about Muhammad's formal education.

When Muhammad would receive the revelations, he would write them down himself immediately. The following verses also helps to endorse the above argument by indicating that it is written down in books by the scribe (which is no one else but Muhammad): /*"For it is indeed a message of instruction: "(it is) **in pages** (suhufin*) held in honor, exalted and pure and holy, **(written) by the hands of scribe**—honorable and pious and just"* (Quran 11:16). / *"Everything, small or large, is written down"* (Quran 54:53)

Muhammad was therefore educated, but only unaware of the belief of God and our relationship with the whole:

---

*   suhufin means a written page. Durrani, Zahida. Allama Parvaiz -Lughat-ul-Quran. Toronto: Tulu-e-Islam Trust. 2007, pages,1008-1009 (swaad, hay, fay)

*Those who follow the messenger, the Prophet who was **ummi** [did not know or unaware of God], whom they will find described in the Torah and the Gospel (which are) with them. **[Now that he knows and is aware of God]** He will enjoin on them that which is right and forbid them that which is wrong.* (Quran 7:157) (Square brackets are mine).

ASCENSION OF MUHAMMAD TO HEAVEN

Did Muhammad really ascend to heaven?

*"And they say: We will not put faith in thee till thou cause a spring to gush forth from the earth for us; . . . . **or thou ascend up into the sky, and even then we will put no faith in thine ascension till thou bring down for us a book that we can read. Say (O Muhammad):** My Lord be Glorified! **Am I aught save a mortal messenger?"** (Quran 17:90-93).*

Could this be the reason we made up stories with regards to Muhammad's ascension to heaven? The Quran does not state specifically anything about his ascension, except some ambiguous verses (53:8-18). Those verses could relate to either some supernatural experiences or the seeing of Gabriel the archangel who used to deliver the verses to Muhammad. It is open for any interpretation.

MUHAMMAD'S MARRIAGE TO AISHA

It is known in the Muslim world and has been widely accepted that Muhammad married Aisha (his friend Abu Buker's daughter) when she was only six years of age, and that the marriage was consummated when she was nine. This information continues to be passed down from the *hadith* books (see chapter *hadith)*.

It is highly outrageous to even think about any ordinary man of age 55 marrying a six year-old child (who has no sense whatsoever of right or wrong). How then, can I associate this story with the highly esteemed persona of the Prophet? And to whom Quran states to be having a high moral character (68:4)? True, there have been marriages in the past where the bride was very young, but that is exactly why the Quran came—to modify and better our situation.

In the Quranic Islam whose message Muhammad was to deliver and to emulate, I see no support for this story. In fact, the Quran offers a different picture for marriageable age. It states that marriage is a "solemn covenant", and explains it is for the age when one possesses "sound judgment" and has matured enough to make proper decisions[*α] :

> *"Make trial of orphans until they reach the **age of marriage** (balagh-un-nikah); if then ye find **sound judgment** (rushdan) in them, release their property to them"* (Quran 4:06).

> *"O ye who believe! Ye are forbidden to inherit women against their will. Nor should ye treat them with harshness that ye may take away part of the dower ye have given them . . . and they have taken from you **a solemn covenant** (meesaaq-e-ghaleeza)?* (Quran 4:19-21).

A 'solemn covenant' is a serious pact, an affirmation of an agreement and is of same strength and intensity compared to that taken from the Prophets as well: *"And when We exacted a covenant from the prophets, and from thee (O Muhammad) and from Noah and Abraham and Moses and Jesus son of Mary. We took from them a **solemn covenant** (meesaaq-e-ghaleeza)"* (Quran 33:07).

Balagh means an adult or a matured person or to reach the term[β]. Beyond any doubt, six years old is not the age of adulthood or where one possesses any sound judgment. It is not the time that one would be able to make any solemn covenant, or any pledge including the covenant required in

---

[α]   I owe this understanding to a friend Abdul Fauq who has a PhD in chemical engineering but his passion is his religion—a self student.

[β]   Durrani, Zahida. Allama Parvaiz LughatulQuran. Toronto: Tulu-e-Islam Trust. 2007, pp. 346-347, under bay. laam. ghain

marriage. Hence, Muhammad would do anything against what the Quran says and go about marrying anyone at such a tender age is unimaginable to me. It is a blotch on his esteemed character. It is no wonder that many in the West call Muhammad (God forbid) a pedophile, or one who has nothing better to do but kill with the tip of the sword and molest young children. It is very heavy for me to write about Muhammad or about any Prophet like this.

True, it was the time when people used to have innumerable wives including child brides. But if Muhammad had a polygamous nature or thirsty for a child-bride, he wouldn't have stayed monogamous for 25 long years with his first wife Khadija until she died. He would have had harems filled with women and child-brides. Especially when there is nothing to stop him not even any Quranic verse but he didn't. If he finally had harem after age 50 is because he may have felt responsible for all those widows whose husbands may have died in defence of a religion that Muhammad brought. He may have felt his duty to take care of all the children and their mothers.[٢]

Nevertheless, under this umbrella, the *Mullahs* and the *Pirs* have enjoyed their lusts by marrying many young girls and thus ruining their innocent lives. If Muhammad could do it, the guardians automatically receive the license to do the same.

AWAITING FOR A REDEEMER

I grew up learning that there is a rescuer who will come and bring peace to the world. This rescuer will look just like Muhammad, and his name will be Mahdi. I also learned that Jesus who had ascended to heaven would descend in order to have a natural death, and would bring the Muslims together.

---

[٢] Please refer to chapter 6 'Women's Issues' under 'polygamy issues' for details about more than four marriages of Muhammad.

Then, I also learned that there is going to be an antichrist called Dajjaal who would later be killed by the spear of Jesus. All of this told to us since childhood, the whole meticulous drama of the future. This and many other such stories are still believed by millions.

As I grew, I was astonished to find that it was not only the Muslim world that had these unfounded stories, but almost every religion believes in some sort of similar story: a savior who will save. The Jewish people are waiting for the true Messiah; the Christians are waiting for the second coming of Jesus and the antichrist, the Hindus are waiting for the *kal ki avatar*, and so on. [18]

Coming back to Quranic Islam, I find no advocacy for these stories. There are however certain verses that have been erroneously interpreted to provide support for the story of the descending of Jesus from the heaven (please note the first part *'I am making you die"*: /"*(And remember) when Allah said: O Jesus! Lo! I am **making you die** and **causing you to ascend (Rafi-uka) unto Me,** and am cleansing you of those who disbelieve and am setting those who follow you above those who disbelieve until the Day of Resurrection"* (Quran 3:55).

Yet, there are other verses which disprove the above interpretation such as: *"Muhammad is but a messenger, messengers (the like of whom) have passed away before him"(Quran 3:144*, also see 21:33). This should unambiguously mean that Jesus has passed away as well. But then how can we square this with the word *rafa-a*? The literal meaning of *rafa-a* is the verb to raise, to lift, to exalt, one who raises or exalts, uplifted, and upraised.[19]

There is another verse that talks about the Prophet Idris (Enoch), where the same *rafa-a* has been interpreted "to honour": *"And We **raised (Rafa-a) him to high station"*** (Quran 19:57).

I therefore see no reason why verse 3:144 should be interpreted differently, other than that the influence of stories from the Bible may have been transposed onto the interpretation of Quranic verses. I know that this whole issue may for some be too insignificant to even mention. Nevertheless, I felt the need to mention it, especially when I saw the whole of this as a quandary for not only Muslims but also Jewish, Christians, and many others religions.

The conclusion that I draw from these issues is that whether concerning a Muslim faith or any other, they all seem to be waiting to have their mess cleaned up by someone else. Consequently, they don't have to be accountable for anything, and they can just sit, relax and do nothing to better their present situation.

As for the Muslims, they should know that the Quran plainly says: *"surely Allah does not change the condition of a people until they first change their own condition?"* (Quran 13:11).

HALAAL AND *HARAAM* ISSUES
(allowed/lawful and forbidden/unlawful issues)

And speak not, concerning that which your own tongues qualify (as clean or unclean), the falsehood: "This is lawful, and this is forbidden," so that ye invent a lie against Allah. Lo! those who invent a lie against Allah will not succeed. (Quran 16:116).

MEAT

__Prohibited for you__ are animals that die of themselves, blood, the meat of pigs, and __animals dedicated to other than GOD__. (Animals that die of themselves include those) strangled, struck with an object, fallen from a height, gored, attacked by a wild animal—unless you save your animal before it dies—and animals sacrificed on altars. Also prohibited is dividing the meat through a game of chance; this is an abomination. (Quran 5:03).

The above verse and other verses in the Quran forbid consuming meat that has been immolated in the name of anything other than Allah. My argument therefore, is based here mainly on invoking God's name: first, why it is necessary, and second, how does this relate to the meaning and interpretation of the verse which has no doubt changed over time?

The Quran did not state how to slaughter an animal; it only emphasizes invoking the name of one God and no other deity while slaughtering an animal. Ironically, more emphasis throughout the Muslim world now has been on the method of slaughtering rather than on the invocation of the name of God. I grew up learning that *halaal* meat is the result of the specific way of slaughtering an animal while invoking the name of God. Since childhood, the only time I saw the butchers invoking God's name while slaughtering the animal was on the *Eid* day celebration (more on this in chapter five). For day-to-day meat sales, I witnessed the method of slaughtering but never heard even one butcher invoking God's name while doing this.

During pre-civilization times, there were human sacrifices which were later changed to animal sacrifices. This ritual has always been present. Islam did not abolish what was already in practice but reformed it. The method of slaughtering called *halaal* is done by cutting the jugular vein with a sharp knife, rendering the animal immediately unconscious. Later, when the blood is driven out of the body due to convulsion, the animal is slaughtered completely.* The Jewish and the Arabs both performed this method even before the advent of Islam. This method was also performed by pagans of the past who used to sacrifice animals for their gods on the altar. The process used to include "bloodletting", the cutting of the jugular vein. The sacrificial animal after the sacrifice was not to be eaten at all. This ritual was mainly done to give power

---

* Note: Many may find this method as inhumane to the animal. Research has been done that proves it is more humane than the stunning method widely used in North America. Stunning usually does not render the animal unconscious but paralyzed. The animal can therefore feel every bit of the pain.[20]

to their deity or deities. Blood was considered the life force; hence "bloodletting" was giving life force to their gods.

The first question is why is this so-called *halaal* method of slaughtering completely missing from the Quran? Especially when it became widely accepted as *halaal* and as synonymous with having had invoked God's name. Second question is why is it necessary to invoke God's name at all?

Since the method of slaughtering was already practiced, it was of no significance (as much as the one God concept was). That is the reason why the method of slaughtering is missing from the Quran. The invocation of the name of God was important in order to instil the "one God" concept. When the people turned from being polytheist into believing in and worshipping only one God, it was hard for them to let go of the past customs and rituals. As I mentioned earlier, the Quran did not come to introduce anything new but it came to improve the quality of life and take the human race to the next level of civilization. It did not abolish the sacrificial custom, because Quranic method for enlightenment is a gradual process: To educate them from within their comfort level. Consequently, the sacrificial ritual remained but the reforms were (a) to think of only one Creator. (b) to eat the meat and share it with the less fortunate instead of letting it rot near an altar: One more step out of the *jahiliyah* (ignorance)./ *"It is neither their meat nor their blood that reaches Allah: it is your righteousness that reaches Him . . . ."* (Quran 22:37)

The Quran further reiterates that even after people had turned into Islam, they would hesitate before eating the meat. As they were not used to eating sacrificial meat and still were not completely comfortable with the practice of invoking only one God and not the other gods, Quran questions:/*"How should ye not eat of that over which the name of Allah hath been mentioned, when He hath explained unto you that which is forbidden unto you?"* (Quran 6:119).

SEAFOOD

Since childhood, I learned that shellfish are not *halaal* because they do not contain blood. But it is something which is allowed and yet not allowed called *makrooh.* This is a preposterous statement. The Jewish scripture states the same thing: shellfish are forbidden and the other fishes are allowed:

> *These shall ye eat of all that are in the waters: whatsoever hath fins and scales in the waters, in the seas, and in the rivers, them shall ye eat And all that have not fins and scales in the seas, and in the rivers, of all that move in the waters, and of any living thing which is in the waters, they shall be an abomination unto you: They shall be even an abomination unto you; ye shall not eat of their flesh, but ye shall have their carcases in abomination. Whatsoever hath no fins nor scales in the waters, that shall be an abomination unto you."* (Leviticus 11:9-12).[21]

Quran on the other hand, states that all seafood is lawful: /*"Lawful to you is the pursuit of water-game (seafood) and its use for food,—for the benefit of yourselves and those who travel"* (Quran 5:96). Yet shellfishes are labelled as non-*halaal.* Further, the Quran says:

> *Say: See ye what things Allah hath sent down to you for sustenance? Yet ye hold forbidden some things thereof and (some things) lawful."* *Say: "Hath Allah indeed permitted you, or do ye invent (things) to attribute to Allah?* (Quran 10:59).

> *O ye who believe! make not unlawful the good things which Allah hath made lawful for you* (Quran 5:87).

I wonder if once again Biblical Quran has been transposed onto the Islamic Quran through *Shariah?*

DOGS

Please refer to the section *hadith* narrations in chapter three where I discussed that in none of the Quranic verses is there any instance where an animal is labelled as a disadvantage to humans, nor are they forbidden for religious matters. The Quran also states:

They consult you concerning what is lawful for them; say, 'Lawful for you are all good things, including what hunting animals (jawaareh*) like trained dogs (mukallibeen*) catch for you.' You train them according to GOD's teachings. You may eat what they catch for you, and mention GOD's name thereupon (Quran 5:04).

Also see the verse 18:18 (about the cave people and their dog in chapter 3).

It has been added through the *hadith* that the dogs are *haraam*:

"Allah's Apostle said, 'Whoever keeps a dog, one Qirat of the reward of his good deeds is deducted daily, unless the dog is used for guarding a farm or cattle"[22] (Narrated by Abu Huraira)

and

"The Prophet said, 'Angels do not enter a house which has either a dog or a picture of a living creature, human being or animal." [23] (Narrated by Abu Talha)

This above *hadith* appears very irrational and contradictory to what Quran reveals in verse 18:18 referring to the story of cave people/ *"and We caused them to turn over to the right and the left, and their dog (kulbuhum) stretching out his paws on the threshold"*. When there appears to be the Divine presence Itself despite the presence of dog, it is absurd to consider that angels would not enter one's house if a dog was present.

Question is why all the fouls have been attributed to dogs when Quran never attributed anything like that? One theory could be connected to Abu Hurayra, who used to hate dogs but love cats and hence his name 'Abu Hurayra' 'father of

___

* Durrani, Zahida. Allama Parvaiz -Lughat-ul-Quran. Toronto: Tulu-e-Islam Trust. 2007, pages,1449-14450 and 424-425 (kaaf, laam, bay and jeem, ray, hay)

kitten' (please see chapter 3 'About Abu Hurayra). Because the foul only comes from the source of *hadith*, especially the ones narrated by Abu Hurayra, it could be that he inserted such hadith so that Muslims could hate the dogs too? *Hadith* literature is filled with sayings about love for cats and hatred for dogs. Abu Hurayra converted from Judaism to Islam, the Jewish community to date hate dogs and consider it evil with demonic powers. It could be that Abu Hurayra couldn't get rid of his negative feelings for dogs.

One of the reasons for their hatred could be linked to one of the gods of the ancient Egypt: Anubis or Hermanubis, a black dog faced god whom people used to worship *(see photo below). Jewish community probably needed to hate the dog in order to divert people from the worship of Anubis and toward the worshipping of only one God. If that so, I may not see them wrong in their justification for harbouring negative feelings for the dogs but should such rationalization survive in today's world too?

Anubis

I would like to add here some feedback sent to me by one of my friends, the late Shaheen Zafar. She was a teacher and business woman by profession, and a passionate self-student of the Quran. Shaheen wrote in an email to me (p.c, January 25, 2008) (please note that it is not necessary that I am agreeing with her understanding completely):

---

*   http://en.wikipedia.org/wiki/Anubis

"i— According to the Quran in the story of Sura Kahf, The most righteous people of their time had a pet dog . . . . **We turned them about to the right and to the left, while their dog (lay) outstretching its paws in their midst … 18:18** Some clever scholars have opted to translate "at the entrance" or "at the threshold" instead of **"in their midst"**. This mention of dogs is repeated each time the number of these people is speculated. However, according to the mainstream "Arabic Islam" the story would have been even better to the taste of mainstream without the mention of the pet dog. But God Almighty-Wise spoke every word with clear and simple meanings; to erase confusions and lies from the minds of the readers. As you have been taught that the angels do not come to the place where there is a dog—and I have come across some cruel hadiths (in Bukhari) confirming this dogma.

ii— **They ask you as to what is allowed to them. Say: The good things are allowed to you, and what you have taught the dogs and birds of prey, training them to hunt—you teach them of what Allah has taught you . . . 5:04** Please read the Arabic text, and you will find the Arabic word **"mukallibeena"**. Kalb means dog, and Mukallabeen is the plural; whereas our scholars have yet again deceived us by translating "beasts of prey ". Now think about it. When the dog follows its prey all *worked up and exited—its saliva foams out of its* mouth. When the dog grabs its prey for its human master, the dog's teeth would pierce the flesh of this prey with its foaming saliva and mucus. Yet, God declares it halaal, and the scholars condemn dog's saliva as haram!"

MUSIC

*'This is a warner of the warners of old. The threatened hour is nigh. None beside Allah can disclose it. Marvel ye then at this statement, and laugh and not weep, **while ye amuse yourselves**? Rather fall prostrate before GOD, and worship".* (Quran 53:56-62).

Many believe (especially the *hadithist*) that the above bolded portion of the verses means that it is forbidden to listen to music or to sing. I am bewildered how anyone can come up with such an interpretation. Even when an average intelligent person reads this verse, they would not pick such a meaning. If the Quran has to be so complicated that an average person who reads it cannot comprehend the plain meaning, then the Quran would have no meaning to me.

Traditionally speaking, there is also a well known *hadith* that when Muhammad came to Madina, the people were so overjoyed that they welcomed the Prophet with songs and music on the street! Even the Quran itself is full of rhythm. Each and every verse resonate music, and it is even read in a melodious way. On a larger scale, the whole natural world of God has music imbed in every grain of it: the sound of the waves, the rustling of the leaves, the patting of rain drops, and the whistling of the wind. These are but a few examples of music that echo the presence of the very God whose Quran *we* say forbids the music.

NOTES:

1. Armstrong, Karen. *A History of God, the 4000-Year Quest of Judaism, Christianity, and Islam.* New York: Alfred A. Knopf Inc., 1993, pp. 132, 135

    Armstrong, Karen. *Islam, A Short History.* London: The Orion Publishing Group, 2000, p. 3

2. Armstrong, Karen. *A History of God, the 4000-Year Quest of Judaism, Christianity, and Islam.* New York: Alfred A. Knopf Inc., 1993, pp. 14, 135

3. Armstrong, Karen. *Muhammad: A Biography of the Prophet.* New York: HarperCollins Publishers Inc., 1992, p. 168

4. Irshad, Manji. *The Trouble with Islam: A Wake Up Call for Honesty and Change.* Toronto: Random House Canada, 2003, p. 57

5. Lehaz, Ali. "41 Dead as Suicide Blast Hits Northwest Pakistan". *Google News*, AFP. October 12, 2009. Date accessed: February 22, 2010. http://www.google.com/hostednews/afp/article/ALeqM5hmW-7E-he09DFvg3gq5inLcspUJQ

6. Armstrong, Karen. *A History of God, the 4000-Year Quest of Judaism, Christianity, and Islam.* New York: Alfred A Knopf Inc., 1993, pp. 118, 346-376

7. Armstrong, Karen. *Islam, A Short History.* London: The Orion Publishing Group, 2000, p. 61

8. Ibid., pp. 41-77, 120, 133-4

    Brown, Daniel. *Rethinking Tradition in Modern Islamic Thought.* Cambridge: Cambridge Middle East Study (for Students). Cambridge University Press, 1996, p. 96

    Rahim, Sir Abdur. *Principles of Mohammadan Jurisprudence.* Karachi Pakistan: Mansoor Book House, 1911, p. 18 (first paragraph)

9. Transparency International. "Surveys and Indices, CPI (Corruption Perceptions Index)", 2009 Table. Date accessed: February 19, 2010. http://www.transparency.org/policy_research/surveys_indices/cpi/2009/cpi_2009_table

10. Durrani, Zahida. *Allama Parvaiz-Lughat-ul-Quran.* Tulu-e-Islam Trust. 2007, (seen, laam, wow), pp.1037-1039, 1045-46

    Hanna, E. Kasis. The Concordance of the Quran (Foreword by Fazlur Rahman) University of California Press Berkley, Los Angeles, London, n.d, p. 1079.

11. Durrani, Zahida. *Allama Parvaiz-Lughat-ul-Quran.* Tulu-e-Islam Trust. 2007, (seen, laam, meen) p. 898

12. Brown, Daniel. *Rethinking Tradition in Modern Islamic Thought.* Cambridge: Cambridge Middle East Study (for Students). Cambridge University Press, 1996, pp. 60-63

13. Bucaille, Maurice. *The Bible, The Quran, and Science: The Holy Scriptures Examined in the Light of Modern Knowledge.* New York: Tahrike Tarsile Quran, Inc., 2003, p. 130

14. Grun Bernard. *The Time Table of History.* Third edition, 1991. New York: Simon and Schuster / Touchstone, pp. 51, 70

15. Durrani, Zahida. *Allama Parvaiz-Lughat-ul-Quran*. Toronto: Tulu-e-Islam Trust. 2007, (alif, meem, meem), p. 262, 2nd paragraph

16. Ibid., p. 452, 2nd paragraph

17. Ibid., p. 262

18. Shabbir, Ahmed. "When is the Messiah Coming?" Our Beacon. Accessed February 28, 2010. PDF from http://www.ourbeacon. com/wp-content/uploads/admin2/2007/08/messiah.pdf p. 11

19. Hanna. E. Kasis. *The Concordance of the Quran.* Berkley: University of California Press, n.d., p. 997

20. Philip G Chambers, Temple Grandin (compilers). "Guidelines for humane handling, transport and slaughter of livestock" (Chapter 7, Slaughter of Livestock, Stunning methods, Electrical stunning) p. 66; 2nd paragraph (PDF version). "Malpractice in immobilization of livestock" pp. 69-70 (PDF version). *FAO (food and Agriculture Organization of the United Nations), HSI (Humane Society International)*, 2001. Date accessed: March 3, 2010, FAO corporate document Repository. http://www.fao. org/DOCREP/003/X6909E/x6909e09.htm

21. University of Michigan Digital Library. *Holy Bible, King James Version,*_Leviticus 11:9-12. Date accessed: October 3, 2010. http://quod.lib.umich.edu/k/kjv/browse.html

22. Khan, M. Muhsin (translation). "Translation of Sahih-Al-Bukhari". Los Angeles: Center for Muslim Jewish Engagement. University of Southern California. Book 39 (Agriculture),Volume 3, number 515. Date accessed: February 13, 2010. http://www.usc.edu/ dept/MSA/fundamentals/hadithsunnah/bukhari/

    Date Accessed: October 20, 2012. http://www.usc.edu/org/ cmje/religious-texts/hadith/bukhari/

23. Ibid., Book 54 (Beginning of Creation),Volume 4, number 448. Date accessed: February 13, 2010. http://www.usc.edu/dept/ MSA/fundamentals/hadithsunnah/bukhari/

    Date Accessed: October 20, 2012. http://www.usc.edu/org/ cmje/religious-texts/hadith/bukhari/

CHAPTER FIVE

RITUALS ౨

It is human nature to partake in ritualized forms of behaviour. Perhaps these rituals assist us in understanding the abstract realms that are interwoven with our physical reality, the dominion unseen but felt. They could also help us build a connection with this conceptual realm, a connection that furthers our progression to becoming whole as individuals within the human collective, while bringing us to a state of peace. Such a state transforms life into a beautiful experience. But, as with anything in the world or the universe at large, there has to be a balance, some kind of benefit and reason for everything; and so it is with rituals. When they become too complex or bypass any benefit to human beings or common reasoning, they are thus devoid of meaning and become a burden rather than a blessing.

Today, we have reduced Islamic *deen* to a hollow, burden-filled religion of complex rituals and "do's and don'ts: *"if you repeat so and so verses of the Quran or God's name 100,*

1000, 1000000 times you will get this or that reward or relief from your pain." We argue that the beard of a man should be 4 or 6 or 8 inches long, that the hair of a women must be all covered (not a single strand of hair should come out), and about how much filth makes the prayer or fast nullified: the equivalent of the size of a pea, or a 50 cent coin, or a dot! And the list goes on.

INNOVATIVE RITUALS

Many non-Muslims became Muslims during the advent of Islam. Some of them yet succumbed to repeating many rituals they had previously performed, and they tried to incorporate those rituals into Islam with some modifications. This is the reason we see so many rituals associated with Islam that have nothing to do with it. Some examples of this is *Shab e baraat*, similar to the Hindu Diwali, or a marriage with a tree or the Quran, a similarity to Christian celibacy; and the giving out of *nayaaz* (sweets in the name of God), similar to the Hindu "*parsaad*". Later, all these different rituals came to be considered "holy".

The above mentioned and many more such rituals came from Hindu, Buddhist, Jewish, Christian and other religious traditions. Another example is *Koonday*, a symbolist ritual that signifies the so-called miraculous act of an Imam. By following this ritual, the followers believe that the same miracle would incarnate in their own lives. Then, there is the visitation to *mazaars* (shrines) and *Dargahs* (monuments), where people invoke saints' names, hymn their praise, perform specific rituals, and ask the saint to answer their prayers.

Performing female circumcision is another of the many "innovative" rituals that have no bearing with the Quran, yet have come to be associated with Islam. Just like Muhammad, Jesus and Moses also preached a simple way of life void of complexities and absurdities. These and other ludicrous

113

and redundant rituals were created later by the "manmade" religions.

QURANIC RITUALS

And for every nation have We appointed a ritual (Quran 22:34).

The Quran has stated a few rituals, all of which I find to be rational and beneficial to us. Nevertheless, to my dismay, even those few simple rituals have been adulterated by human concoctions. I myself grew up knowing and observing them. I am therefore a living witness to such concoctions.

SALAAT

In the Quran the meaning of *salaat* is not limited to a ritualistic activity only, but it is also referred to as a communal activity for societal reform and care. I shall delve into these two subjects separately.

Salaat, which is derived from the root word *sallu or Sallee,* in literal sense means to follow, to bend, nourish, or adhere to the laws, or to advise, hence the word *salaah.* It further means to honour, encourage and appreciate, to exercise resilience and to remove faults*.

Salaat is not something originally introduced by Muhammad, but was already established during the time of Abraham. Muhammad's part was to revive the *salaat* as a way of life and as a ritual. It was followed by those of Jewish and Christian faiths, but was later forgotten or performed in a way that there remained no meaning to it. Still today some orthodox Jewish sects will be seen performing *salaat* and ablution exactly the way Muslims do.

---

*   Durrani, Zahida. Allama Parvaiz -Lughat-ul-Quran. Toronto: Tulu-e-Islam Trust. 2007, (suaad, laam,wow and yeh), p. 1034-1047.

SALAAT A RITUAL ACTIVITY

Ritualistic *salaat* as per the Quran is very simple, neat, and short. It is kind of like a meeting with God (see point # 2 & 3 below). People later made it too complicated and long to even think of performing. As a consequence, many started to avoid it completely. This is indeed sad! Instead of calling people to the way of God we have actually made them flee.

(He) has placed no hardship on you in practicing your religion—the religion of your father Abraham. (Quran 22:78).

Muslims in general pray five daily prayers at certain intervals: *fajr* (dawn), *zohor* (mid-day), *asr* (late afternoon), *maghrib* (evening), *Isha* (nightime). But before starting a prayer one has to wash oneself (ablution)—a symbolic cleansing—before they come to the meeting with God. Some schools of thoughts differ in the way the *salaat* is performed and the number of *salaats* per day. Quran never specifies detailed methods of the *salaat* and leaves it to its readers to interpret. It only specifies to commemorate and remember God while standing, bowing, sitting and prostrating; and these positions must be done at certain intervals throughout the 24 hours in a day. There are many verses scattered all over the Quran about this. Please see appendix C for some detailed verses that specify the *salaat* times and their numbers.

What could be the reason for practicing *salaat* in this way?

1. Physically, all of the *salaat* positions, uttering certain words, and breathing in and out are techniques of exercise and stress release for the body. It has been proven that such exercises are important for healthy lifestyle. Today, many people use yoga techniques to receive the same benefits.

2. Spiritually, God always has Its channel built within us. It is rather our communication that is often disrupted and distracted. *Salaat* is one way of connecting back

to the channel of God, of finding ourselves one with our Creator. It may sound silly though, it is the natural propensity of human beings to crave for a connection with the intangible dominion of the Creator. We humans want to perform some sort of rituals in order to strengthen the belief in the unseen. This helps us to acquire and maintain calmness and serenity in our lives. When we bow or prostrate, it makes us humble and down-to-earth. It develops compassionate feelings in us for others, and makes us realize how very small and vulnerable we will always be. It makes us thank our Creator, and to be complete with It.

3. Ritualistic *Salaat* helps to embody the affirmation of the communal *Salaat*[α]: that our whole life will be toiling around (*tasbih*[β]) in fulfilling our responsibility of righteous deeds (*amle-swaleh).*

4. Lastly but importantly, it helps one to be organized, and teaches the discipline of daily regimes and hygiene.

Conditions for *Salaat* as per the Quran

As per the Quran, the following verses explain the conditions for *salaat*. The Quran states that these conditions, including ablution, must be applied before beginning the prayers. (Note: those conditions are not something only ordained by the Quran but also by the previous scriptures, and, the People of the Book initially used to follow them):

O ye who believe! Draw not near unto prayer (salaat) (1) when ye are drunk, till ye know that which ye utter, (2) nor when ye are in a state of sexual impurity (janabah), save when journeying upon the road, till ye have bathed. (3) And if ye be ill [or have disease](mard), (4) or on a journey, (5) or one of you cometh from the toilet, (6) or

---

α   see below '*Salaat* a Communal Activity'
β   see below after Communal *Salaat* for detail explanation on *tasbih.*

ye have touched women (sexually), . . . Lo! Allah is Benign, Forgiving. (Quran 4:43)

> *O ye who believe! When ye rise up for prayer (salaat), wash your faces, and your hands up to the elbows, and lightly rub (muss-han) your heads and (wash) your feet up to the ankles. And if ye are unclean, purify yourselves. And if ye are sick or on a journey, or one of you cometh from the closet, or ye have had contact with women (sexually), and ye find not water, then go to clean, high ground and rub your faces and your hands with some of it. Allah would not place a burden on you, but He would purify you and would perfect His grace upon you, that ye may give thanks.* (Quran 5:6)

Conditions for *Salaat* as per Past Scholars

Apart from what the Quran had already stated (outlining in entirety what conditions must be met for *salaat*), past scholars have for some reason violated verse 4:43 by adding more conditions to the prayers. These may nullify the *salaat* or the ablution for *salaat* to the extent that it may let people take flight from observing this simple *deen*. Examples of how one may be unfit for *salaat* apart from what the Quran states includes situations such as passing gas, running blood, sleeping, simply touching ones wife (not sexually), eating, having a dirty spot on a shirt, menstruation, and more.

Another condition is about the missed *salaat* times, which must be fulfill as a *qada salaat* (literally a *salaat* that is gone, disconnected, dead), at any other time. The Quran is silent about this condition. Quranic silence in this regard, makes me conclude that there is no need to say any such *salaat*. Nevertheless, if one wishes to say and feel at peace, I don't think there is any harm either. However, as the Quran states, *salaat* is only to "remember God for helping us to do *aml-e-swaleh*" (righteous deed) and is on "time ordinance" (4:103), it shouldn't matter if you miss one (but one should not intentionally miss them). Once the time is gone, it's gone; you can catch up with the next as it is something you perform daily on a regular basis like eating food. Prayers should be a pleasurable ritual in which one finds peace and tranquility. It should not be a burden that is too hard to follow. It should be easy, accommodating and should seamlessly integrate into one's life.

Shortening of *Salaat*

Once again the direct command of God has been violated in verse 4:101 (below). Through this verse, Quran gave allowance to shorten the prayer when one is in fear for his or her life (especially in times of war and oppression) and is in the course of traveling (principally to leave the oppressed land [4:97]). This ruling is not extended for regular or vacation traveling. Yet, *Shariah* have extended it as such, along with the addition of variable distances depending on which scholar one is consulting.

> *When ye travel through the earth, there is no blame on you if ye shorten your prayers,* ***for fear the unbelievers may attack you****: For the Unbelievers are unto you open enemies* (Quran 4:101).

Recent Schools of Thought and their Methods for Ritualistic *Salaat*

There are some recent schools of thought that have emerged who believe there is no prostration or bowing in *salaat*. *Salaat* to them merely means the reading of the Quran. Their argument is that the specific ritual as is observed by mainstream Islam (which includes bowing and prostration) has no meaning whatsoever. They say that it does not make any connection with God or give them any "food for thought". They believe that the bowing and prostration as mentioned in the Quran is not to be taken in the literal sense.

Everyone is entitled to their own interpretation of the Quran, just as I am. This has some drawbacks when considering some of the recent interpretations. Because of such unacceptable interpretations that are unfortunately prevalent, some choose to retreat to old schools of thought, preferring to remain with the mainstream man-made Islam, and thus to avoid confusion.

This retreat strategy leads to no answer or solution with our task of understanding the true meaning of Islam. Instead, we come all the way back to square one. The old schools of thought were no better than some of the present alternatives. Considering the above, I had to spend a little time re-thinking the assertion as put forth by some recent groups. What makes them so sure of their claims? Is there any cogency in their reasoning? My conclusion was the following:

Firstly, we all know that belief in a God is an abstract thought. No one has seen God, yet people believe. We humans are earthly creatures; we are bound by this earth and its phenomena. We are so chaotic on the inside that we need some sort of consoling force to embalm us. The idea of a God, helps us understand our inner chaos and puts it at peace. As I have mentioned previously, it is we who need God more than God needs us. Bowing, prostrating and doing the set rituals in a prayer (or any other form) helps us create a relationship with this abstract thought of a God. It helps us symbolize God and ground this belief to the earth. It helps us to comprehend and find meaning in something that is beyond our intellectual capacity. It even helps us to break our arrogant self, and become humble and compassionate.

Secondly, if the Quran (as the group asserts) does not mention the terms of bowing and prostrating for *salaat* in its literal sense, then the Quran is too complex to understand. This would mean that we are limiting the access of understanding of the Quran to only those who have perhaps an above average intelligence quotient. And, if one simple average person cannot understand the meaning of the Quran, then to me the Quran has no purpose to serve.

Thirdly, Muhammad spent 25 years of his life in Islam. It is therefore quite unimaginable to think that if he never prayed with bowing and prostrating (let alone five times prayer), and everyone else started doing as such right after his demise, doesn't make proper logical sense.

SALAAT A COMMUNAL ACTIVITY:
(For Societal Well Being)

Communal *salaat* has a wider nuance that encompasses all of our activities in general. The different literal meanings that I wrote in the beginning can be collectively spoken herewith. Such as the verse 11:87 of the Quran where Madian people questioned Shu'aib the messenger:/ *". . . O Shu'aib! does your* **salaat** *(prayer) enjoin you that we should forsake what our fathers worshipped or that we should not do what we please with regard to our property? . . ".* Here, by associating *salaat* with the activity of their material goods or possessions and being instructed through the *salaat* how to conduct activities, this verse demonstrates that s*alaat* is not simply limited to the ritualistic prayers, but has a wider meaning and application. Muslims in general, have reduced this *salaat* to only one ritualistic form and have thus devoid themselves from its many benefits. (for more detail please also refer to the topic *tasbih/ibaadat* after *salaat* as they all are in conjunction in the Quran).

Salaat therefore, has a wider spectrum than what we generally perceive. We are also performing *salaat* when we simply think about God at any moment, when we feel from deep within the desire to thank God. *Salaat* is also performed when we do any good deeds or make any sort of positive differences. All such examples are in a way of remembering and praising our Creator, becoming close to It and having our lives revolve around it. To reduce the *salaat* only to its physical bowing prostrating at certain intervals of the day is to make it a hollow ritual without understanding the underlying meaning behind it. Many Muslims consider that a person who does five daily ritualistic prayers is a "true" Muslim. This is a very narrow definition of a true Muslim. The Quran states:

> *Have you observed him who denies the deen (way of life)? That is he who repels the orphan, and does not feel the urge to feed the needy.* ***Ah, woe unto those who pray (musalleen), who are heedless of their prayers (salaat); Who make just a show, yet refuse small kindnesses!*** (Quran 107:1-7).

Having said that, it does not mean that the ritualistic five daily *salaat* is not important, it is important. But practicing one form of *salaat* without the other does not produce a holistic sense of the definition of *salaat.* When our daily conducts are not aligned with the command of God, but we are doing daily ritualistic prayers, how can we say we are true Muslims? It is performed for our own well being and we must also not forget the next step in the *salaat* that incorporates taking care of each other, being kind with each other, doing all the righteous deeds, which shows the "best conduct" within us.

When we do the ritualistic prayers we are in essence affirming that we are taking care of our communal prayer.

Tasbih/Ibaadat

Tasbih and ibaadat are the two oft repeated words in the Quran, but its meaning has been construed very narrowly such as: *Tasbih:* to praise God or repeat God's name on a rosary *(tasbih),* and *Ibaadat:* servant of God or serving God *(abd, aabid, ibaadat).*

Tasbih has been derived from *sabha* or the term *sabbaha* from root S.B.H, which literally means to swim, other meanings construed: to struggle, toil, to make effort, to revolve, to complete a revolution, or tightly woven, strong etc.* and *ibaadat* is a word derived from the root A.B. D, which means an effort with benefits. In literal sense, it is a type of a flower that has many benefits but is obtained with hardship*. Generally speaking, *ibaadat* means to abide by the law of God in order to receive its benefits. It can be interpreted as 'a law abiding citizen'—to abide by the law requires greater efforts but the benefits outweighs the struggle.

---

* Durrani, Zahida. Allama Parvaiz -Lughat-ul-Quran. Toronto: Tulu-e-Islam Trust. 2007, (seen, bay, hay S.B.H), p. 834-837 and (ain, bay, daal A.B.D) p. 1120-1127.

When we put two together, it actually means to keep toiling and making efforts towards doing the righteous deeds (*aml-e-swaaleh)*, it is the deed toward which, Quran has extensively instructed to observe. In thus doing, one revolves and struggles to swim around to complete the revolution of life, while at the same time one also keep reaping its many benefits. After that, one finishes his/her life cycle and becomes one with the Creator. This is what our final destination is, this is what God's law is, what God's worshipping and praising is. God is not hungry for praise; God doesn't need it, neither the worshipping (*pooja)* like idols, but rather abiding by the laws, the rules of right conducts throughout our lives until the end. That is why Quran uses the word *zikr-allah* more often but it is loosely translated as 'praise Allah'. Z*ikr* broadly means to 'remind' oneself regularly of God's command, in order to do *amle-swaleh*. Even the Quran itself means 'a reminder, a reading'.

By having narrowly defined the word *sabha* or the *abd*, we have portrayed God as hungry for Its praise and deification. We have made God appear a warrior god, a barbaric and callous god. A god that to whom should we not praise or be servant to in literal sense, we are calling ourselves to "burn in hell". Such God to me is not merciful, is not caring or compassionate. Such is not my Creator.

FASTING (Ramadan)

Traditionally, *fasting* is observed on the ninth month of the lunar calendar called *Ramadan*. It is again nothing newly introduced, but was already a standing tradition:/ *"O ye who believe! fasting is prescribed for you,* **even as it was prescribed for those before you***"* (Quran 2:183). The People of the Book have changed the way it was practiced before; they observe it in a rather different or easier way than what is stated in the Quran. Specifically, they observe *Ramadan* by giving up certain things that they enjoy, like choosing to walk instead of driving or abstaining from eating one certain food for the duration of *fasting*, etcetera.

In the Quran however, it is written that one should fast for the entire month of *Ramadan* (that is, those who can fast). The *fasting* is observed by not eating, drinking, or having sexual intercourse from dawn until dusk. The following three verses elaborate on this ritual:

(Fast) a certain number of days; and (for) him who is sick among you, or on a journey, (the same) number of other days; and for those who can afford it there is a ransom: the feeding of a man in need—but whoso doeth good of his own accord, it is better for him: and that ye fast is better for you if ye did but know. (Quran 2:184).

The month of Ramadan in which was revealed the Qur'an, a guidance for mankind, and clear proofs of the guidance, and the Criterion (of right and wrong). And whosoever of you is present, let him fast the month, and whosoever of you is sick or on a journey, (let him fast the same) number of other days. Allah desireth for you ease; He desireth not hardship for you; and (He desireth) that ye should complete the period, and that ye should magnify Allah for having guided you, and that peradventure ye may be thankful. (Quran 2:185).

It is made lawful for you to go in unto your wives on the night of the fast. They are raiment for you and ye are raiment for them. Allah is Aware that ye were deceiving yourselves in this respect and He hath turned in mercy toward you and relieved you. So hold intercourse with them and seek that, which Allah hath ordained for you, and eat and drink until the white thread becometh distinct to you from the black thread of the dawn. Then strictly observe the fast till nightfall and touch them not, but be at your devotions in the mosques. These are the limits imposed by Allah, so approach them not. Thus Allah expoundeth His revelation to mankind that they may ward off (evil). (Quran 2:187).

Many of today's scientists agree that *fasting* is something very beneficial to our physical bodies. Our body is working like a machine, it therefore, need some time off to rest so that it can rejuvenate and perform better. It is thus a requirement of a healthy body to fast. During the present time, many non Muslims or even atheists will perform *fasting* but only under a different title, such as the 'Body Cleansing Process'.

Spiritually, *fasting* teaches us to have self-discipline. It helps us to realize the value of food, and to empathize with those less fortunate than ourselves who do not have regular access to food. It therefore helps to build a bridge between the fortunate and the less fortunate, so that we can take care of each other, look after one another, and be thankful for what we have.

THE ABUSE OF QURANIC *FASTING*

Muslims have made *fasting* a more complicated ritual than it was supposed to be. It is very astonishing to note that the more the Quran states to make religion easy to follow (22:78), the more we are constantly striving to make it as hard to follow as possible. Islam is suppose to be our *deen* (way of life), and it cannot be as such if it is not in harmony with the natural rhythm of day-to-day life. We Muslims are therefore responsible for this discord and will eventually be accountable for it and bear the consequences thereof.

In order to make it hard enough for people to consider following the tradition of *fasting*, we have dictated in detail what would nullify the fast (just the same way we dictated what would nullify the *salaat*). For example, the wearing of perfume or make up, the smelling of food, touching one's spouse (not sexually), and bleeding or vomiting are but a few of the things that are supposed to "nullify" our *fasting*.

Whereas, Quran only says that we are to stay away from eating, drinking, and sexual intercourse while *fasting* from dawn to dusk. It would be interesting to note that these direct commands (especially no eating or drinking) have been softened by the scholars of Islam. For example, letting a women taste food if she is cooking for her "husband" and allowing one to eat and drink and 'not to fast' while on travel and continue this option while staying in a destination away from home. Quran only states not to fast while one is on a *journey,* and not when one reaches a destination. /*"(Fast) a certain number of* *days; and (for) him who is sick among you, **or on a journey,** (the same) number of other days"* (Quran 2:184-85).

It is quite logical and reasonable for the Quran to provide this space and these alternatives, especially because while traveling, one may not know when to start or break the fast due to the time differences, or, if on a tedious journey one may need to eat and drink—a natural body requirement. Nevertheless, to continue this option even after reaching a destination is an abuse and exploitation of the verses of the Quran.

MOON SIGHTING

This is a very trivial issue but it has caused much mayhem. To date (especially in North America), Muslims still remain disorganized in the fast. They do not start *fasting* or celebrating *Eid* together on the same date, because some may or may not have sighted the new moon in their present location.

It is preposterous to see people "locked up" in 7th century Arabia in what is now the 21st century. Today, we have the technology at hand to know in advance when the new moon will emerge, yet Muslims prefer to sight the moon with their naked eyes as per the *hadith* because the Prophet did that way. If Muhammad had access to the technology as advanced as it is today, he definitely would have benefitted from it. And, if the Quran had taught against acquisition of knowledge and leading to the advancement of technology (which it does not), our Prophet would have lived his pre-civilization era in a cave—but he didn't.

Aga Muhammad Shafi, the author of *Islamic Principles of Economics* (please see chapter seven) pointed me to a Quranic verse that states:/ *"They ask thee concerning the New Moons. Say: They are fixed periods of time for humankind"* (2:189). He argued a point on the basis that had the Quran wanted the Muslims to "sight" the moon to begin and end the *ramadan*, the Quran would not have stated that "it is already a fixed time" which can be determined beforehand.

Recently, there has been organizations such as the "global moon sighting" for Muslims who have taken the scientific approach to moon sighting. The organization measures to a very precise degree the course of the moon, and suggests the date for *Eid* and *Ramadan*. Those measurements have helped to bring out a 10-year calendar with fixed timings for new moons. The Islamic authority regards this organization as "prone to error", and consider sighting through the naked eye to be more accurate! I believe that they feel threatened by the potential of losing their guardianship when science seeps back into Islam.

LITERAL MEANING OF *RAMADAN* AND ITS ISSUES

Ramadan means "the hottest day, extreme heat" or "heat of the day".[1] Some therefore believe it should take place in the summer, starting on the summer solstice and continuing for the 10 days when it is the hottest time. This argument appears convincing; however, there are couple factors which need to be addressed before we jump into accepting it:

> **The month** *(shahar-u) of Ramadan in which was revealed the Qur'an, a guidance for mankind, and clear proofs of the guidance, and the Criterion (of right and wrong). And whosoever of you is present, let him fast **the month**, and whosoever of you is sick or on a journey, (let him fast the same) number of other days. Allah desireth for you ease; He desireth not hardship for you; and (He desireth) that ye should complete the period, and that ye should magnify Allah for having guided you, and that peradventure ye may be thankful.* (Quran 2:185)

The Quran has stated *Ramadan* as one of the months (*shahar—month*). A "month" as we all know can be from 28 to 31 days, but never 10 days. Similarly to what I discussed in the *salaat* section, if Muhammad (who spent 25 years of his life in Islam) did not observe *Ramadan* for more than 10 days, and immediately after his demise, all the Muslims throughout the world started observing it for almost 30 days, the mention of the word "month" in verse 2:185 in the Quran seems to be senseless and out of place.

There are many schools of thought with variant understandings of the meaning of *Ramadan*: some take it in a metaphoric sense that while one is *fasting* he or she is going through tough turmoil, hence the "heat". Others may say that since *fasting* is from dawn to dusk, it is the "heat" of the sun that is mentioned. Others, as stated above, do not take a holistic meaning.

HAJJ (PILGRIMAGE)

Perform the pilgrimage and the visit (to Makka) for Allah (Quran 2:196).

To every people have We appointed rites and ceremonies which they must follow (Quran 22:67).

Just as Jewish people visit the Wailing Wall and Christians visit Bethlehem in Jerusalem, Muslims visit the Kaba (house of God) in Saudi Arabia. Other religions also have similar pilgrim rituals. It is simply a ritual to make you feel that you are connected with your Creator.

The Muslim's visitation is called the *hajj* (pilgrimage). It is the last month in an Islamic calendar. This ritual is another that has become complicated and more valued from what was ordained in the Quran. As it is clear from the above verse (22:67) and many other verses, *hajj* is only one of the rites and rituals that we have to perform, and nothing more (I shall come shortly to my own explanation regarding this ritual).

We have added value to *hajj* by making people believe that over time, the one who performs *hajj* (noun: *hajee*) receives a "clean slate" afterwards. A *hajee* is cleansed from all sins and receives a re-birth like a newborn baby and his or her prayers are also accepted more readily. Hindus undertake the pilgrimage to Banares for the same reason: to wash away their sins by bathing in the Ganga River, thus receiving a clean slate. All of these are only whimsical dreams and wishful thinking. They have no bearing or endorsement from the Creator. It is God's discretion to forgive the sins of whomever God may, and to say on the part of Muslims that *hajj* can endorse such a clean slate is pure conjecture.

DAY OF THE *HAJJ* ISSUE

In mainstream Islam, *hajj* ritual has been reduced to only one day. After this, the *Eid* celebration takes place. We shall see now what Quran says in regards to this.

"The pilgrimage is (in) the well-known months (ash-harun)" (Quran 2:197). Please note "months" (plural: *ash-harun*) and not "month" (singular: *sharun*). When the Quran explicitly states "months" for the pilgrimage, why have we reduced it to a day? The ramification of this has been the loss of human lives every year due to *hajees* being stampede during the performance of the *hajj* rituals. Considering this, it is no wonder that the outside world sees Islam as a crude and barbaric religion.

In verse 2:197, it is clear that God Itself did not intend such consequences but we made it so. If the message of the Quran was only for the Arabs, a day for *hajj* would have been fine, but the message of the Quran is not only for the Arabs but universal. Quranic message being considered as universal, how would we expect nearly 7 billion people on earth to perform the pilgrimage in one day, should they all become Muslims?

HAJJ RITES AS PER THE QURAN

And (remember) when We prepared for Abraham the place of the (holy) House, saying: Ascribe thou nothing as partner unto Me, and purify My House for those who make the round (thereof) and those who stand and those who bow and make prostration . . . . and mention the name of Allah on appointed days over the beast of cattle that He hath bestowed upon them. Then eat thereof and feed therewith the poor unfortunate. Then let them make an end of their unkemptness and pay their vows and go around the ancient House (Quran 22:26-29).

This is where we get the rites of pilgrimage: starting not from Muhammad, but from Abraham. The basic rites as per the Quran includes: no fighting (war) or animal hunting, no wrongdoing or aggression and no sexual intercourse. *Hajj* rites include travelling the distance between *Saffa/ Marwa* mountains and *Arafat* if one wishes to perform. Moreover, there are rites to abstain from shaving hair during pilgrimage and finally sacrificing an animal.*

The animal sacrifice *qurbani* (offering or sacrifice as stated in the above verse) is slaughtering of an animal usually cow, goat, lamb or camel. The meat of the sacrificial animal is eaten thereof and is shared with the poor (See also *halal/ haraam* issue in chapter 4). The Quran does not command to all Muslims to slaughter an animal after *hajj* except those who go for pilgrimage and are present at the *Kaba* for *hajj.* It says in relation to the pilgrimage rites in chapter Hajj:

"And the camels! We have appointed them among the ceremonies of Allah [like the Hajj]. *Therein ye have much good. So mention the name of Allah over them* **when they are drawn up in lines** [at the ceremony]. *Then when their flanks fall (dead), eat thereof and feed the beggar and the suppliant. Thus have We made them subject unto you, that haply ye may give thanks."* (Quran 22:36). Square bracket is mine.

But it is a common practice among the Muslim world to do animal sacrifice, whether they went for the pilgrimage or not. This innovation has created more trauma than a day of celebration with peace of mind. Many people cannot afford to do *qurbani* but feel the urge and obligation to do one and consequently put themselves into financial hardship. Many people, who can afford, may want to compete in this ritual

---

* See also Quranic verses: 5:1-2, 2:158, 196-203, 22:26-37, (there are more verses on hajj but these are specifically associated with the rites)

to spend more than their neighbours, but then this is not the principle of the Quran. We live in a 21st century now, it is time that we should rise above these petty thinking and rather do something that can benefit the other humans especially those who are in distress.

It would be interesting to note though that in all the verses related to *hajj* ritual of slaughtering an animal, the word used is not *zabiha slaughtering* or *qurbani* sacrifice but *hadiya,* which in literal sense means a gift without thought of gain, or to guide.[2] Gift can have a wider connotation: at the pilgrimage—animal sacrifice as a ritual, and at your home—anything that you can easily afford according to what your means are and so be content that you participated in the *qurbani.*

*"Perform the pilgrimage and the visit (to Makka) for Allah. **And if ye are prevented, then send such gifts (hadiya) as can be obtained with ease****, and shave not your heads until the gifts have reached their destination. And whoever among you is sick or hath an ailment of the head must pay a ransom of fasting or almsgiving or offering. And if ye are in safety, then whosoever contenteth himself with the visit for the pilgrimage (shall give) such gifts (hadiya) as can be had with ease. And whosoever cannot find (such gifts), then a fast of three days while on the pilgrimage, and of seven when ye have returned; that is, ten in all. **That is for him whoso folk are not present at the inviolable place of worship***. Observe your duty to Allah, and know that Allah is severe in punishment."* (Quran 2:196)

REASONS FOR QURANIC *HAJJ* RITES

I recognize *hajj* as being nothing more than a ritual. Some rituals help us to create a relationship with the incomprehensible phenomena of this material earth. *Hajj* rites build a feeling of proximity to our God who we have never seen. It also helps to ground our belief from a religio-historical

---

* It can apply for both: who went on pilgrimage and those who were prevented.

perspective. It makes us see things that are apparently invisible to us, and hence it aids in the strengthening of our belief. Being around the house entitled to God, helps us to make a connection with the incomprehensible dominion of God. When we put a symbolic representative for God in this spatial earth, we feel God and Its presence, hence we believe.

It also makes us become one race of humankinds under one umbrella where every people from all around the world cast their differences aside and become united.

CRUDE AND INNOVATIVE *HAJJ* RITES

We have already made *hajj* rites appear savage by reducing it to a one day event, resulting in **stampede deaths,** and now we have added more: **kissing of the Black Stone** and **pelting stones to the devil**—resulting again in the merciless death of many who are accidentally hit by the stones thrown by others. The reason we give for this rite is to remember how Abraham pelted stones to the devil when he was tempted.

When the Quran stated the detailed *hajj* rites, it could have stated kissing the stone and pelting stones to the devil, but it didn't. There is no verse that talks about the stone or the story of Abraham pelting stones to the devil. It only states the following verses about sacrificing his son (these verses are also open to numerous interpretations, not relating to pelting stones at the devil).

And when he attained to working with him, he said: O my son! surely I have seen in a dream that I should sacrifice you; consider then what you see. He said: O my father! do what you are commanded; if Allah please, you will find me of the patient ones. Then, when they had both submitted, and he had flung him down upon his face, We called unto him: O Abraham! Thou hast already fulfilled the vision. Lo! thus do We reward the good. Lo! that verily was a clear test. (Quran 37:102-106).

Even if historically such an incident happened, it cannot be a part of *hajj* rites if Quran does not make it one.

ZAKAT (WELL-BEING TAX)

> *Those who believe, and do deeds of righteousness, and establish* **regular prayers and give zakat,** *(aqamus-salaata-wa-atuzzakata) will have their reward with their Lord: on them shall be no fear, nor shall they grieve. (Quran 2:277)*

Before Islam, in both the Semitic religions—Judaism and Christianity—there was *zakat*, just as there was *salaat* and *fasting*. Quran stresses *salaat* and *zakat* together many a times in its verses: / "establish *salaat* and give *zakat*" (*aqamus-salaata-wa-atuzzakata*). We have already discussed the meaning of *salaat;* let's see what is *zakat.*

The word *zakat* has been translated interchangeably with "charity", "alms-giving", and payment for the poor due. All of these are not the correct translation of the word itself, which means "to nourish", "to help grow", and "well-being".[3] So when the Quran states *aqamus-salaata-wa-atuzzakata*, it in spirit means to care for the well-being of the society. In a nutshell, it means to roll our resources whether tangible or intangible, in order to be used for a better purpose. From economic standpoint, *zakat* can be another form of taxation in order to fund public services. It is due to these services that a country is able to progress and run its economic system. *Zakat* helps to nourish a society in a healthy manner, and to support the infrastructure of a country. It actually promotes the same concept what commonly is associated as the saying of Jesus *Eesa*: "give a man a fish and he will eat for a day, teach a man to fish and he will eat for life".

Charity or alms-giving on the other hand is not equivalent to *zakat*, but those English terms have been used in conjunction with the *zakat* word whenever translated. While *zakat* is mandatory, charity is not. Charity is something that you do at will. *Sadaqa* is the word used in the Quran to clearly identify and differentiate *zakat* from charity or alms-giving. The word *feqoon* used in the Quran only means "to spend", "to give", or "to keep it open from all sides" (from the root *infaaq*).[4] Hence, *feqoon* can be used for both *zakat* and charity. We shall see further below how it is used in the Quranic verses.

When non-Muslims were taxed *Jizya* during the time of the Ottoman Empire, it was because Muslims couldn't charge *zakat* from them. So, in order to take the responsibility *zhimma* of looking after their well-being and providing them with public services, they were charged a tax. There has been much uproar about this tax, but I don't see any wrong with it. I give tax in Canada because I live here and abide by its rules. *Jizya* simply came from the root word "*jiza'a*" which means "to compensate"*. Umar, the second caliph after the demise of Muhammad, established a proper system of collecting and distributing *zakat* money. This system was called "*bait-ul-mall*" or "house of wealth". Umar used to redistribute this wealth as needed accordingly for the betterment of the public.

When we pay tax, or give alms or charity in any form, we are in essence making sure that the system for the security and existence of our society not only remains but also runs smoothly. Rolling over our resources is far better a purpose than letting it stagnate, which serves no beneficial purpose for the society that we live in.

WHAT PART OF OUR INCOME IS *ZAKAT*?

In the current Islamic world, the part of our income allotted to *zakat* money has been calculated to be 2.5 percent of our excess income weighed in gold. Quran did not specify any numbered amount for *zakat* that one should set aside, but it says:/*"they ask thee what they ought to spend (yun-feqoon). Say: **that which is superfluous**"* (Quran 2:219).

Other translators have written that it is the amount "in excess" or beyond one's needs. But how can one measure what

---

*   Zahida Durrani, Allama Parvaiz -Lughat-ul-Quran. Toronto: Tulu-e-Islam Trust. 2007, (jeem, zay, yea), pp.429-431.

is beyond one's need or superfluous? Some may possess more than one house, or even cars, boats, and more (on which one may be paying mortgages and or instalments). Consequently, those people may have all their money tied down in payments and could consider themselves not capable of having extra (a superfluous amount) of income for *zakat* or charity. Should a situation like this be considered as no excess income? Should these people be waived from giving *zakat* or charity?

It is very difficult in this material era to distinguish what one wants and what one needs. It depends on our standard of living, and the bare necessities required for living a decent life. This standard of living can be very subjective. But unless we deceive our own conscience, this and our common sense should effectively be able to tell us what is luxury and what is required, in order to know what amount to spend (*feqoon*). We should be able to easily discern what we can live without and what we cannot.

Verse 70:24-25 states that a known part of possession which includes money is to be set aside for *zakat*, but the specific percentage is missing: "*A known part of their possession (amwalayhim haqqun ma'loom) is for those who ask and those who are deprived.*" As stated earlier, in mainstream Islam, this amount has been accepted to equal 2.5 percent. If God left the exact amount out of the Quran, it could be that God in Its infinite wisdom left us to decide what the amount should be according to our circumstances and also the dire needs of our country at large. Nevertheless, the Quran do give us certain criteria for judging what must be considered the right amount to set aside: "*And let not your hand be chained to your neck nor open it with a complete opening, lest you sit down blame worthy and insolvent.*" (Quran 17:29). A percentage that can provide a win-win situation: Not a financial burden to those who give and also enough for those are in need.

WHO SHOULD GIVE *ZAKAT*?

*"Those who spend **in ease and in adversity**"* (Quran 3:134).

This verse has some interesting issues. Islam as practiced today with its *Shariah* rules creates a situation that is very lenient for those who are not economically sound. The rule exempts these people from giving *zakat*. It would be a disservice to a society if the poor were exempted from contributing their share of *zakat*. What incentive is there for the poor to better their situation when they are already enjoying the benefits of receiving *zakat* without participating in the efforts to contributing in it? Consequently, we are helping the society not towards betterment but towards becoming crippled.

True, *zakat* is for the poor who are not stable in their lives, but only to help them to a certain degree and not to cripple them. It is there to provide a safety net. It is reminding me of the welfare system in British Columbia, Canada, which is quite similar to what is written in the Quran. In this system, the government supports the poor by giving them welfare cheques. Previously, this provision was provided without any time limit. Hence, the poor would not think of making their lives better by themselves because (a) they are getting their livelihood for free, and (b) the money that they are receiving was never earned by them, and therefore does not possess any value in their eyes. Sometime back, the government made changes and reduced the welfare provision to five years only.

The above verse (3:134) states distinctly to give even during the state of adversity. I therefore think that every one of us has to give *zakat* and charity in any form, regardless of our circumstances or poverty level. No one is relinquished, but it should be given according to ones means. I think this is the only way we can ensure the growth, survival and the safety of our society.

WHEN TO GIVE *ZAKAT*?

From the following verse it may be understood that when one receives income, one must give zakat or charity. I believe it is based upon our own circumstances and our country's decision as to how we consider our income calculation: daily, weekly, monthly or yearly:/ *". . . and give its due (haqqah) thereof upon the harvest day (or income), and be not prodigal"* (Quran 6:141).

WHOM TO GIVE *ZAKAT* AND HOW TO QUALIFY THEM?

It would be of interest to note that the Quran states first to give to one's parents: *"that which ye spend for good (must go) to parents and near kindred and orphans and the needy and the wayfarer"* (Quran 2:215). This does not mean that if parents or relatives are well-off one shall still give them the *zakat* or alms, but only if they are destitute. In fact, verses 9:60 and 17:26 below state some of the qualifications for receiving *zakat* or alms: that it should go to:/ *"the poor, the needy, the workers who collect them, the new converts, to free the slaves, to those burdened by sudden expenses, in the cause of God, and to the traveling alien"* and *"give the kinsman his due, and the needy, and the wayfarer, and squander not (thy wealth) in wantonness."* There are many other verses such as these that can be found in the Quran.

The Quran also outlines for us how we can recognize those who actually deserve and qualify for alms, or for that matter *zakat*: /*"The unaware may think that they are rich, due to their dignity. But you can recognize them by certain signs; **they never beg from the people persistently**"* (Quran 2:273).

People tend to give overwhelmingly to those who come near to them begging with importunity, but considering verse 2:273, the Quran seems to be indicating otherwise. This brings up the question, should beggars be given any charity or be allowed in the streets? I think they should be given *zakat* in the form of help toward a permanent solution for their better life.

To the end of this discussion, I'd like to leave my readers to consider the verse 57:7 of the Quran where it says to/ "*spend of that which He has made you* **trustee**". This seems that from anything to our own money and earnings as well, all but belong to God, we are not the owners at all. How can then we keep more for ourselves and nothing or less for others? As a trustee how should our conduct be in this matter?

EID CELEBRATION

Eid is a Muslim celebration that occurs after the month of *Ramadan* and the month of *hajj* (see section *Hajj* above for detail). It is no more than a celebration, similar to those seen in many other religions.

Muslims have varied opinions about celebration. Some may celebrate not only *Eid*, but also many other (holy) days. Some only celebrate *Eid*, and yet some celebrate nothing at all and consider these activities totally unnecessary or indulgent.

Celebration is a natural tendency of human beings. It is human nature to celebrate, and it is in our blood. We cannot escape what is embedded in our nature by God: we feel ultimate happiness when we celebrate. As with anything else, celebrations also can lead to indulgence; just the way being overzealous in religion can lead to indulgence and lead us farther away from the truth. The key is moderation in everything. Life without any kind of celebration is very dull and boring. The Quran does not mention *Eid* or any celebrations, but it does not forbid them either. If Allah left out mentioning the *Eid* celebration, I think it is because God wanted us to decide: according to our different cultures, what and how we want to celebrate. Nonetheless, God did say that *"for every nation have we appointed a ritual"* (Quran 22:34).

137

Celebration is another form of ritual, and rituals have to exist to create meaning within the incomprehensible world. What we have to know is how to maintain a balance, and how to reap some benefit or have some meaning within those rituals. We do feel happy and joyous when we celebrate. Happiness is an innate behaviour in human beings and it benefits us: it keeps us healthy, and it also makes us able to thank God for our happiness. I don't believe God wants us to remember, praise, and thank God without the joys of celebration. When we are happy, "thank you" automatically comes from the deep core of our heart. Those who void themselves from every legitimate pleasure are hurting themselves; they are running away from something that is inherently present in them. In the long run, it does not do any good, but harms them and their well being.

The universe at large itself is so beautiful. Every single thing in this world is so full of life and radiance that should God have wanted us to remain dull and boring, our world would have reflected the same.

NOTES:

1. Zahida Durrani, *Allama Parvaiz-Lughat-ul-Quran.* Toronto: Tulu-e-Islam Trust. 2007, (ray, meem, duwad), p. 781

2. Ibid., (hay,daal,yeh), p. 1757

3. Ibid., (zay, kaaf, wow), pp. 808-810

4. Ibid., (noon, fay, Qaaf), p.1652

CHAPTER SIX

WOMEN'S ISSUES ৫১

Women's issues relating to the Quran have been much debated in recent times. There are verses in the Quran that have been either grossly misinterpreted or translated in a biased way. During my course of study I have found that overall the Quranic Islam provides immense rights to women; more than what women later acquired during the 20th century that is some 1400 years after.

While the "man-made"* Islam may be considered to have brought the devaluation of women, "man-made"* Judaism and Christianity as well have not done any better in the past with regards to women's issues. There are innumerable passages in

---

*   I have termed the main stream Semitic religions as man-made because all three have been seized and brutally succumbed by the hands of men and not by the hands of the holy books, the interpretations of which has been mainly controlled and dictated by men.

the Bible (both the Old and New Testaments) that are alleged to have brought on misogynistic attitudes towards women, and consequently curbed their rights. It is not the intent of this book to offer a comparative study of women's rights in the Bible and the Quran, but readers are encouraged to go through the Bible references at the end of this book.

Those Biblical misogynistic attitude and curtailment of women's rights has now been brought into the present day Islam, especially through the *ahadith* that are interpolated into the Quran. All three religions (Islam, Judaism, and Christianity) emerged during the patriarchal era and hence are in essence patriarchal doctrines. My discussion mainly focuses on examining my own choice of the Quran, which though I accept is a patriarchal doctrine; it has adopted the female perspective in-depth and has attempted to create a balance by observing egalitarian principles. As we go through this chapter, we will come to know through some comparisons why the Quran is still my choice.

Recently, there have been innumerable attempts by progressive or rather liberal Muslims and also by conventional Muslims to clear many misconceptions about women in Islam. I myself have argued on this topic many times. The addition of women's issues in this book may therefore seem not to be something especially new. Nevertheless, in my exploration of this subject, I have tried to avoid being apologetic and have made an attempt to remain as neutral as possible.

Before I go into a lengthy examination of what the Quran states about women, I would like to briefly touch on the state of women in the Muslim world at present, and also discuss the state of women before the advent of Quranic Islam.

MUSLIM WOMEN'S DILEMMAS IN TODAY'S WORLD

It is noteworthy to mention that the first person to become a Muslim after the dawn of Islam was a woman. This was Khadija, Muhammad's wife. This is one more reason why it is heart breaking for me as a Muslim woman to see the dismal state of women in so-called Islamic societies.

There are many claims by various Muslim groups (from liberal to conventional) regarding how just or fair the Quran is to women. Also, many have opinions regarding how a Muslim woman is in a far better position than a non-Muslim woman. But in reality, we see a rather bleak picture overall for Muslim women living in Muslim countries. Fundamental rights of women can be found in books and in sermons, especially with reference to the Quran, but we will find it completely void from what is being practiced in Muslim countries. I therefore would not blame non-Muslims if they were to call Muslims hypocrites and Islam as a patriarchal sexist religion or even if they were to blame the Quran for promoting these views. If we have not fulfilled the principles of Quranic Islam in general (as we have discussed in the previous chapters), how can we progress and work on women's issues?

Broadly speaking, women have hardly any rights in Muslim countries. The classical *Shariah* law in all Muslim countries is filled with misogynistic attitudes. The overall literacy rate is very low to be of any significance and the female literacy rate is even lower than that of men. Considering only the case of Pakistan (a Muslim state where I was born and brought up), over 70 percent of the population is in villages and the remaining 30 percent in urban centers. From this 30 percent, only approximately 5 percent have access to decent schools and are in a financially secure situation. According to the CIA fact-book, the female literacy rate in Pakistan is 36 percent, compared to the male rate of 63 percent (2005 stats).[1] This literacy rate is not a true picture of education though, it is determined by using the criteria of the ability to only read and write—and does not consider whether citizens have acquired any degree or certification. One might wonder why these are such low percentages when the Quran and even some of Muhammad's *ahadith* however fabricated they may be stress the fundamental rights of education, and the imparting of it?

Some Muslim countries such as Saudi Arabia and Iran have employed "religious police", these in place mainly to take care of the females in their societies. More specifically, the religious police are in place to make sure that women remain subservient and abiding to men. One example of the consequences of having the religious police in place is the tragic case of a girl's dormitory that had set fire in Saudi Arabia in 2002. Approximately 15 Muslim girls were burned to death in a situation where they could have easily been saved. In this case, the religious police did not allow the male firefighters to enter the female school on the preposterous pretext that they were non-*mehram* (with whom one can marry)! Neither did they allow the girls to escape from the blazing building because they were not fully covered according to their *Shariah* rule.[2]

Another example of the lack of women's rights are job and study limitations imposed, as well as a ban on women driving automobiles and traveling alone (this on top of the dress code which is dictated to women).[3] It is very ironic to note that during the time of the Prophet, women used to ride camels, take part in community affairs, make decisions, actively participate in wars, and tend to the wounded.

The *jehadis* (holy warriors) on the other hand consider themselves to be the "chosen ones". In truth, many have no idea what *jehad* really means, but know that they are "God's soldiers". Because of this, they believe that they will receive "voluptuous" women in heaven as a gift for their *jehad* efforts. They also believe that while in this world, they have the right and are even justified in raping a woman, exemplified in the many cases in Darfur, Africa as well as other "Muslim" countries including Algeria. These men feel proud of committing rape, as if they are doing a just deed. After all, they would contend that a "Muslim" child will be born from the loins of "those black Darfur women". As they see it, they are doing a favour for these black "filthy" women by raping them. As they understand it, these women will be receiving greater *sawaab* credit from God for bringing a "Muslim" child into the world. To these "holy warriors", all these actions have been approved and sanctioned by God because these warriors have become "God's Soldiers".[4]

The *Karo Kari* system in Pakistan (which I am myself a witness to) is another example of 6th century savage Arabian culture, reminiscent of a time when vendetta upon vendetta with blood baths was the norm.[5] In Pakistan, under this system, an innocent female of a tribe "A" who has nothing to do with tribal issues but if needed can be sanctioned by the *jirga* (community court) to be gang raped by the men of the tribe "B" in order to avenge the honour of tribe "B". An example of this in practice was the case of Mukhtaran Bibi in 2005, which caught the attention of media worldwide. This practice also reminds me of an Assyrian Law (1200 BCE) where the penalty for a married rapist was to have his own wife "dishonoured"[6] even when the wife had nothing to do with her husband's raping activities. This was acceptable from the point of view of Assyrian culture, especially at a time when women were nothing but "things". However, this sort of behaviour should be unimaginable for the 21st century. Unfortunately, *Karo Kari* is happening today not only in Pakistan but also in many other parts of the world.

Women generally, are therefore in an abject state in any Muslim country. Even basic human rights are negligible, not to mention the practice of stoning to death women in cases of adultery (while men are acquitted, such are the many cases in Nigeria) (see also *Hadith* chapter). The Muslim countries have even declined to ratify the United Nations Convention on the Elimination of All Forms of Discrimination Against Women (CEDAW). In the view of Muslim countries, these rights are interpreted "differently" according to religion.[7]

143

These are some of the many dilemmas that a woman living in a so called Muslim country must face. It is beyond the capacity of this book to describe every single issue, but the main question is: if the Quran is so egalitarian and impartial with justice, and has so immensely adopted the women's perspective, then why are we faced with this hopeless state of Muslim women today? How could we not then accept the idea that the "man-made" Islam as a religion is inherently a sexist and barbaric religion?

WOMEN'S DILEMMAS BEFORE QURANIC ISLAM

In this section, I have mainly referred to the extensive research of Leila Ahmed in her book *Women and Gender in Islam*. She is a professor of women's studies and near Eastern studies, and a director of the women's studies program at the University of Massachusetts, Amherst. I have also used information from other sources such as Wikipedia, and Bryan Sykes's genetic research in tracing our genetic makeup all the way back to prehistoric times.

ANCIENT MESOPOTAMIA

During the 1960's, archaeological findings (especially by James Mellaart) revealed much about the prehistoric societies such as the Neolithic (New Stone Age) settlement of Catalhoyuk in Turkey, dated circa 7500 BCE. Based on these findings, it was observed that women once held highly esteemed and dominant positions in their society.[8] As per Ahmed, worship of a mother goddess during the Neolithic period is not only evident from the Catalhoyuk excavation but other archaeological findings as well done throughout the Middle East.[9] People lived very egalitarian lives where there was hardly any gender-based social distinctions. Mellaart's findings further revealed that there were mainly female deities, this based on his discoveries of female figurines and their details.

Perhaps that time was the time of matriarchy (rather a better period). As we moved from the Stone Age to the Iron Age at about the 12th century BC, the patriarchal era established deep roots with the rise of complex urban societies, and women's positions thus declined. Instead of goddesses, there were now gods. At this time, physical strength and use of tools came to be recognized as power, and men's positions therefore started to become more prominent. While women were once looked upon as powerful deities, they were later reduced to weak sexual beings. Their reproductive capability, which was once seen as a miraculous power of life, was regarded as merely a function for which women were born. Why this transition happened? According to Gerda Lerner (a prominent historian and currently a professor emerita of history at the University of Wisconsin Madison) is due to the need of increasing the population and the labour power.[10] I agree with this view of Lerner's because it is understandable how when we moved from the time of hunters and gatherers to the time of farmers, the demand for increased labour and population escalated,[11] and thus the women were viewed as a commodity to be used for producing labour power. This eventually resulted in a woman becoming merely the property of men: before marriage she would be the property of her father, brothers, or uncles, and after marriage she was the property of her husband.

As male dominance increased due to the demand for labour and eventually military power, women's functions were reduced to only procreation. They were gradually excluded at large from being contributors to the society. Their status thereafter was further marginalized. Under a patriarchal family, they were subordinated and controlled by men and were forced to owe full submission to them.

Many harsh restrictive laws against women were codified. In the Mesopotamian region (present day Iraq), the restrictive harsh code of *Hammurabi* was created by the sixth Babylonian king called *Hammurabi* (circa 1760 BC). It was written down in stone tablets standing six feet tall and it is one of the earliest and well-preserved recorded codes.[12] These harsh Hammurabi codes were later followed by harsher Assyrian laws.

Even animals by today's standards are not treated in such ways as women were treated at that time. For example, men were historically allowed by the code to use women and children as debt pawns or even to sell them to pay off debts. Men could divorce women easily if they were unable to bear any children. Later, in Assyrian law (which was much harsher), it was permitted to beat the "debt pawns" mercilessly. Also, this same law permitted husbands to mutilate the ears of their wives or pull their hair out for any disobedience, and this was done without any liability to the men.[13] Women who were virgins became economically "valuable" property that could be negotiated. It has been argued that this may have led to the emergence of prostitution, according to Ahmed.

During the Zoroastrian laws around 500 BC (occurring in a monotheistic religion in Iran and Iraq) and continuing during the Sasanian period (AD226-651),[14] Ahmed says that wives were required to give total obedience to their husbands. Failure to do so would lead to divorce. Every morning, a Zoroastrian wife was to present herself in front of her husband with full submission. Bringing in a male heir was the religious duty of every woman. A man therefore could loan his wife to another in order to produce a male heir, or, for sexual pleasure. If a wife would not submit completely to her husband, she would receive a "certificate of disobedience" by the court and could be divorced without any consent required on her part.[15] On top of this, if a man was to divorce his wife, he would acquire everything she owned and the divorced wife would be left penniless even if she were a rich woman before marriage[16] (more on this later in the chapter).

THE PRE-ISLAMIC MIDDLE EAST

Such practices and misogynistic attitudes towards women as described above were silently seeped into Jewish and then later Christian religions of the Middle East. When Quranic Islam arrived, it continued this patriarchal system, but with some modifications in order to help reform societies. However, with the rise of Arabic Islam after the 7th Century, the Mesopotamian practices to some extent became part and participle of Islamic religion the same way it was handed down by the Judaeo-Christian traditions.

As we go through some of the salient features of the laws of that time in Persia, Mesopotamia, Syria, and Greece, many of my Muslim, Christian, Jewish even Hindu readers will find a parallelism in the mores that were practiced then and what is now being practiced under the guise of religion.

During the Byzantine Empire, approximately 306-337 AD, studies by the 11th century Byzantine historian and philosopher Michael Psellos indicate that preference was given to the birth of a boy, (a much more celebrated occasion than the birth of a girl). At the age of twelve or thirteen, children could be betrothed. Education for boys was more important than that of girls. Rather, girls were to learn the education of cooking and sewing. "Honourable" women were those who would remain silent, submissive, and within the four walls of their homes. Their being "invisible" would be a mark of respect. Hence, they were supposed to wear veils to distinguish themselves as respectable women and not prostitutes. Women's clothing would be such that it would not show any part of their flesh, including their hands which would be covered with gloves.[17] This practice even went so far as to cover the legs of tables and chairs due to their resemblance of a female leg. Both sexes were segregated in order to guard the contained world of women—they should neither be seen nor heard by other men.

In classical Greek society and especially in ancient Athens (the home of philosophers like Plato and Aristotle), women were marginalized the same as they were in the Byzantine culture (the Greek and Roman Empire). Women were not to be seen by any men except their relatives. Men would spend most of their time in public places, and as Ahmed says, the "respectable" women stayed at home. They were only to manage the household duties including caring for children, were to keep to themselves, and were to be veiled from head to toe in front of any strangers. Examples of similar practices were evident in Syrian societies as well. Inter-family marriages were required in order to produce a male heir for the family. Even an already married woman would be required to bring in a male heir for another member if this was necessitated. Women had no say in the family or in outside affairs, and they were not allowed to go outside the house or engage in any sort of financial transactions. They were treated as "infants" for whom decisions were made by men or the patriarch. In Greek and Roman societies, it was a law to raise only one daughter and dispose of any extras that were born (this rule did not apply to multiple sons).

ARISTOTLE'S THEORIES ABOUT WOMEN

Aristotle (384-324 BC) was an influential Greek philosopher who was the student of Plato and the teacher of Alexander the Great. Apart from writing about physics, metaphysics, and poetry, he wrote theories on women's issues that shaped the Athenian laws and further augmented women's marginalization. His misogynistic theories were codified and became the norm of that time. According to him, the primary function of women is to bear children. He also said that women were by nature defective and inferior to men because of their deficiency in mental and physical capabilities, and therefore must be ruled by men. Moreover, Ahmed while quoting Aristotle, wrote that women are "more jealous, more querulous, more apt to scold and strike . . . more void of shame and self respect, more false of speech, more deceptive".[18]

While writing about the male and female contribution in conception, Aristotle considered the female aspect in the conception as inferior, as it only provides a body mass while men's secretion provides the main soul and shape. He thought that females were actually impotent males, deformed in this way due to a lack of "something" or interference within the womb.[19]

In his well-researched book "Seven Daughters of the Eve", the geneticist Bryan Sykes traces the genetic make-up of humans and has written startling evidences regarding our genetic makeup. He was able to narrow down DNA into seven main sequences that trace our ancestral history. He called these DNA sequences the "Seven Daughters of Eve". His research resulted in the evidence that we humans receive nuclear genes from both parents, but only one mitochondrial gene (this comes down only from the mother and it remains unchanged). Because of its unchanging nature, this mitochondrial gene helped Sykes to determine the seven DNA sequences and hence the female names—Only through mothers one can truly trace and recognized oneself.

As for Aristotle's claim with regards to conception as stated above, Sykes explains that "the natural course of events is for the human embryo to develop into a female".[20] We all are by nature supposed to be females; we become male only due to the introduction of a "Y" chromosome. His research indicated that the "Y" chromosome is "full of 'junk' DNA" [21] and that it is also "small and stunted".[22]

It is very interesting to observe how God plans what God plans!

Eventually, as Judaism and then Christianity adopted these misogynistic attitudes, the church itself started to vociferously impart such tendencies through the Bible and writings of the church fathers. Women's sexuality became such a shameful thing that they were veiled, segregated, and considered a corrupted and evil temptation who would lead men astray from the path of God. It is distressing to note that even church fathers like Saint Augustine and Tertullian severely imparted misogyny, and wrote about it. For example, when Saint Augustine pondered why God created women, he finally concluded:

149

"I fail to see what use woman can be to man . . . if one excludes the function of bearing children".[23]

Tertullian wrote about woman:

"You are the Devil's gateway. You are the unsealer of the forbidden tree. You are the first deserter of the divine Law. You are she who persuaded him whom the devil was not valiant enough to attack. You destroyed so easily God's image, man. On account of your desert, that is death, even the son of God had to die".[24]

Arabic Islam later adopted almost all of these misogynistic attitudes towards women, especially through other sources like the *ahadith*. Most of these have close parallels with the Bible. Quranic Islam continues the patriarchal system; however it does not advocates any of what is written above. We shall see as we go through each topic in this chapter how Quranic Islam is much more prone to advocating the betterment of women's conditions. I shall now concentrate on what Quranic Islam dictates, and I shall compare that with what the *Shariah* edicts of the Arabic Islam currently advocates.

QURANIC ISLAM AND WOMEN

Western women have historically experienced the same dilemmas as Muslim women do now with their impasse into the present world. It is only recently (in the 20th century) that Western women have been able to acquire equal rights. In contrast to other religions, Quranic Islam gave many rights to women as long ago as 1400 years in the past. This is one of the deciding factors for my choice of being Muslim. There are many specific details about women's rights outlined in the Quran. As I go along discussing other issues related to women, I shall highlight some major rights that the Quran provided during a time when women in other religions were considered mere chattels.

Since Quran deals with issues in a patriarchal world, it mostly addresses men and not women. However, unlike other holy books, Quran has lifted the state of women from nothing to something. It even compliments in many ways with the contemporary world views of women. For me therefore, it has been easy to accept its dictates in general and adopt them in my everyday life without changing anything in my life style. And that is something I recognize and appreciate.

Below I have discussed under separate headings some salient features of the Quran with regards to the recognition of women's rights as stated by the Quran. They are those rights that other religious books have failed to recognize or due to wrong interpretations have been unable to recognize. I have also discussed alongside parts of the Quran that yet pose a question mark because of its ambiguousness and wrong interpretations. Some women's issues in those rights are also discussed and what concerns still surround the women of today have also been dealt with.

SPIRITUAL EQUALITY ISSUE

After the advent of Islam, Quranic Islam gave women spiritual rights that were never before given to them:

*And whoso doeth good works, **whether of male or female** (zakaran-au-unsa), and he (or she) is a believer, such will enter paradise and they will not be wronged the dint in a date-stone.* (Quran 4:124).

Lo! men who surrender unto Allah, and women who surrender, and men who believe and women who believe, and men who obey and women who obey, and men who speak the truth and women who speak the truth, and men who persevere (in righteousness) and women who persevere, and men who are humble and women who are humble, and men who give alms and women who give alms, and men who fast and women who fast, and men who guard their modesty and women who guard (their modesty), and men who remember Allah much and women who remember—Allah hath prepared for them forgiveness and a vast reward. (Quran 4:33-35).

151

QURAN SAVED EVE FROM ALL SINS

The Bible suggests in the story of Adam and Eve that it was not Adam but Eve who sinned, and because of her sin, all mankind is sinful—and that is the reason why women are cursed with menstruation and child bearing.[25] The church has long associated women with Eve, the one who is responsible for the 'original sin' in the world and the fall from grace.[26] Muslims have adopted this idea and superimposed it onto the Quran via the *hadith*. On the other hand, Quranic Islam actually removed the idea of women bringing sin to mankind through Eve when it directly states that / *"Each soul earneth only on its own account, nor doth any laden bear another's load"* (Quran 6:164). Further in regards to the story of Adam and Eve, the Quran puts the accountability equally on both sexes:/*"But the Devil whispered to him, saying: O Adam! Shall I show thee the tree of immortality and power that wasteth not away? Then they **both ate** thereof . . . He said: Go down hence, **both of you**"*(Quran 20:120-123).

The Quran also removed the concept that menstruation is a "curse" when it stated that the phenomenon is nothing more than an ailment occurring when one is not to have sexual intercourse (Quran 2:222). The idea of the childbearing curse was also lifted when the Quran honoured motherhood and raised it to the level of revering God alongside mothers:/ *"reverence Allah, through whom ye demand your mutual (rights), and (reverence) the wombs (That bore you): for Allah ever watches over you"* (Quran 4:1).

The Quran also suggests that one should be generous in performing duties for one's mother, and should thank one's parents in the same way that we would thank God:/ *"And We have enjoined upon human (insaan) concerning his parents—His mother beareth him in weakness upon weakness, and his weaning is in two years—**Give thanks unto Me and unto thy parents**. Unto Me is the journeying"* (Quran 31:14).

QURAN SAVED WOMEN'S MENSTRUATION FROM BEING A CURSE

They question thee (O Muhammad) concerning menstruation. Say: It is an illness, so let women alone at such times and go not in unto them till they are cleansed. And when they have purified themselves, then go in unto them as Allah hath enjoined upon you. Truly Allah loveth those who turn unto Him, and loveth those who have a care for cleanliness. (Quran 2:222).

In the past, menstruating women were considered a curse and untouchable; even eating with them would be considered a curse. This practice became common with the observance of Bible teachings (the Old Testament). After this, when certain Bible verses were superimposed onto the Quran through the *hadith*, it became part of the Muslim practice as well. Even today, many Muslim countries and many Arabs diligently follow the Bible verses[27] acquired from *ahadith* and consider them Islamic. In the Quran, it is written that menstruation is an ailment, and does not mention anything concerning the idea that menstruation is a curse or would make women untouchable—only the blood is dirty. The restriction as per the Quran is only for sexual intercourse. Medically speaking, this may be correct because menstruating blood is unclean as it contains dead tissue. Also, if a couple copulates during menstruation, the woman is potentially at risk of acquiring dangerous diseases.

QURAN SAVED *HOOR* ACQUISITION FOR WOMEN TOO

(Misconceptions of Companions in Paradise *Hoor*)

The idea of beautiful, voluptuous, wide-eyed females called *hoors* waiting for good "men" in paradise has long been associated with the Quran. Question is, if the Quran is governed by egalitarian principles, then why such incentives only for men? What about women? What do they get in paradise for their good works, and why such sensual enticements to begin with? Could it be that the translations of those specific verses

153

related to *hoor* have been done in such a way that it draws out such renditions? Let's take another look:

As stated before, the Arabic language has polysemic attributes that enables different interpretations of the Quran in different settings. One can therefore extract both the worst meanings of verses as well as the best, and thus there exists the Quranic advice to find the "best meaning" (39:18). Now the onus is upon us to do justice to this advice.

Before I delve into the in-depth analysis of the verses related to *hoor*, I would like to discuss what "*hoor*" literally means in Arabic. It is the plural genderless form of the words *ahwar* (masculine) and *haura* (feminine).[28] The literal meaning of *hoor* is "extreme whiteness".[29] In Quran, it is generally used in conjunction with *ayin* or *zawj*. *Ayin* in a literal sense means "eyes", whereas *zawj* has a wider definition including everything in pairs. It literally means "pair or together",[30] and not "wife" as it is generally translated, however, it certainly can imply as wife too. Thus, the word *hoor* is genderless in its literal sense and means "extreme whiteness", and cannot be associated with wives or female figures at all.

I shall now breakup in point forms below the various verses related to *hoor*, what their literal meanings translate to, and how differently they have been translated by the traditional exegetists. Later, I shall join the pieces together to make a holistic sense of all those verses related to the mysterious afterlife experiences:

The verses related to *hoor* can be found in chapters: 44:54, 55:72-74, 56:22-23, 78:31-34.

1. *"Wa-zawaajunahum-behoorin-a-ayinin"* (Quran 44: 54). It means "to pair or join them with whiteness of the eyes". This literal meaning may not seem to make any sense; we shall see later one possible understanding that could help to make sense. This verse has been translated differently by different exegetists:

154

Yusuf Ali—*"We shall join them to fair women with beautiful, big, and lustrous eyes"*

Pickthal—*"We shall wed them unto fair ones with wide, lovely eyes"*

Shakir—*"We will wed them with Houris pure, beautiful ones"*

Khalifa—*"We grant them wonderful spouses"*

2. *"Wa-hoorun-ayinun* (whiteness of the eyes)—*ka-amsaalay* (like, similar, for example) [31]—*oolu-ul* (pearls)-*maknoon* (shelter, enclosed)"[32] (Quran 56:22-23). It means "whiteness of the eyes is similar to the pearls within its shell", but it has been translated as:

   "And (there are) fair ones with wide, lovely eyes,—Like unto hidden pearls" (Quran 56:22-23)

3. *"Hoorun* (whiteness)—*maqsooraatun* (settled place)[33]—*fil-khayaam* (shelter, tent)[34] . . . *lam* (negative past term)—*yathmis-hunna* (to touch, slander, filth or corruption)[35]—*insun* (human)—*qablahum* (before)—*wala-ja-aan* (supernatural being—jinn) (Quran 55:72-74). It means "This whiteness is settled in a shelter untouched by either humans or *jinns*" but it has been translated as:

   "Fair ones, close-guarded in pavilions . . . whom no man or jinn before them has touched" (Quran 55:72-74)

4. *"Wa-kawa-ib*—Has various meanings coming from the root *ka-ab*, which means the joints in the body or projection, swell or high stature, clear, honourable, or a solid high square building. Hence the meaning for *Kaaba,* which is the "the house of God in Islam"[36]—*Atraaba*—from *turab*—dust, earth to similar type or equal. It also means friends or people with similar ranks[37]—*Wa-kasa* (filled, full)[38]—*Dahaqa* (drinking cup)"[39] (Quran 78:33-34). Together, they literally mean "and similar high statured

friends, and a filled cup". The verse before this state: /"*Indeed! for the righteous is achievement—Gardens enclosed and vineyards*" (Quran 78:31-32). All of the verses from 78:31-34 together could mean "*Lo! For duteous is achievement—Gardens enclosed and vineyards, and similar high statured friends, and a filled cup*".

To Summarize:

In summary, "those who are successful in the end will receive fruits of the gardens, its drinks as well as similar ranking honourable friends". But it has been translated as:

"*And voluptuous women of equal age; And a cup full (to the brim)*" (Quran 78:33-34), as translated by Yusuf Ali, Pickthal, and Shakir and, /"*Magnificent spouses. Delicious drinks*" (as translated by Khalifa). Even some have also translated it as "*full breasted women of same age*" and others have translated it as "*round ripe similar grapes*". Interesting part is the word *kawa-ib* that has been translated to mean voluptuous or full breasted women in 78:33 has been translated as 'goblets or bowls' in verse 56:18 related to *hoor* concept.

We can see how variant the renditions are and one can draw out many different meanings ranging from worst to best. We must therefore not disregard the thematic structure of the verses and the *matn* (substance) so that we can come to a meaning that is '*ehson*' (best), otherwise it may not cohere together with the matrix of all the verses. Such as the translation of the verses related to hoor in chapter 78 starts with stating that:/"*Indeed! for the righteous is achievement—Gardens enclosed and vineyards*"(78:31-32), and immediately after that, it entices and describes carnal/sensual pleasures that too for men only (78:33-34), does not enmesh with the matrix. This breaks up the *nazm*, the thematic structure of the overall verses and its rightful meanings.

The traditional translations have been done by men at a time when women were of no significance other than sexual, hence the masculine sexist tone in all the verses related to this mysterious afterlife reward and the portrayal of women as voluptuous sex objects. The idea of the afterlife is only what one can perceive—no one has ever come back from death to tell us exactly what really happens and how. Such verses therefore can only be interpreted by us using what we are accustomed to in our earthly surroundings: what we can see, hear, touch and feel; but this would still remain our wild imaginations or best inference, and not proof.

Even if we consider the traditional translations done by the exegetists above as correct, it still doesn't make sense, because in any of the verses related to *hoor*, the Quran does not uses the word "men" (*rijaal*) who would receive the gift, but instead the word "those" *(mun)* or the "duteous" or "righteous" *(mutaqeen)* or "humans" *(ins)*, hence must include both the male and female genders. Yet the traditional translations have excluded women altogether from receiving the reward. When verses 78:31-34 promise the reward to both righteous men and women, what then women will get? Luxurious gardens and "voluptuous women" or "full breasted women"? Does this make sense? The traditional translations therefore, do not harmonize with the thematic structure of the overall Quran.

In a traditional translation, all the verses related to hoor, would read together as follows:

"for those" (wal-e-mun) "for righteous"(mutaqeen):

". . . We shall wed them unto fair ones with wide, lovely eyes (44:54); *"Fair ones, close-guarded in pavilions . . . whom no man or jinn before them has touched"* (55:72-74); *(there are) fair ones with wide, lovely eyes,—Like unto hidden pearls"* (56:22-23); *"Indeed! for the righteous is achievement—gardens enclosed and vineyards, and voluptuous or full breasted women of equal age; And a cup full (to the brim).* (78:31-34).

I put together all the literal meanings of the specific words in Arabic from the above verses, it reads together as follows:

"for those" (wal-e-mun) "for righteous"(mutaqeen):

we shall pair or join them with whiteness of the eyes" (44:54), *"This whiteness is settled in a shelter untouched by either humans or jinns"* (55:72-74) *""whiteness of the eyes is similar to the pearls within its shell"* (56:22-23)," *indeed! for the righteous is achievement—Gardens enclosed and vineyards, and similar high statured friends, and a filled cup.* (78:31-34).

It is as if the Quran is meaning to say: "Once you follow the right conduct, you come to know the truth. Within your hearts you will be able to see the extreme purity (whiteness) of the *deen* which is like hidden pearls and only you got the chance to own them first. Everything will be then manifested to you in pure black and white".

I am not a scholar, but this is my common sense understanding based on the literal meanings of those specific words. Can we rule out the possibility of such a meaning as I just translated?

It is true that Only God knows what the actual meaning of Its words are, our efforts should only be to find the best thereof. Due to worst interpretations of verses stated as above and many other, we see how Quranic message has been abused and exploited to recruit "jehadis" "suicide bombers" calling them "God's Soldiers" and thus their reception of reward awaits in the heavens in the form of "full breasted voluptuous women" for their services.

POLYGAMY ISSUE

In antiquity, polygamy was commonly and freely practiced and many men had innumerable wives. When Quranic Islam rose, it did not abolish polygamy but laid restrictions on it. This issue is the center of an ongoing debate as to whether the practice of polygamy or the practice of monogamy is the ideal in Islam. Although Quranic Islam permitted restrictive polygamy, it advocates monogamy:

You shall hand over to the orphans their rightful properties. Do not substitute the bad for the good, and do not consume their properties by combining them with yours. This would be a gross injustice. If you deem it best for the orphans, **you may marry from the women (nissaa) (that is their mothers)—you may marry two, three, or four. If you fear lest you become unfair, then you shall be content with only one, or with what you already have** *(ma-malakat-aimanukum[α]). Additionally, you are thus more likely to avoid financial hardship* (Quran 4:2-3).

The overall theme of the above verses is related to the situation of orphans but traditionally, these verses have been interpreted out of context, (discussed below). It appears that only one marriage is sanctioned, and other marriages are only to support orphans, the divorced, or widows. That too has a condition to it: one has to deal justly with all of them, otherwise only one is sufficient. *"If you fear lest you become unfair, then you shall be content with only one"*. This is further backed by verse 4:129, *"****Ye will not be able to deal equally between (your) wives, however much ye wish*** *(to do so)"* (Quran 4:129).

Despite the fact that polygamy was rampant at the time of the inception of Islam, up until the age of 50, Muhammad remained married to only one wife, Khadija (he was 25 years of age and she was a 40 years old widow). He devoted all of his attention, love, and care towards her.[40] After she died, he married widows to support them (the only exception is Aisha, who was not previously married).[41][β]

More than one marriage is therefore only to support women at a time of their dire need, such as during a time of war when many women had lost their husbands and were left alone with children. It is indeed very sad to see people exploiting this verse as a tool to satisfy their own libido.

Going back to verses 4:2-3, the out of context interpretation has led to marrying not the mothers of the orphans but the

---

[α]   See below 'Mistresses' for its explanation.

[β]   Please refer to 'Muhammad's Marriage to Aisha' in chapter 4 "Islam and Its Issues"

orphan girls themselves (including virgin women). This traditional interpretation cannot be right because: (a) Quran uses the word 'women' (*nissaa*) not girls (*bint*), so it could very well be referring to the mother of the orphans. And (b) The verses instructs to provide care and protection to the orphans, if we assume that the verse actually meant to marry the orphans in order to provide care then what about the male orphans? Who would provide protection to the male orphan, if the men go about marrying orphan girls to protect them?

MORE THAN FOUR WIVES OF MUHAMMAD

Having mentioned Muhammad's married life, it would be important to address here that it is also alleged that even though Muhammad was married to one wife until the age of 50 (c.620) and did not marry any other until his first wife died, why is it that Muhammad had more than four wives when the Quran only allows four marriages? Verse 4:2-3 came after the battle of Uhud[42] at the end of c. 626.* Muhammad had three more marriages as per the traditional history.[43] Why did he have more marriages? There are many answers to this question, but it has always been debated as to how many wives Muhammad actually had. So what if he really didn't have more than four wives at a time? But traditionally speaking, why a Prophet should even have four wives? Is it becoming to a Prophet to be involved in such sensual pleasures? May be not, but doesn't it show that he was very much a human just like anybody else, yet a Prophet?

---

* The revelation order of surah *Nisa*, which contains the four marriages verses (4:2-3) is between 90 and a 100 (traditional order 4, *see appendix A*), thus a range of between c. 626-c. 630 (from 4th to 8th *hijri* migration calendar) is given by different historians for the commencing and completion of this *surah* chapter. It may therefore be that Muhammad may have acquired more than four wives as per the traditional culture before the verses for marriage restrictions were even revealed.

It has been reasoned that he needed to set alliances in order to build a strong hold of Islam and the tribal custom dictated to strengthen and build relationship through marriages. It could also be that he felt responsible toward all those women whose husbands died fighting for a religion that he brought, hence the verse 4:2-3.

I personally think if he was a man of lust he would have had harem from the age of 25 when he married a 40 year old but he choose to remain monogamous throughout the primetime of his age. And if he was a man of not craving for lust but for worldly possessions through crafty methods and thus married a wealthy old widow, he wouldn't have hold the title of *ameen* (a trusty) and *sadiq* (truthful) given to him by the disbelievers at a very early age. Quran wouldn't have endorsed him as an *'honourable'* man with *'great moral character'*. (69:40, *68:4)*

MISTRESSES

It is common among many Muslims including Arab Muslims to hold mistresses. These could be women living outside of the home, or they could be living in a household (such as maids or servants). These mistresses can be had regardless of whether the man is married or not. This behaviour is wrongfully justified by stating that the Quran itself allows having mistresses and also to fornicate with them. They quote the following verse:

The believers must (eventually) win through—Those who humble themselves in their prayers; Who avoid vain talk; Who are active in deeds of charity; Who abstain from sex, Except with those joined to them in the marriage bond, **or (the captives) whom their right hands possess** *(malakat aymanuhum***)* [generally translated as maid servants that one owns or hires],—**for (in their case) they are free from blame**, *But those whose desires exceed those limits are transgressors.* (Quran 23:1-7) (square bracket is mine).

---

*   Discussed below.

Please note that having slaves during the time of the revelation of the Quran was very common and the Quran did not abolish it but its teachings gave way for gradual eradication of slavery. There are overwhelming verses which state to release slaves and give them their freedom, and to deal kindly and justly with them. Even if they seek emancipation, one must provide them in writing. (Quran verses 90:13, 58:3, 5:89, 4:92, 24:33 and more) I find this a reform by the Quran, a gradual process to wipe out slavery completely.

As for the above translation (23:1-7), it doesn't make sense that the first five verses speak about the high character of a believer. It states that those who believe in a Creator are humble, pious and full of morality. It assigns those characters as the crux of success, but then immediately after that, the same God allows having extra marital sex or unlicensed sex with other women and maidservants and that too without any blame. This doesn't seem to congeal very well. It also does not cohere with the thematic structure of the majority of the verses in the Quran.

If that is really the meaning of the bolded portion in the above verse, then why does the Quran speak about guarding one's chastity except with their spouses, and call those who cross this line "transgressors" (Quran 70:29-31)? And, what shall we make of the verse where the Quran encourages and advises to marry maids and slaves:/*"And marry such of you as are widowed or single (al-ayaami) and the pious of your slaves and maid-servants. If they be poor, Allah will enrich them of His bounty. Allah is of ample means, Aware."* (Quran 24:32). Even regarding the women who became refugees seeking asylum with the Prophet, the Quran urges Muslims to marry these women, /*"and there will be no blame on you if ye marry them upon providing their dower to them."* (Quran 60:10).

In addition, there is a verse in the Quran that says anyone who cannot find someone to marry "must remain chaste":/ *"Let those who find not the wherewithal for marriage keep themselves chaste, until Allah gives them means out of His grace."* (Quran 24:33). Further in the same verse, the Quran exhorts not to force one's maidservants to whoredom, but rather to release them of their slave bonding:

> *And if any of your slaves ask for a deed in writing (to enable them to earn their freedom for a certain sum), give them such a deed if ye know any good in them: yea, give them something yourselves out of the means which Allah has given to you.* **But force not your maids to prostitution when they desire chastity, in order that ye may make a gain in the goods of this life.** (Quran 24:33).

If verses 23: 1-7 are meant to allow unlicensed sex and extra-marital sex, then why are there these other verses that speak otherwise: Advising and urging Muslims to marry these women (whether they be widows, singles or slaves)?

Aimaanuhum in 23:7 is generally translated to mean *right hand*, the plural of which is *aimaan* (faith or belief). It is from the root *ya-meem-noon (Y.M.N)*, which has diversified meanings—from "faith or belief" to "toward the right side or right hand" or "strength or strong" to "solemn oath or solid contract".[44] The verses 23: 1-7 above where it says "or (the captives) whom their right hands possess" is the translation of *ma-malakat-aimaanuhum,* which is always referred to in the past tense meaning that had already gone through before. *Lughat-ul-Quran* gives many diversified meanings along with stating that usually *aimaanaykum* means the subordinates, including slaves. But it points out that this has come in connection with marriage ties when one takes a solemn oath, and that the Arabs had the custom to lifting their 'right hand' when taking an oath.[45] This is also a common practice in today's courtroom. So why should it be difficult to interpret verses 23:6-7 as /"*Except with those joined to them in the marriage bond, or (the captives) with whom they have taken solemn oath (with their right hand) to betroth?"*

Having so many diversified meanings, I find myself unable to affix the translations as done for verses 23:1-7 to the specific Arabic words. These translations also do not square well with the whole theme within the Quran, neither promote the 'best meaning' (39:18). When there already had existed rampant and uninhibited sex, the Quran need not provide a license to continue this, but rather advice to curb it for a better community. Therefore, those verses could be speaking of maids or women whom they have already married or are betrothed to marry.

MARRIAGE RIGHTS / RELATIONSHIP ISSUES

In the past, women were considered 'property' that was to be transferred from father to husband, and so on. Hence, women would lose their family name after they were married because they were after all only a property. Judaism and Christianity as well as Hinduism also enforced this custom. After marriage, a woman would lose her individual identity and would not be able to divorce or remarry. If her husband died, the woman would have to remain widowed all her life; she would become untouchable and be reduced to a living corpse.

On March 14, 1913, the British in South Africa enforced and legalized only those marriages that were solemnized according to Christian rites. All marriages based on other beliefs (whether in the past, present or future) were considered "outside the pale of legal marriages", and instantly all these married women became concubines.[46] Gandhi religiously fought this sanction and helped legalize marriages which were solemnized according to other religious rites. But this reprieve was only given provided the family name of the bride was changed to the husband's family name, as in the Christian tradition.

Sadly, we Muslims adopted some of these customs as well. This is partly due to the ignorance about our own proper religious rites as dictated in the Quran. The Quran did not only help curb the reducing of women to nothing, but also gave women an identity and a voice that even Western women were unable to acquire up until the mid 20th century.

Below I will highlight a few marriage rights that the Quran provided during the 6th century when women were simply nothing.

MARRIAGE REQUIRES THE BRIDE'S CONSENT TO BE VALID

"O ye who believe! It is not lawful for you forcibly to inherit the women" (Quran 4:19). In reality, many women are still forced into marriage in Muslim countries.

DOWRY REQUIREMENT

And give the women (on marriage) their dower as a free gift; but if they, of their own good pleasure, remit any part of it to you, take it and enjoy it with right good cheer (Quran 4:4). This dowry system is still in practice in some places. Before the advent of Islam, provision of a dowry by the woman was a common practice. As pointed out earlier, whatever a woman owned became the property of her husband. Because of this, people started assigning properties in the name of their daughters so that they may be able to attract suitors, hence the birth of the idea of a dowry. On the other hand, the Quran reversed the idea of the provision of a dowry from a woman to a man, and it became a gift that honoured the woman for accepting and starting her life with her chosen man.

This is an improvement in the quality of a gender specific life, as many women in the past remained unmarried only because they were unable to provide a hefty dowry. By shifting the dowry toward men, the Quran not only raised the status of women but also removed the heavy burden from the shoulders of those families who were financially challenged to provide a large dowry and would have otherwise seen their daughters remain unmarried.

Ironically, in present Islam, women are still burdened to provide the dowry and this verse 4:4 (above) has been generally interpreted (rather trimmed down) to mean "*haq mahr*": This is not dowry, and is interpreted to give in the form of money and that too only at the time of divorce (though the amount is settled on at the time of marriage). Consequently, many women are forced to provide the dowry, and if they are not divorced (which many wouldn't want to be), they never get the chance to receive their marriage gift or dower. This is despite the ruling provided in the Quran that dowry is a gift to be given at the beginning of marriage by the would-be husband and not when he divorces. If women were to provide dowry then why Quran is silent about it?

WIFE BEATING ISSUES

Men are in charge (qawwamun ala) of women, because Allah hath made the one of them to excel the other, and because they spend of their property (for the support of women). So good women are the obedient, guarding in secret that which Allah hath guarded. As for those from whom ye fear rebellion (nushuz), admonish them and banish them to beds apart, and scourge them (idribuhunne). Then if they obey you, seek not a way against them. Lo! Allah is ever High, Exalted, Great (Quran 4:34).

Due to the above translation, it has been alleged that the Quran itself teaches us to torture women and subdue them (please also refer to the section "Woman as Leaders" for more discussion on the same verse). The old translations fit their age of exegesis, the age when it was not difficult to accept men as superior to women and therefore allowed to beat a disobedient wife. Women themselves used to accept such a situation during those times. During the present time also, there are women who may still think this way, but their numbers are minimal.

Because of the polysemic attributes of the Arabic language, the rendering of verse 4:34 should reflect the best meaning in accordance with our time. It is the time when no abuse is tolerable, let alone the beating of a woman. I would therefore like to concentrate on two key questions related to 4:34: One, whether the reading of the Quranic verse as above is in harmony with the whole thematic structure of the Quran for our time, and two, if not, what would be the "best meaning" (39:18) of the verse in terms of the Quranic premise of teaching for today's society?

Quran came to reform and not to remove what was already being practiced at a certain time. Its teaching becomes dynamic within each verse's multi-meaning capabilities. These offer an ongoing mode of interpretation to reform whatever is needed at every time and age.

The word *qawwamun 'ala* means "those who provide a means of support or livelihood", and "to keep a balance, fairness" and to "fulfill needs".[47] It therefore means that men are **responsible** for supporting and caring for women through their monetary means, and not because they are physically stronger (or superior or in charge of them). Otherwise, as Abdul Fauq pointed out to me[48], the Quran would not have appointed men and women to be each other's guardians *awlia* (Quran 9:71).

But why the need for men to remain responsible when today women can equally be financially secured on their own? If the Quran had not made one of us responsible for the other, our very system of bonding together as a society would have been threatened (as there would be no family concept and no obligations whatsoever). But such a rendering would only be conditioned upon a man being economically capable of doing so and woman not.

As a married woman with children myself, I know that there is a natural inclination and affinity within a woman towards nurturing. I have always been very ambitious and active, I have studied and worked, and I am also now a business woman and serve as a tribunal member. Yet, I find myself crawling back to my natural desire to care for my children, my home, and my husband, and to see that everything runs smoothly without any of these coming into harm. Despite being career oriented, I would prefer my husband be responsible and obligated, especially in financial matters, to take care of us rather than myself. I would want my career only to satisfy my ambitious nature, and not for it to become an obligation for taking care of my family, unless this was needed. Nevertheless, there are factions of women who are different and do not think or act the way I do.

Coming back to the verse at hand, if we look at the last part where it is assumed that men are supposed to "beat their wives" if the wives disobey (*nushuz*), this is due to the word *idribuhunne* which has the root word *daraba*. Again, this would best be suited for 6th century culture. The translation of *daraba*, "to beat", would be acceptable during such an age, and would be considered an act of reforming the society when it is restricted to use only as a last resort. The culture at this time was such that beating a woman for anything was the norm, so much that a woman herself would consider it something normal despite her resentment for it.

Daraba comes from the root *darab (zarab)*, which apart from meaning to "beat or strike", also means to "counsel, prevent, travel, leave, set up, [or] take away".[49] Considering the verse, if a man is responsible for taking care of his wife and family and his wife is indifferent, disloyal, of ill conduct, or of lewd character (all of which are also the meanings of *nushuz*) [50], she should be "left alone or counselled" as a last resort. As Barlas says:

"At a time when men did not need permission to abuse women, this Ayah simply could not have functioned as a license; in such a context, it could only have been a restriction insofar as the Quran made daraba the measure of last, not the first, or even the second, resort. And if the Quran meant to restrict abuse even during those most abusive of times, there is no reason to regard this Ayah as an authorization at a time when we claim to have become more, not less, civilized."[51]

RIGHT TO AFFECTION AND KINDNESS FROM EACH OTHER

*And of His signs is this: He created for you mates from yourselves that ye might find rest in them, and **He ordained between you love and mercy**. Lo! herein indeed are portents for folk who reflect.* (Quran 30:21).

MUTUAL CONSENT A NECESSITY

If they desire to wean the child by mutual consent and (after) consultation, it is no sin for them; and if ye wish to give your children out to nurse, it is no sin for you, provide that ye pay what is due from you in kindness. Observe your duty to Allah, and know that Allah is Seer of what ye do. (Quran 2:233).

Nowhere in the Quran did I find a verse saying that household chores are the duty of a woman only. The above verse should be enough to interpret in a wider sense. Historically, we know that Muhammad always helped in household chores. If the Prophet of the Muslims himself helped and did household chores, then other men (who are not at all superior to the Prophet) must do the same. The idea that household chores are the duty of women has simply been imbedded in our culture. There is no harm in both the husband and wife mutually deciding to practice this. But, to call it a part of Quranic Islam would be something of an innovation.

CONTRACEPTION RIGHTS

There is no verse in the Quran that says one must not practice Planned Parenthood. The orthodox Muslims believe that the Quran forbids contraception based on the verse/ *"and that ye slay not your children because of penury—We provide for you and for them"* (Quran 6:151). The only thing that is taken from the verse for their purpose is the part that states *"God is the provider"*, thus, they believe we should have as many children as we want.

They overlook or ignore the part where the Quran says *"and slay not your children".* This is what Barlas explains as "reading out of context".[52] The part of the verse *"and slay not your children"* is enough to conclude that this verse is not even remotely suggesting not to use contraception, and is instead speaking about children who have already come into this world. Verse 6:151 is advising parents: once you already have a baby, do not slay it out of fear of poverty, for God provides for everyone. The Quran did not advise that one must keep having babies and do no planning. It has no connection whatsoever with contraception. It is simply a pretext for many Muslim men to satisfy their libidos and nothing more.

INCEST PROHIBITIONS

And marry not those women whom your fathers married, except what hath already happened (of that nature) in the past. Lo! it was ever lewdness and abomination, and an evil way. Forbidden unto you are your mothers, and your daughters, and your sisters, and your father's sisters, and your mother's sisters, and your brother's daughters and your sister's daughters, and your foster-mothers, and your foster-sisters, and your mothers-in-law, and your step-daughters who are under your protection (born) of your women unto whom ye have gone in—but if ye have not gone in unto them, then it is no sin for you (to marry their daughters)—and the wives of your sons who (spring) from your own loins. And (it is forbidden unto you) that ye should have two sisters together, except what hath already happened (of that nature) in the past. Lo! Allah is ever Forgiving, Merciful. (Quran 4:22-23).

MUTA MARRIAGE ISSUES (Temporary Marriage)

The *Shiites* in Islam mainly follow the *muta* marriage tradition. In literal sense, *muta* means "enjoyment or pleasure". In this temporary marriage custom, a man and a woman can marry for a short period of time for enjoyment purposes. When the marriage term expires, it dissolves automatically. Herein, they do not acquire the titles of husband or wife. When the term expires, the man can give the woman wages for her sexual services.

In other words, it is much like legalizing prostitution in the name of religion. If the Quran was to promote prostitution via *muta* marriages, then why did it put restriction on polygamy in the first place? Why did it talk about guarding one's chastity except with spouses and called those who cross this limit "transgressors" (Quran 70:29-31)?

It is argued that the Quran itself supports this custom. A specific sentence (in bold print) in this following verse is being used to justify this custom:

Also prohibited are the women who are already married, unless they flee their disbelieving husbands who are at war with you. These are GOD's commandments to you. All other categories are permitted for you in marriage, so long as you pay them their due dowries. You shall maintain your morality, by not committing adultery. ***Thus, whoever you like among them, you shall pay them the dowry decreed for them.*** *You commit no error by mutually agreeing to any adjustments to the dowry. GOD is Omniscient, Most Wise.* (Quran 4:24).

Pickthal has put the words in another way: "and those of whom ye seek content (by marrying them), give unto them their portions as a duty", whereas Yusuf Ali has put the sentence in the following words: "desiring chastity, not lust, seeing that ye derive benefit from them, give them their dowers (at least) as prescribed". However, the rendition given by the proponents of *muta* marriage is rather different: "so those of them, whom you enjoy, give them their appointed wages".

Considering the variant readings of the Quran, how can we come to an agreement on the "best meaning" (39:18) of verse 4:24 based on reasons and common sense? Those traditional readings cannot be the 'best meaning' otherwise, it is a legalization of prostitution under the guise of religion. It therefore must have been taken out of context. So we should look at the verses that precede and follow verse 4:24 (please see all the verses 4:19-25 at the end of the chapter). We find that it is with reference to only marriage ties and the dowry issue and nothing to do with paid sex service. Such a rendition of one specific sentence in a verse, not even the whole verse, appears not to fit with the whole matrix of the verses that precede and follow it, which are related only to legal permanent marriages (please see all the verses 4:19-25 at the end of the chapter). It reminds me of the verse where the Quran states:

> He it is Who hath revealed unto thee (Muhammad) the Scripture **wherein are clear revelations—they are the substance of the Book**—and others (which are) allegorical. **But those in whose hearts is doubt pursue, forsooth, that which is allegorical** seeking (to cause) dissension by seeking to explain it. None knoweth its explanation save Allah. And those who are of sound instruction say: We believe therein; the whole is from our Lord; **but only those of understanding really heed.** (Quran 3:7).

DIVORCE ISSUES

Before the rise of Islam, the concept of divorce in Christianity was abhorrent. It was believed that since the marriage is made in heaven, it couldn't be broken once it was tied down. Later, people started living together discreetly without marriage to see how it would work. Consequently, many children were born out of wedlock and many women remained unmarried. There was not even any moral and legal obligation on either party. This quandary is still prevalent.

As a reforming book, the Quran came up with the concept of divorce in a marriage. It not only legalized divorce, but promoted the concept of marriage as a contract. It further allowed women to retain their family name after marriage as an individual identity (33:5), which previously women would lose once they were married. This innovation in the Quran is something I would like to acknowledge and honour. Whether the Quranic divorce concept is fair for both genders is something I leave with my readers to decide.

RIGHT FOR WOMEN TO INITIATE DIVORCE

Marriage is considered a contract in the Quran that can be dissolved by either party.

If a wife fears cruelty or desertion on her husband's part, there is no blame on them if they arrange an amicable settlement between themselves" (4;128), *"But if they disagree (and must part), Allah will provide abundance for all from His all-reaching bounty: for Allah is He that careth for all and is Wise.* (4:130).

Quran outlines in detail only men's divorce procedure and not women except what is mentioned as in the above verse. When all the relevant verses are put together of marriage life and its responsibilities, there is a pattern we see, where more responsibilities are put on the shoulders of men (as apparent by the many rights a woman can enjoy). It is conceivable that since men have overwhelming obligations to maintain, providing and caring for his wife and family, his divorce procedure needed to be outlined in detail so that he cannot get away from his huge obligations very easily. But that is just another way one can view the issue, and it may sound apologetic to some, yet one cannot deny that at least Quran did give many rights to women at a time when they had none.

RIGHT FOR MEN TO INITIATE DIVORCE
(A Triple Divorce Issue)

I am considering only two points here: one, the Quran provided the right to divorce and remarry which other religions failed to provide, and two, to analyze whether the Quranic concept of men divorcing women is just and fair, or otherwise.

Just like polygamy, Quran permitted divorce, but it does not advocate it. It made divorce a procedure so lengthy and intricately elaborate that it is essentially as difficult as not getting a divorce. This way, it also made it clear that marriage is surely a *"solemn covenant"* (Quran 4:19-21), and a serious obligation from which one cannot simply get away.

In today's "Arabic Islam", men can free themselves from an unwanted wife in a blink of an eye—all they have to do is say "I divorce you" three times, and in an instant they are free of any obligations whatsoever. They can also free themselves instantaneously from any kind of provision towards the wife or the ex-wife under different divorce circumstances. Is this what the Quranic precept of divorce is for men? I had also believed in the past in this verbal "triple divorce" rule for men, but my continuous studies of the Quran and various literary discussions made me later be able to comprehend the concept of the "triple divorce" better: divorce is in fact not as easy and as short as it has been made into, but instead is a complicated and a lengthy procedure.

I shall go through the divorce procedure in detail below. To summarize: after each divorce there is a time lapse and the couple goes through an interim period. Each divorce in the "triple divorce" procedure is itself a complete divorce, and a couple can part ways if they so wish to. However, the first two divorces are revocable: /*"Divorce may be retracted twice"* (Quran 2:229), so if a couple reconciles, they can remain married. When the couple goes through the divorce procedure the third time, it is then that the divorce procedure becomes irrevocable. In addition, through every step of the divorce, the Quran has laid a heavy emphasis on the provision, maintenance, and the residence of the woman regardless of whether she is still the wife of the man or the ex-wife. In the present "Arabic Islam", the woman instantaneously becomes homeless and without provisions the moment she is divorced three times verbally.

The reduction of the divorce procedure into the "triple divorce" rule—a quick, verbal, three times repeated "I divorce you"—has made a jest of Quranic Islam and has insulted the Quranic message. Consequently, the Quranic idea of divorce seems dated, preposterous and inapplicable. The Quran thus became static rather than dynamic.

Below I have put down the step-by-step procedure of divorce as it is outlined in the Quran, with reference to relevant verses:

Step 1: Arbitrator Requirement

If a couple finds that they are unable to live together in a marriage relationship, the first step is to appoint an arbitrator for each of the parties:

If a couple fears separation, you shall appoint an arbitrator from his family and an arbitrator from her family; if they decide to reconcile, GOD will help them get together. GOD is Omniscient, Cognizant. (Quran 4:35).

Step 2: First Divorce Initiation and Witness Requirement

If after appointing arbitrators, differences don't resolve and the couple still wishes to continue going through the process of divorce, the man initiates the divorce in the presence of two witnesses. /*"You shall have two equitable witnesses witness the divorce before GOD"* (Quran 65:2). (In the Arabic Islam, which is practiced today, there is no need to have any witness; a man can verbally divorce at any time).

Step 3a: Provisional Period

After step two, the couple goes through an interim period in which the woman waits three monthly courses: /*"Women who are divorced shall wait, keeping themselves apart, three (monthly) courses. And it is not lawful for them that they should conceal that which Allah hath created in their wombs if they are believers in Allah and the Last Day"* (Quran 2:282). *"O you prophet, when you people divorce the women, you shall ensure that a divorce interim is fulfilled. You shall measure such an interim precisely"* (Quran 65:1).

In this period, as per verse 2:282, it is ascertained whether there is any pregnancy (see step 4). This period also provides a cooling-off period so that both parties may ponder whether they really should go through with the divorce procedure or not.

Step 3b: Woman to Remain in the Same Home During the Interim

During this interim period, the woman can remain in her married home if she wishes, which the Quran calls *"their home"* (Quran 65:1). Although the first divorce is complete, it is still a revocable divorce. During the interim period when the wife is living in the same house, the Quran warns the husband not to make life so miserable for his wife that she is forced to leave her married home. It also warns men against using force to make them stay in the same home should they decide otherwise (see verse 2:231 below).

*Do not evict them from **their homes**, nor shall you make life miserable for them, to force them to leave on their own, unless they commit a proven adultery. These are GOD's laws. Anyone who transgresses GOD's laws commits an injustice against himself. You never know; maybe GOD wills something good to come out of this.* (Quran 65:1).

*You shall allow them to live in the same home in which they lived with you, and **do not make life so miserable for them that they leave on their own**.* (Quran 65:6).

The divorced woman shall be allowed to live in the same home amicably, or leave it amicably. (Quran 2:229).

*If you divorce the women, once they fulfill their interim (three menstruations), you shall allow them to live in the same home amicably, or let them leave amicably. **Do not force them to stay against their will, as revenge.** Anyone who does this wrongs his own soul. Do not take GOD's revelations in vain. Remember GOD's blessings upon you, and that He sent down to you the scripture and wisdom to enlighten you. You shall observe GOD, and know that GOD is aware of all things.* (Quran 2:231).

Step 4: Reconciliation or Parting Ways

If it is established that the wife is pregnant, and after knowing this fact the couple decides to reconcile, they can remain married (as the first divorce is revocable). Moreover, in this instance of discovered pregnancy, the Quran advises the husband to revoke the divorce and take his wife back:/ *"And their husbands would do better to take them back in that case if they desire a reconciliation"* (Quran 2:282).

If the wife is pregnant but the couple still decides to continue with the divorce procedure, the provisional period extends until the infant is born. The wife remains in her married home and the husband is required to provide for his wife while she is pregnant: /*"If they are pregnant, you shall spend (your substance) on them until they give birth"* (Quran 65:6). The extended interim period provides the couple with long enough time to consider revoking the divorce, as now, there is another life involved.

However, if after the baby is born the couple still decides to separate, the ex-husband is still required to provide for the ex-wife and the child: /*"If they nurse the infant, give them their recompense. You shall maintain the amicable relations among you. If you disagree, you may hire another woman to nurse the child"* (Quran 65:6).

If on the other hand the wife is not pregnant, the couple may continue through the provisional period steps 3a and b (which would work as a cooling off period), and at the end of the provisional period, they may decide whether to part ways or remain married: /*"Once the interim is fulfilled, you may reconcile with them equitably, or go through with the separation equitably"* (Quran 65:2).

Step 5: Dowry Settlement

After the divorce, some negotiations are required with regards to the dowry that was given to the wife (bride) at the time of marriage by the husband (bridegroom). It is a gift given to the bride in order to honour her for accepting and starting a married life with her chosen man, the Quran legislates that the dower once given cannot be taken back even if one divorces his wife. It was historically a common practice by husbands to take from divorced women whatever they had given to their wives along with whatever she herself may have acquired. Quran states: /*"It is not lawful for the husband to take back anything he had given her"* (Quran 2:229).

In other verses, the Quran strongly urges the husband to refrain from committing such acts and considers them as abomination:

> *O you who believe, it is not lawful for you to inherit what the women leave behind, against their will. You shall not force them to give up anything you had given them, . . . But if ye decide to take one wife in place of another, even if ye had given the latter a whole treasure for dower, Take not the least bit of it back: Would ye take it by slander and manifest wrong? How could you take it back, after you have been intimate with each other, and they had taken from you a solemn pledge?* (4:19-21).

If the wife herself foregoes or gives back anything at her own will, only then a husband can enjoy part of the dower given back to him: /*"they commit no error if the wife willingly gives back whatever she chooses"* (Quran 2:229).

Step 6: Second Divorce Initiation

Since the second divorce is also revocable (*"Divorce may be retracted twice"* 2:229), a couple can go through the same process from steps 1 through 5.

Step 7: Third Divorce Initiation

The third divorce is the divorce which is irrevocable. Once it is initiated, the couple goes through the divorce procedure without reconciliation and eventually part ways./ *"If he divorces her (for the third time), it is unlawful for him to remarry her"* (Quran 2:230).

Addendum to Step 7: Provision to Re-Marry the Divorced Wife by the First Husband

The Quran states that after the third initiation of the divorce, if the couple wishes to re-marry, they can do so only under one condition: the wife must first marry another man and have this second husband divorce her. Only then can the first husband re-marry his divorced wife:/ *"unless she marries another man, then he divorces her. The first husband can then remarry her"* (Quran 2:230).

For a long time, I have raised questions as to why it is the woman who has to go through a second marriage before re-marrying her ex-husband and not the other way around. Also, what is the reason for this weird condition for re-marrying once divorced? My reasoning below may sound apologetic to some but it provides much needed peace for my belief.

For the first question, there is perhaps justification if we look at the natural psychology present. I would reason that if a man were also given the condition to marry another woman before he could re-marry his ex-wife, he probably would enjoy his temporary sexual pleasures with another woman. On the other hand, women are generally less sexually oriented and more family oriented by nature, so it could be anguish for her to go through this predicament. At the same time, there would be more anguish for a man to know that another man is having sexual pleasure with a woman who used to be his wife (whom he now wishes to have back).

For the latter question, I understand that this condition may sound strange, but perhaps it would help deter treating divorce like a pastime. A couple would have to think twice or thrice about the repercussions before they decide to divorce each other. Marriage in the Quran, is considered a *"solemn covenant" meesaaqan-ghaleeza* (Quran 4:19-21) and a serious obligation from which one cannot simply get away.

Nonetheless, when a couple has already gone through the three lengthy steps of the divorce procedure (which adds up to a minimum of nine months and a maximum of 18 months to decide to part ways), it is better for them to remain apart rather than be together again. If both the man and the woman remorse after the third irrevocable divorce and wish to reconcile, the Quran would fairly speak that you were given ample of time to make up your mind and yet you decided to go with the divorce. So, now stay separated.

When a couple cannot find themselves staying together throughout the three long divorce procedures, what guarantee is there that they won't do it again if united a second time?

Step 8: Special Provisions

The Quran stipulates special provisions for divorce under different circumstances:

1. If a woman has reached menopause, her interim period depends not upon her being pregnant: /*"As for the women who have reached menopause, if you have any doubts, their interim shall be three months. As for those who do not menstruate, and discover that they are pregnant, their interim ends upon giving birth. Anyone who reverences GOD, He makes everything easy for him"* (Quran 65:4).

2. If a couple is divorced before consummating the marriage, there is no interim period for them. However, the husband is still supposed to maintain and provide for his ex-wife, just the same way he would have to in a divorce with an interim period:/ *"O you who believe, if you married believing women, then divorced them before having intercourse with them, they do not owe you any waiting interim. You shall compensate them equitably, and let them go amicably."* (Quran 33:49).

3. As with #2, if the dowry was also not settled before the couple was divorced, the ex-husband is still responsible for providing for his ex-wife, but according

> to his means:/ *"You commit no error by divorcing the women before touching them, or before setting the dowry for them. In this case, you shall (provide) compensation to them—the rich as he can afford and the poor as he can afford—an equitable compensation. This is a duty upon the righteous."* (Quran 2:236).

4. Regardless of the circumstances, the ex-husband is responsible and liable for the provision of his ex-wife:/*"The divorcees also shall be provided for, equitably. This is a duty upon the righteous. GOD thus explains His revelations for you that you may understand."* (Quran 2:241-242).

Another question is why the Quran gave the divorce procedure so many twist and turns. As an example, in the Canadian legal system, provisions for divorce are there but the procedure is very simple. While it has the same views as the Quran where child support and alimony are concerned, it does not have anything like the triple divorce system.

Armstrong says, that it came to create "a decent and a just society",[53] the Quran therefore, had to do more than just implementing equitable solutions. The Quran was to establish a society where each and every person is taken care of within the lines of each society's culture. If it had left the divorce procedure as simple as the Canadian divorce system is (for example), this would not have helped in keeping the balance of the society. There would have been no deterring factor from a divorce, ensuing higher rate of divorce among marriages. This higher rate of divorce is evident in Canada since the system does not deter a person from going through the divorce. Many in Canada may treat divorce with not much more reverence than a pastime.

The Quran therefore (along with fitting itself into the very fabric of each society's culture) is making sure that there remains a balance in the society and that the weak and vulnerable are taken care of. Women at all times have been subjugated. They have also been treated unfairly and inequitably not only in the recent past, but also in the present time. Only the gravity of subjugation has taken different modes, depending upon the times.

Speaking of divorce system, Quran is at the least making an effort to see that women's rights are being met by making sure that women are being thoroughly taken care of while going through the ordeal of divorce.

RIGHT TO RE-MARRY

*(In the case of) those of you who are about to die and leave behind them wives, they should bequeath unto their wives a provision for the year without turning them out, **but if they go out (of their own accord) there is no sin for you in that which they do of themselves within their rights.** Allah is Mighty, Wise. For divorced women a provision in kindness: a duty for those who ward off (evil). Thus Allah expoundeth unto you His revelations so that ye may understand.* (Quran 2:240).

Even though the Quran speaks about re-marriage in the verse above, in the Muslim world, a widow or divorced women will have lost all the luxuries of life to enjoy further. If she ever decides or intends to re-marry, she is looked upon as a woman with no dignity or honour. Some may consider such a woman as being equal to a prostitute. As a result, in order to avoid this stigma, many women would never think of re-marrying. Men on the other hand are encouraged to re-marry.

LEGAL ISSUES

Just as women's rights were akin to very little in many areas of life, so it was historically in the legal arena. Despite the fact that in the past a women had no right to even claim to have a soul, or that women in the United States did not have voting rights until the early 20th century, the Quran had already reformed and provided many legal rights for women 1400 years back, some of which I will describe below.

RIGHT TO PROVIDE LEGAL TESTIMONY

Historically, women living in many different societies were not allowed to bear witness or to provide any testimony. During such a time it is only the Quran that allowed women to do both, but to a degree.

As I wrote in the beginning of this chapter, the Quran was a book revealed in the patriarchal era and hence mainly addresses men when it describes reforming anything. In terms of legal rights, the Quran has done the same. It is true that when it comes to financial transactions, the Quran accepts a man and two women as witnesses. However, it is also true that in other instances, the Quran accepts one male and one female witness. In some cases, women's testimony invalidates men's testimony (24:6-11). Here, it is not my effort to justify the Quran, but I appreciate the fact that compared to other religions and the cultural impasse that women have faced and still are facing, Quran at its minimum provided more than a woman could dream of.

*O ye who believe! When ye contract a debt for a fixed term, record it in writing. Let a scribe record it in writing between you in (terms of) equity. No scribe should refuse to write as Allah hath taught him, so let him write, and let him who incurreth the debt dictate, and let him observe his duty to Allah his Lord, and diminish naught thereof. But if he who oweth the debt is of low understanding, or weak, or unable himself to dictate, then let the guardian of his interests dictate in (terms of) equity. **And call to witness, from among your men, two witnesses. And if two men be not (at hand) then a man and two women, of such as ye approve as witnesses, so that if the one erreth [tudil] (through forgetfulness) the other will remember.** And the witnesses must not refuse when they are summoned. Be not averse to writing down (the contract) whether it be small or great, with (record of) the term thereof. That is more equitable in the sight of Allah and more sure for testimony, and the best way of avoiding doubt between you; save only in the case when it is actual merchandise which ye transfer among yourselves from hand to hand. In that case it is no sin for you if ye write it not. And have witnesses when ye sell one to another, and let no harm be done to scribe or witness. If ye do (harm to them) lo! it is a sin in you.*

Observe your duty to Allah. Allah is teaching you. And Allah is knower of all things. (Quran 2:282) (square bracket is mine).

Quran talks profoundly about men and women's equality and considers itself to hold a universal message, yet in certain parts it seems to be unjust or unclear. Could it be that we are still unable to comprehend the "best meaning" (39:18)? Anyone can ask this question, especially when he or she compares these verses with the overwhelming number of verses that have stood up to high principles and fairness, and are harmonized with science.

I have had long discussions and arguments about this and other controversial verses with some well educated people, professors, and scholars. I noticed that even those who vehemently talk about the rights of women could not justify this verse. Some might stretch the issue to mean that in the past, women were not much into financial transactions or that the women have other obligations (such as, one may be a witness but could be pregnant or taking care of a baby and thus unavailable to testify). Some would even go further to say that women are very emotional so it is possible that they may forget and err (*tudil*), or some would say that women might also be bias(!).

It is troubling to hear such justifications, because in today's world, can we rule out the possibility of a man being equally prone to the same mistakes or being in a same predicament as a woman? It would hold true if it were the 7th century Arabian culture or a culture before that. But, in today's scientific age when human physiology has been so thoroughly explored, it is unfathomable for any educated person to accept the arguments mentioned above.

If in fact this kind of justification is accepted in the present time, then we might as well also accept the *hadith* that says women are deficient in intelligence.[54] One scholar asked me to look into the fact that the Quran calls for two men and not one. But, then the Quran could have called for two women to substitute two men. A better understanding could have resulted had the Quran continued and had stated that if not one man is available, then four women would be needed. This would have beyond doubt implied that one man is equal to two women. But, the Quran stayed silent, and left us with all possibilities for interpretation. Even if the Quran did not mean what we understand it to mean, the vague terms have resulted in unlimited possibilities of interpretation. How can we then fit the single verse 2:282 within the universal message of the Quran?

Having said all that, I do not mean to assert in any way that I am a feminist or that men and women are equal from all aspects. I fully acknowledge and understand that both sexes have different roles to play which help both genders to complement each other and in turn allow a society to flourish. Nevertheless, the justifications as given above by different scholars seemingly make half of the human population less human.

In order to find the best meaning of this verse, one solution could be to look into the purpose of the witnesses. This verse calls for witnesses to a contract or dealing where usually, two contractual witnesses are required and not one. When it comes to a crime such as murder, even one witness is enough. But, when there is a contract or a deal taking place, there is a need for a minimum of two witnesses. This is because the dealing may have an effect on both contractual parties in the future. The two witnesses under the legal system serve as the following: (1) One witness witnesses the other witness witnessing and vice versa, (2) one witness will congeal the contract when the other witness fails to do so, and (3) one witness can vouch for the other witness and vice versa.

It could be therefore that the two women witnesses are needed not because one will err or forget, or that two women "equal" one man, but because it is a legal requirement as per the above argument. The Quran initially asked for two men as well and not one man and one woman. As we have established that two witnesses are a legal requirement, it could be that the Quran asks for a pair of the same gender as "two witnesses" (either two men or two women). This way, if one man is substituted, there should then be a pair of two women as contractual witnesses. Perhaps the difference in gender psychology initiates such a requirement, or is it so I am hoping? Also the Quran left the verse wide open for interpretation, we thus cannot rule out a logical or a sensible possibility.

Some may say that this is purely a conjecture on my part—fair enough—but an educated one. We may not have used (or are currently incapable of using) the proper hermeneutic techniques to analyze the verse(s). After all, it was strongly agreed upon in the past that according to the Quran men are allowed to beat women, but this is not the case anymore.

RIGHT TO MUTUAL CONSULTATION

And <u>*those*</u> [means both men & women] *who answer the call of their Lord and establish worship, and whose affairs are a matter of counsel, and who spend of what We have bestowed on them.* (Quran 42:38) (square bracket and underlining is mine).

ECONOMIC RIGHTS

RIGHT TO EARN AND OWN PROPERTY

Unto the men (of a family) belongeth a share of that which parents and near kindred leave, and unto the women a share of that which parents and near kindred leave, **whether it be little or much—a legal share.** (Quran 4:7).

Before Islam, women did not have any share in owning property. They themselves were considered property of a man (before marriage the property of their father, then gradually, that of their husband). If a woman owned property or had any wealth or earnings, these were taken by the husband.[55] When

Quran came, it provided for cases such as this a legal share to each person, male and female both.

RIGHT TO PROTECTION, FOOD, CLOTHING, AND SHELTER

Concerning these, it is the father and not the mother who has the responsibility of looking after the family. Even when a couple is going through a divorce, the man is to provide for the family, including the woman whom he is divorcing. Not only that, she is also to live in the same home until the final divorce.

The duty of feeding and clothing nursing mothers in a seemly manner is upon the father of the child. No-one should be charged beyond his capacity. A mother should not be made to suffer because of her child, nor should he to whom the child is born (be made to suffer) because of his child. (Quran 2:233).

RIGHT TO ALIMONY, CHILD SUPPORT, AND WIDOW'S MAINTENANCE

It is ex-husband's responsibility to provide for his ex-wife according to his means:

You commit no error by divorcing the women before touching them, or before setting the dowry for them. In this case, you shall (provide) maintenance for them—the rich as he can afford and the poor as he can afford—an equitable compensation. This is a duty upon the righteous. (Quran 2:236).

You shall provide maintenance for them equitably, and let them go amicably. (Quran 33:49).

(In the case of) those of you who are about to die and leave behind them wives, they should bequeath unto their wives a provision for the year . . . The divorcees also shall be provided for, equitably. This is a duty upon the righteous. (Quran 2:240-241).

If a pregnancy is discovered while going through a divorce procedure, the husband is to provide for the wife and she also stay in the same home:/ *"If they are pregnant, you shall spend (your substance) on them until they give birth."* (Quran 65:6). Even, if after the baby is born and the couple still decides to part ways, the ex-husband is still required to provide for his ex-wife and the child: /*"If they nurse the infant, provide maintenance for them. You shall maintain the amicable relations among you."* (Quran 65:6).

RIGHT TO INHERITANCE (A MAJOR ISSUE)

Allah (thus) directs you as regards your Children's (Inheritance): **to the male, a portion equal to that of two females:** *if only daughters, two or more, their share is two-thirds of the inheritance; if only one, her share is a half. For parents, a sixth share of the inheritance to each, if the deceased left children; if no children, and the parents are the (only) heirs, the mother has a third; if the deceased Left brothers (or sisters) the mother has a sixth.* **(The distribution in all cases ('s) after the payment of legacies and debts. Ye know not whether your parents or your children are nearest to you in benefit.** *These are settled portions ordained by Allah; and Allah is All-knowing, Al-wise.* (Quran 4:11).

This verse has been a hot issue in debates focused on whether the Quran is unjust. I would reiterate here that compared to other religions, the Quran ranks favourably when you consider that it gave women rights that they previously hadn't dreamed of. Similarly to how women in the past were not allowed to bear witness, and then were granted this right by the Quran, they even previously had no share in their family assets. (How could they when they themselves were considered an asset?) Bearing these in mind, the Quran at least provided a legal share to women at a time when they had none at all.

Because we expect Quran to be just, why we might find an "unjust" rule could actually be an instance where we haven't found the "best meaning" (39:18) of the verse yet. One opinion is that because a man is given much more responsibility than a woman, the man is entitled to a "double share", especially considering monetary assets. Another opinion is that a man needs to share a portion of wealth with his family, including relatives. In contrast to this, a woman's share is for her to keep—she doesn't have to share with anyone not even with her husband. In addition, her earnings are also hers to keep, and she is not responsible for providing for her family either; only her husband is. Yet other opinions go further to say that this is done in order to create a better bond between husband and wife, an interlocking relationship of responsibilities, care, love, and support—not just a "mine" and "yours" situation.

I could agree with the above arguments, as their proponents strive for an ideal society following the "best meaning" of the Quranic verses, and thus ideally no woman should be exploited or subjugated. The reality is that societies everywhere are not ideal, and we often see women deprived of their rights. Today when women are working shoulder to shoulder with men and are also actively providing for their family, how can we square the 1:2 ratio of shares for women and men?

If God had willed it, God could have called for a 1:1 ratio, but It did not. Unless there is an alternate meaning, I believe that verse 4:11 is only applicable when there exists an ideal society. It is like saying in legal terms that the ration is "subject to or conditional upon all other rules being strictly followed", otherwise, the above verse cannot be applied in today's society, and we are left to decide its best meaning according to what suits the present time. There is one point to note though:

WRITING A WILL—A MANDATORY DECREE

Despite the above arguments, one point to note in verse 4:11 is that it advises the said ratio to be in effect *only* after taking into account any money bequeathed or debt acquired: /"after any legacy he may have bequeathed (*waseeyat—Will*), or debt (hath been paid)". It is repeated again in verse 4:12 of the Quran. Writing a Will has been mandated as a "written law" *((kutiba) and* "duty" *(huqqa)* in chapter two of the Quran, which has the revelation order before chapter four. This means that before the inheritance law was passed, the law for 'writing a will' was enacted: /*"It is prescribed (kutiba) for you, when death approacheth one of you, if he leave wealth, that he bequeath (waseeyat) unto parents and near relatives in kindness. (This is) a duty (huqqa) for all those who ward off (evil)."* (Quran 2:180). Yet Muslim world choose to ignore this first injunction of the Quran.

The mandatory writing of a Will is necessary because every family situation can be different. Based on one's circumstances, one may even provide a daughter more shares in the inheritance than to a son by exercising the power of writing a Will. After all, what if the son is financially well-off but the daughter is financially struggling? This is further confirmed by the following sentence within the same verse 4:11 (which could mean that the testator may not know which child or parents of his is in dire need to benefit well with an appropriate and just Will):/ *"Ye know not whether your parents or your children are nearest to you* (through your Will) *in benefit."*

Moreover, in order to keep a check on the fairness of a Will, the verses further goes and grants protection to the heirs from a wrongful or unjust Will if such made by the testator. The verses state that in such cases there is no blame if one who is charged with the execution of the Will, alters it. However before this command, it warns not to alter the Will unless it is justified: /*"If anyone alters a Will he had heard, the sin of altering befalls those responsible for such altering. GOD is Hearer, Knower. If one sees gross injustice or bias on the part of a testator, and takes corrective action to that (restore justice to the Will), he commits no sin. GOD is Forgiver, Most Merciful."* (Quran 2:181-182)

CLOTHING

THE BEST APPAREL

"O ye Children of Adam! We have bestowed raiment upon you to cover your shame, as well as to be an adornment to you. But the raiment

of righteousness,(taqwa)—that is the best. Such are among the Signs of Allah, that they may receive admonition." (Quran 7:26).

As I described in chapter one, we have essentially created an Arabic Islam. This Islam is reflected in our clothing as well. Once people become too involved in this particularly Arabic Islam, they are expected to reflect Arabic clothing in their choice of wardrobe; otherwise, they will not be considered "real" Muslims. If the message of the Quran is universal, then everyone must be allowed to wear clothing according to his or her own culture rather than becoming an Arab. Even the Quran in this instance, approves the diversity of humans and it states that:/ *"O mankind! Lo! We have created you male and female, **and have made you nations and tribes that ye may know one another**"* (Quran 49:13). From the above verse (7:26), it can be deduced that modest but beautiful attire is the apparel that Quran advises us to wear, however, deeds of righteousness is given precedent over any apparel. In a broader sense, clothing is of less important compared to conduct: *"Lo! the noblest of you, in the sight of Allah, is the best in conduct. Lo! Allah is Knower, Aware"* (Quran 49:13).

As a result of the introduction of various religious cultures and the *ahadith* books into Islam, women were forbidden even little pleasures such as laughing or giggling. And it does not stop here—some Muslims have gone as far as to completely forbid women from any kind of beautification, and those who wear adornments are considered evil. Contrasting this, the Quran states/ *"Say: Who hath forbidden the adornment of Allah which He hath brought forth for His bondmen, and the good things of His providing?"* (Quran 7:32). Even Muhammad was questioned for forbidding things that God did not: /*"O Prophet! Why holdest thou to be forbidden that which Allah has made lawful to thee?"* (Quran 66:01).

HIJAB OR HEAD COVERING ISSUE

Traditional *Hijab* and its History

The word *hijab* has become synonymous with Islam. It has been so deeply rooted into Islamic culture that to call it un-Islamic is comparable to calling oneself a renegade to Islam; however, one is entitled to the choice of whether or not to wear a head covering. Before I go into what the Quran says concerning *hijab*, I would like to share a brief history on this subject.

In literal sense, *hijab* means a cover, partition, barrier, and/or a curtain or drape,[56] and *khimar* means a piece of cloth, usually worn over the head as a cover;[57] in the Arabian cultural norm as the climate dictates. The wearing of a *khimar* is generally associated with the advent of Islam. The idea of a veil (that is heavily associated to *hijab* today) was actually practiced extensively before Islam, not only in the Mediterranean regions but also in the Christian Middle East.[58] Very discreetly, it assimilated into Islam once Islamic conquests began to take place. These conquests allowed converts to Islam to bring along aspects of their cultures and mores, resulting in the deep groundwork for Islamic ideology based intrinsically upon already established cultures that predate Islam.

While mentioning the detailed Assyrian law regarding veiling during the 12th century BCE, Leila Ahmed in her book *Women and Gender in Islam* explains that the veil "served not merely to mark the upper classes but, more fundamentally, to differentiate between 'respectable' women and those who were publicly available".[59]

As such, when Islamic conquests began, these practices gradually became the part and participle of Islamic mores and the wearing of a veil came to denote respectable Muslim women. After all, what harm is there in a veil providing distinctions for women? Regrettably, this did not distinguish women as distinct individuals, but allowed the subjugation and subordination of women. Under the past exegesis of the Quran, Biblical transposition to the Quran and Muslim traditional practices (including later to Hindu customs), this veiling forced women to remain "silent" and "indoors", keeping themselves covered from head to toe. In the present time, we can see Afghani Muslim women for example, covered in burqas (clothing that covers a female from head to toe, loosely resembling a shuttle cock).

Later, this practice extended further resulting in women not studying or becoming educated, and soon their only appropriate activity was to procreate. Essentially, they did not acquire any outside occupations, and instead kept to their housework (as women were considered a source of evil and sins).[60] In the present day, the expansion of this clothing custom requires a women to literally walk behind a man. These examples are only a few of the many women's rights nearly vanquished in the Muslim world in particular.

Quranic *Hijab*

There is only one verse with the word *hijab* in it and I shall come to that later. Let's now look at what the Quran has to say about veiling or *hijab* in general (in this context, I will cover each verse separately):

Say to the believing men that they should lower their gaze and guard their modesty: *that will make for greater purity for them: And Allah is well acquainted with all that they do.* **And say to the believing women that they should lower their gaze and guard their modesty;** *that they should not display their beauty and ornaments except what (must ordinarily) appear thereof;* **that they should draw their veils (khimar) over their bosoms.** (Quran 24:30, 31).

Notice that even before women, men are commanded to lower their gaze (24:30). But this part (deliberately) escapes attention. If only the first line of this verse is recognized and given the attention it needs, many of the social evils would already be solved: no man 'gazing' at a woman to see how she is dressed, and hence no sexual arousal in him to begin with. Nevertheless, if both genders apply modesty in their behaviour, most of these evils will be no more.

When considering the popular meaning of the above verses, especially 24:31, I find myself perplexed with the strong emphasis put on the covering of one's head, as it is not stated in this verse. The only word mentioned that has been translated to mean *hijab* (veil or curtain) is *khimar*. *Khimar* as I explained earlier means a piece of cloth that would hang over the shoulder from the headgear worn traditionally at that time and had nothing to do with Islam. Women used to leave their breasts bare to attract suitors, but they would wear the headgear as per their tradition. Considering this, the Quran in verse 24:31 appears to be referring to this loose practice, and advising women to cover their "breast" with the piece of cloth that is hanging from their headgear. Hence, the emphasis here is not on covering the head but covering the breasts: *"draw their khimar **over their bosoms (**breast, **ju-yoob)**".*

By shifting the emphasis from covering the breast to covering the head, we are essentially changing the commandment in the Quran to something that is (a) not stated in the book and (b) only benefits our own desires from a subjective point of view.

In another verse, the Quran states that women should "cast" their *jilbab* (dress), but it is translated differently by different exegetists: to cast it on their faces, over them and their person (Yusuf Ali); to draw it close around them (Pickthal); to let down (Shakir); and to lengthen it (Khalifa).

O Prophet! Tell thy wives and daughters, and the believing women, alay-hin min jalabehin, that is most convenient, that they should be known (as such) and not molested. And Allah is Oft-Forgiving, Most Merciful. (Quran 33:59).

Due to the varied readings and renditions of the verses, we can come to appreciate the dynamism of the Quran. At a time when women are working shoulder to shoulder with men enjoying their rights and freedoms legally bestowed to them, modesty in dressing, guided by our conscience would better suit the purpose. The interesting part is, the verse itself only states "*alay-hin min jalabehin*," which means "over, a cover or attack".[61] This opens a wide range of interpretations.

There is only one verse that has the word *hijab* in it within the context of women, however, it does not reflect what is generally understood and followed:

> O Ye who believe! Enter not the dwellings of the Prophet for a meal without waiting for the proper time, unless permission be granted you. But if ye are invited, enter, and, when your meal is ended, then disperse. Linger not for conversation. Lo! that would cause annoyance to the Prophet, and he would be shy of (asking) you (to go); but Allah is not shy of the truth. **And when ye ask of them (the wives of the Prophet) anything, ask it of them from (hijab) behind a curtain.** That is purer for your hearts and for their hearts. And it is not for you to cause annoyance to the messenger of Allah, nor that ye should ever marry his wives after him. Lo! that in Allah's sight would be an enormity. (Quran 33:53).

This verse is only connected to Muhammad's wives and surprisingly it is directing not the wives but the "men", to *hijab* or "to ask from behind a curtain" when they ask for anything. Hence, this *hijab* command is only limited with reference to Muhammad's household and that too not to his wives but his companions. If it wasn't limited to Muhammad's household, the Quran could have extended the verse and added "and with all the believing women, men should ask from behind the curtain" (as we have observed in other verses), but it didn't.

The most sexually arousing parts of women psychologically are the buttocks and the breasts and not the hair or the face. It therefore doesn't make sense to force women to cover each and every single strand of hair or to wear a full *niqab* (face cover) in order to curb sexual arousal in "men" and make it a distinguishing mark for Muslim women.

In any case, Quran states that/ *"The believers are naught else than brothers and sisters (to each other)"* (Quran 49-10), and also that /*"the believers, men and women, are protectors*

195

(aulia) of one another, they enjoin the right and forbid the wrong" (Quran 9:71), then why would one Muslim man worry about his Muslim woman being harassed, molested or raped by another Muslim man when we are supposed to be protectors and brothers and sisters to each other, and look after the well-being of the whole *ummah* (community at large)? Truth of the matter is that, there is no protection for a woman in a Muslim state. We may hold the title of "Muslim' officially but our conducts are that of a hypocrite.

The word *hijab* thus has been blown out of proportion, and has been distorted to the extent of marginalizing the natural rights of women. This weakens the very fabric of a social structure of any nation where both men and women are crucial players toward the integrity and strength of that nation.

We should look into the main purpose behind each and every verse of the Quran, instead of being clout by our own subjective natures. In conclusion, I see the gist of all this "covering" issue in just one verse:

> *"O Children of Adam! We have revealed unto you raiment to conceal your shame, and splendid vesture,* **but the raiment of restraint from evil, that is the best***"* (Quran 7:26).

EDUCATION

In today's Muslim world, there are those who still believe that women should not be allowed to acquire a higher education. These views are either religiously oriented or culturally oriented. Their argument is something similar to "we don't intend to have our women-folk work". It is no wonder that the Islamic world is decaying into radicalism when the whole world is moving forward. It reminds me of what Benazir Bhutto (the late Prime Minister of Pakistan) wrote in her book *Reconciliation—Islam Democracy and the West* with regards to women's education: "Islamic societies that fail to educate women condemn their children to a vicious cycle of ignorance and poverty. From illiteracy and poverty stem hopelessness. And from hopelessness come desperation and extremism".[62]

Historically, Muhammad himself used to teach classes specifically for women. He also hired a tutor for his wives, and even ordered his companions to go home and teach their families what they had been taught. Even if one were to consider this piece of historical information untrue, there is a well known canonical *hadith* that states: *"Education is obligatory on both man and woman".*

"Quranically" speaking, there is no verse to be found that even remotely suggests that women should not be educated. The Quran has many verses in support of education for both genders. The Quran did not use any specific gender related terms when it states "those who have knowledge", or "those who learn", or "those who read", or "those who ponder", or even when it says "to seek help from those who know". The absence of a gender term should be enough evidence that the Quran refers to both genders.

SOCIAL STATUS

MEN AND WOMEN ARE EQUAL

*Their Lord responded to them: "I never fail to reward any worker among you for any work you do, be you male or female—**you are equal to one another**.* (Quran 3:195).

*And whoso doeth good works, **whether of male or female**, and he (or she) is a believer, such will enter paradise and they will not be wronged the dint in a date-stone.* (Quran 4:124).

***Each soul** earneth only on its own account.* (Quran 6:164).

It is true that men and women have different roles to perform; they cannot call themselves equal from every perspective. But, to call one more superior than the other is something that is unthinkable in this present age. To consider women (half of the human population) "less of a human" or "less favoured" (and hence not equal to men) is preposterous and irrational.

It has been mainly due to the misogynistic *ahadith* that the social status of Muslim women has regressed, and continues to regress. Women who were once at the forefront of every field during Muhammad's time are now being confined within the four walls of their homes. Consequently, the disempowerment, subjugation, and segregation of women came to pass.

Some opinions are that the Quran itself calls men better than and superior to women. To support this claim, they quote a partial verse:/ *"men have a degree (of advantage) over them. Allah is Mighty, Wise"* (2:228). This is a classic example of how the meaning of a verse can change completely if taken out of context.

Here is the entire verse:

Divorced women shall wait concerning themselves for three monthly periods. Nor is it lawful for them to hide what Allah hath created in their wombs, if they have faith in Allah and the last day. And their husbands have the better right to take them back in that period, if they wish for reconciliation. And women shall have rights similar to the rights against them, according to what is equitable; but men have a degree (of advantage) over them. And Allah is exalted in power, wise. (Quran 2:228).

As we can see, the verse above is in connection with divorce, and is advising men to take their wives back if they find them pregnant:/ *"and their husbands would do better to take them back in that case if they desire reconciliation"*. In this context, the Quran at first states that women have the same right to be treated well with what is known or accepted *ma'aruf,* which has several meanings: 'known or accepted as correct', 'back to back' 'one after the other', 'similar or a mid-point'[63] : /*"and they (women) have rights similar to those (of men) over them in ma'aruf"*. Second, the Quran states that men are a step ahead of women in the matter of divorce perhaps by initiating the divorce /"*men have a (darajah) degree (of advantage) over them. Allah is Mighty, Wise*". By reading this last sentence of the verse out of context and inferring that all men are a degree above women, is to undermine and deny the Quranic concept of equality (Please refer also to the topic 'Women as Leaders'). This concept of equality is vehemently supported in countless other instances within the Quran.

From the Quranic perspective, when it comes to considering men or women individually, there is no distinction among them to qualify one as superior or more favoured than the other: "***you are equal to one another***" (Quran 3:195). There is only one distinction: by "conduct" (*taqwa*):

O mankind! Lo! We have created you male and female, and have made you nations and tribes that ye may know one another. **Lo! the noblest of you, in the sight of Allah, is the best in conduct.** *Lo! Allah is Knower, Aware.* (Quran 49:13).

Blessed is He in Whose hand is the Sovereignty, and, He is Able to do all things. Who hath created life and death **that He may try you which of you is best in conduct**; *and He is the Mighty, the Forgiving.* (Quran 67:1-2).

FORBIDDING OF FEMALE INFANTICIDE

Female infanticide was rampant before and during the 7th century Arabian culture, and hence there appears another reforming verse in the Quran:

When if one of them receiveth tidings of the birth of a female, his face remaineth darkened, and he is wroth inwardly. He hideth himself from the folk because of the evil of that whereof he hath had tidings, (asking himself): Shall he keep it in contempt, or bury it beneath the dust. **Verily evil is their judgment.** (Quran 16:58-59).

And when the girl-child that was buried alive is asked, For what sin she was slain, . . . (Then) every soul will know what it hath made ready. (Quran 81:8-14).

MOTHERHOOD AND PARENTHOOD HONOURED

If the Islamic countries had upheld the Quranic principles to their "best meaning" (39:18), we wouldn't see the abject state of the women in these countries. In practice, a woman is treated less than a human. All she has to do is stay home, work, cook, or even work in the field. When it comes to eating food, she is left with only the gravy to savour, regardless of whether she is pregnant. This is despite the Quranic rule: /"***A mother should not be made to suffer because of her child***" (Quran 2:233). It is no wonder that the malnutrition rate of mothers in those countries is high, and a maternal mortality rate is disgraceful.

Many schools of thought have regarded the merciful and compassionate nature of God to that of a mother. In this context, it would be intriguing to observe the root of the word *ar-rhman-ir-rahim* (the compassionate and the merciful) that is associated with God: Schimmel in her book *My Soul is a Woman* explains that the root word of *rahman* and *rahim* is *rahma* (mercy), which is derived from the same root *rahm*, "mother's womb".[64]

The Quran in its overall theme appears to be very masculine due to the patriarchal age, but it has emphasized and protected the rights of women who previously were considered nothing but chattels. It has even stressed the care of the mother more than that of the father. In the verse below it has likened the duty toward one's mother to the duty toward God: /"***Be careful of your duty toward Allah*** in Whom ye claim (your rights) of one another, ***and toward the wombs (that bare you)*** [i.e mother]. *Lo! Allah hath been a watcher over you*" (Quran 4:1). (square bracket is mine)

And, in the following verse, it has again associated thanking parents with thanking God, yet again the mother's position is highlighted more than the father's:

And We have enjoined upon man concerning his parents—**His mother** beareth him in weakness upon weakness, and his weaning is in two years—**Give thanks unto Me and unto thy parents.** Unto Me is the journeying.* (Quran 31:14).

The Quran puts significant emphasis over the respect, honour and care of both the parents. It has emphasized the showing of kindness, care, and obedience toward the parents:

*Thy Lord hath decreed, that ye worship none save Him, and (that ye show) kindness to parents. If one of them or both of them attain old age with thee, **say not "Fie" unto them nor repulse them, but speak unto them a gracious word.** And lower unto them the wing of submission through mercy, and say: '**My Lord! Have mercy on them both as they did care for me when I was little.*** (Quran 17:23-24).

Apart from this, the Quran also emphasizes subtle points where one is not supposed to be obedient towards parents if they encourage or force their children to do *shirk* (set partners) with God (yet, even then the kindness toward them is not to be taken away, only the obedience):

We have enjoined on man kindness to parents: but if they (either of them) strive (to force) thee to join with Me (in worship) anything of which thou hast no knowledge, **obey them not.** Ye have (all) to return to me, and I will tell you (the truth) of all that ye did.* (Quran 29:08).

And We have enjoined upon man* concerning his parents—His mother beareth him in weakness upon weakness, and his weaning is in two years—Give thanks unto Me and unto thy parents. Unto Me is the journeying. But if they strive with thee to make thee ascribe unto Me as

---

A subtle change in the translation changes the overall theme or meaning of a verse. As an example, in the verse (31:14), the word "man" is used by Pickthal to translate the Arabic word *Insaan* and thus subsequently he used "his" for its pronoun. This is actually not the correct translation. *Insaan* is a non gender-specific word; it includes all humankind. To restrict its interpretation to mean only man or men is to bring patriarchal rendition of the Quran when it isn't there.

*partner that of which thou hast no knowledge, **then obey them not.
Consort with them in the world kindly,** and follow the path of him
who repenteth unto Me. Then unto Me will be your return, and I shall
tell you what ye used to do.* (Quran 31:14-15).

When it comes to the childbearing function of a women,
the intricate detail with which the Quran mentions Mary
(Jesus' mother) and her delivery pains (19:23-26) is enough
evidence that such a function of a women is not something
insignificant or to be taken for granted,[65] and is not something
that is evil. Judaeo-Christian tradition had long upheld the
notion that childbearing is the curse of women and evil.[66]
Rather, such a great task a women has to perform—bringing
a new life into the world! A mother should be revered and
shown mercy without any conditions attached.

*So she (Mary) conceived him, and she retired with him to a remote
place. And the pains of childbirth drove her to the trunk of a palm-tree:
She cried (in her anguish): "Ah! would that I had died before this! would
that I had been a thing forgotten and out of sight!" But (a voice) cried
to her from beneath the (palm-tree): "Grieve not! for thy Lord hath
provided a rivulet beneath thee; And shake towards thyself the trunk of
the palm-tree: It will let fall fresh ripe dates upon thee. So eat and drink
and cool (thine) eyes.* (Quran 19:22:26).

Please also note below an example of the emotional
attachment that a mother has with her child. This has been
given considerable emphasis when Quran details the feelings
that the mother of Moses went through when she was
separated from her child and how thereafter God consoles her
heart (28:7):

*And We inspired the mother of Moses, saying: Suckle him and,
when thou fearest for him, then cast him into the river and fear not nor
grieve. Lo! We shall bring him back unto thee and shall make him (one)
of Our messengers.* (Quran 28:7).

Also, note in the above verse the fact that Moses' mother
was "inspired". She received the *wahy* (inspiration), which
means it is not only men who used to receive *wahy*.[67]

WOMEN AS LEADERS

In general, the Muslim world denies women's authority as leaders. Ironically, it would be intriguing to observe that some Muslim countries who fervently oppose women's leadership have had women as leaders (such as Pakistan's Benazir Bhutto and Bangladesh's Khaleda Zia, to name but a couple).

Muslim countries in general oppose women being leaders. They do so by misrepresenting the Quran. When Benazir Bhutto stood for her presidency election in Pakistan, the *mullas* (priests) and religious fanatics started distributing pamphlets all over the country against her very nomination for the election. In those pamphlets they had written materials with this message: "'men are in charge of women' (Quran)" in order to moot her claim for electoral right and her standing for the election. As has already been discussed, this is clearly not the message of the Quran.

What they did was cut and paste a portion of one verse related to the husband/wife relationship issue in the Quran and applied it to mean to all men and all women. This is indeed an exploitation and abuse of the Quranic messages. They did this to show that the Quran, upon which the "ideology" of Islam is based and hence also the creation of Pakistan, denies the right of women to be leaders. The whole verse is as follows:

Men are in charge of women, because Allah hath made the one of them to excel the other, and because they spend of their property (for the support of women). So good women are the obedient, guarding in secret that which Allah hath guarded. As for those from whom ye fear rebellion, admonish them and banish them to beds apart, and scourge them. Then if they obey you, seek not a way against them. Lo! Allah is ever High, Exalted, Great. (Quran 4:34).

For detail discussion of this verse, please check the section 'wife beating' in this chapter. Now, let us assume for argument's sake that the 'cut and paste' misrepresentation of the verse in question as mentioned above is rightly represented and that generally "men are in charge of women". Why would a complete stranger on the street that I may happen to pass, be in charge of me when there is no relationship to begin with? The whole verse is connected to a specific relationship between a man and a woman, a marriage relationship where they are each other's spouses. The verses that precede and follow 4:34 are also in relation to family issues. To expand such a verse to mean that all men are in charge of all women is to transpose one's own macho whims and desires into the Quran.

In addition, the Quran itself speaks about one woman leader and commemorates her leadership qualities when it mentions the story of the Queen of Sheba-Bilquis, a ruler who has been *"provided with every requisite; and she has a magnificent throne"* (27:23). Moreover, the Quran itself commends her wisdom and her sound judgment further when it states that after reading Solomon's letter, she indicates the letter to be *"worthy of respect"* (27:29) and takes the course of a peaceful resolution (27:32-35) rather than using might.[68] Despite this example, there are those who say that the Quran denies the right for women to be leaders. This is based on an "out of context" sentence, and would be tantamount to putting words in God's mouth.

I believe, women can be better leaders than men because of their propensity to details, to family orientation, and because of their patience. By comparison, men have more physical strength and are more impatient. Women in general have family nurturing capabilities, and enjoy organizing and looking after every little detail, including protecting their children and family from harm. A country is like a huge family where a leader has the responsibility to look after every single being living within its premise. Such a role requires a great deal of patience and a peaceful resolution on every issue in order to keep the harmony of a country intact, and at the same time allow it to grow and progress, just like a family.

Can we achieve such an objective with the natural predilection of men? Some may call my thoughts feminist, indeed it may be so. But, have we witnessed any better results with male rulers? Aren't we regressing toward a primitive society regardless of how civilized we become due to technological advancement?

CONVERT ISSUES

One may wonder what issues there could be if one converts. There may not be any issues unless a non-Muslim woman is married to a non-Muslim man, and later converts to Islam—then it is quite a significant issue.

Common sense will tell us that a women who is already happily married before converting, who has children in that happy marriage, and whose conversion has no affect on her marriage in any ways, should remain in that marriageable relationship even after she converts. This could be simply for her children's sake, as we all know what havoc it plays upon the lives of those children whose families have been broken. There can be no religion which would force the break-up of a happy family as this would consequently damage the fabric of a healthy society.

I have had real life encounters with women who converted to Islam when they had previously been happily married and had children in that happy marriage. These women had been hounded by the so-called *mullahs* and religious scholars, and had been labelled as whores for sleeping with their non-Muslim husbands who according to their *fatwa* (decree) are *haram* (forbidden) to them once they have converted.

I would like to pause here for a moment and ask my readers to use their common sense and fathom the whole picture, and those poor women's lives that were torn apart. There has already been irreparable damage done to Quranic Islam, and this blow leaves another huge blotch.

The *fatwas* in question had been issued on the context of the following Quranic verses:

O ye who believe! When believing women come unto you as fugitives, examine them. Allah is Best Aware of their faith. Then, if ye know them for true believers, send them not back unto the disbelievers. **They are not lawful for them (the disbelievers), nor are they (the disbelievers) lawful for them.** *And give them (the disbelievers) that which they have spent (upon them). And it is no sin for you to marry such women when ye have given them their dues. And hold not to the ties of disbelieving women; and ask for (the return of) that which ye have spent; and let them (the disbelievers) ask for that which they have spent. That is the judgment of Allah. He judgeth between you. Allah is Knower, Wise.* (Quran 60:10).

Do not marry idolatresses unless they believe; a believing woman is better than an idolatress, even if you like her. **Nor shall you give your daughters in marriage to idolatrous men, unless they believe.** *A believing man is better than an idolater, even if you like him. These invite to Hell, while GOD invites to Paradise and forgiveness, as He wills. He clarifies His revelations for the people, that they may take heed.* (Quran 2:221).

It is argued that verse 60:10 explicitly states that once a woman has converted, she should not be sent back to her family: /*"send them not back unto the disbelievers. They are not lawful for them (the disbelievers), nor are they (the disbelievers) lawful for them."* The second verse 2:221 also states that Muslim women should not be married to non-Muslim men, unless they become Muslim: /*"Nor shall you give your daughters in marriage to idolatrous men, unless they believe".*

A careful look at the verses reveals that 60:10 speaks about a specific circumstance where a woman is a fugitive. One becomes a fugitive only when one's life is threatened. Those women who escaped and went to Muhammad for asylum did so to escape oppression and persecution. Perhaps before coming to Muhammad, they were tortured to the extent that their lives were at stake, and they were left with no choice but to leave their husbands. For that reason, they came to Muhammad's protection. Should they then be sent back? Common sense will say that they should be given asylum, and that is exactly what the Quran instructed Muhammad to do.

On the flip side, if those women's lives were not threatened even after their conversion, they would not have needed to become fugitives. Does then Quran still instruct to break up marriages once such a married woman has converted to Islam when there is no threat to begin with? On chapter 4, verse 22 of the Quran, where it describes unlawful and lawful marriages, it states specifically about the marriages that happened in the past and what to do with it: *"but do not break up existing marriages. GOD is Forgiver, Most Merciful."*

When husbands have such big hearts that they accommodate their wife's religious decisions, and still accept them and live with them happily, then there would be no reason to run away or break up the marriage. In fact, there would be more than a fifty-percent chance that the husbands of these women would receive greater exposure to Islam due to the conversion of their wives, and perhaps later decide to convert. Verse 60:10 therefore only speaks about and passes decree for women who are unable to follow their chosen religion with freedom, and who were left with no choice but to become fugitives.

Verse 2:221 talks about women who are already Muslim and "not yet married". It has no relevancy to verse 60:10, or for that matter to those women who converted after their marriage. These are two very different issues.

Think about the repercussions that were experienced by women I came across. One did not have the courage to tear apart her family for "Islam". She could not live without her children or husband and decided after much careful thought to leave Islam rather than attaching to herself a label of "whore". It may be that she left Arabic Islam, but in her heart she remains a Muslim. Another woman left her very loving and caring husband "for Islam" only to find, much to her dismay, that her "Muslim" husband is nothing more than an anguish.

I leave this topic now for my readers to decide: whether we should read out of context, or whether we should read all relevant verses as a whole and try to find a holistic and just meaning. Whether we should find the "best meaning" of a verse as exhorted by the Quran (39:18), or whether we should simply look at a verse through our own subjective points of reference?

NOTES:

* *O ye who believe! Ye are forbidden to inherit women against their will. Nor should ye treat them with harshness, that ye may Take away part of the dower ye have given them,-except where they have been guilty of open lewdness; on the contrary live with them on a footing of kindness and equity. If ye take a dislike to them it may be that ye dislike a thing, and Allah brings about through it a great deal of good. If you wish to marry another wife, in place of your present wife, and you had given any of them a great deal, you shall not take back anything you had given her. Would you take it fraudulently, maliciously, and sinfully? And how could ye take it when ye have gone in unto each other, and they have Taken from you a solemn covenant (meesaaq-e-ghaleeza)?*

And marry not those women whom your fathers married, except what hath already happened (of that nature) in the past. Lo! it was ever lewdness and abomination, and an evil way. Forbidden unto you are your mothers, and your daughters, and your sisters, and your father's sisters, and your mother's sisters, and your brother's daughters and your sister's daughters, and your foster-mothers, and your foster-sisters, and your mothers-in-law, and your step-daughters who are under your protection (born) of your women unto whom ye have gone in—but if ye have not gone in unto them, then it is no sin for you (to marry their daughters)—and the wives of your sons who (spring) from your own loins. And (it is forbidden unto you) that ye should have two sisters together, except what hath already happened (of that nature) in the past. Lo! Allah is ever Forgiving, Merciful. Also prohibited are the women who are already married, unless they flee their disbelieving husbands who are at war with you. These are GOD's commandments to you. All other categories are permitted for you in marriage, so long as you pay them their due dowries. You shall maintain your morality, by not committing adultery. Thus, whoever you like among them, you shall pay them the dowry decreed for them. You commit no error by mutually agreeing to any adjustments to the dowry. GOD is Omniscient, Most Wise. And whoso is not able to afford to marry free, believing women, let them marry from the believing maids whom your right hands possess. Allah knoweth best (concerning) your faith. Ye (proceed) one from another; so wed them by permission of their folk, and give unto them their portions in kindness, they being honest, not debauched nor of loose conduct. And if when they are honourably married they commit lewdness they shall incur the half of the punishment (prescribed) for free women (in that case). This is for him among you who feareth to commit sin. But to have patience would be better for you. Allah is Forgiving, Merciful. (Quran 4:19-25).

1. Central Intelligence Agency (CIA). The World Factbook, Country: Pakistan, under "People of Pakistan". Date accessed: March 8, 2010. https://www.cia.gov/library/publications/the-world-factbook/geos/pk.html

2. BBC news. "Saudi Police 'Stopped' Fire Rescue", March 15, 2002. Date accessed, April 12, 2010. *http://news.bbc.co.uk/2/hi/1874471.stm*

3. Afkhami, Mehnaz (et al). *Faith And Freedom.* Syracuse NY: Syracuse University Press, 1995, p. 135

4. Ibid., pp. 188-190

5. Armstrong, Karen. *Islam, A Short History.* London: The Orion Publishing Group, 2000, p. 3

6. Ahmed, Leila. *Women and Gender in Islam.* New Haven: Yale University Press, 1992, p. 14

7. Afkhami, Mehnaz (et al). *Faith And Freedom.* Syracuse NY: Syracuse University Press, 1995, p. 103-119,126-129

8. Wikipedia. "Catalhoyuk", section "Religion". Last modified March 10, 2010. Date accessed: March 10, 2010. http://en.wikipedia.org/wiki/%C3%87atalh%C3%B6y%C3%BCk

   Ahmed, Leila. *Women and Gender in Islam.* New Haven: Yale University Press, 1992, p. 11

9. Ahmed, Leila. *Women and Gender in Islam.* New Haven: Yale University Press, 1992, p. 11-12

10. Ibid., p. 12

11. Sykes, Bryan. *The Seven Daughters of Eve.* New York: Norton and Company Inc., 2001, pp.133-134

12. Wikipedia. "Code of Hammurabi". Last modified March 11, 2010. Date accessed: March 12, 2010. http://en.wikipedia.org/wiki/Code_of_Hammurabi

13. Ahmed, Leila. *Women and Gender in Islam*. New Haven: Yale University Press, 1992, p.13

14. Wikipedia. "Sassanid Empire". Last modified March 9, 2010. Date accessed: March 12, 2010. http://en.wikipedia.org/wiki/Sassanid_Empire

15. Ahmed, Leila, *Women and Gender in Islam*. New Haven: Yale University Press, 1992, pp. 19-20

16. Ibid., p. 13

17. Ibid., pp. 15, 26-28.

18. Ibid., p. 19

19. Ibid., p. 19

    Sykes, Bryan. *The Seven Daughters of Eve*. New York: Norton and Company Inc., 2001, p. 23

20. Ibid., p.187

21. Ibid., p.190

22. Ibid., p.187

23. Ahmed, Leila. *Women and Gender in Islam*. New Haven: Yale University Press, 1992, p. 36

24. Ibid., p.36

25. University of Michigan Digital Library. *Holy Bible, King James Version, Genesis 3:6-17.* Date accessed: March 18, 2010. http://quod.lib.umich.edu/k/kjv/browse.html

And when the woman saw that the tree was good for food, and that it was pleasant to the eyes, and a tree to be desired to make one wise, she took of the fruit thereof, and did eat, and gave also unto her husband with her; and he did eat. And the eyes of them both were opened, and they knew that they were naked; and they sewed fig leaves together, and made themselves aprons. And they heard the voice of the LORD God walking in the garden in the cool of the day: and Adam and his wife hid themselves from the presence of the LORD God amongst the trees of the garden. And the LORD God called unto Adam, and said unto him, Where art thou? And he said, I heard thy voice in the garden, and I was afraid, because I was naked; and I hid myself. And he said, Who told thee that thou wast naked? Hast thou eaten of the tree, whereof I commanded thee that thou shouldest not eat? And the man said, The woman whom thou gavest to be with me, she gave me of the tree, and I did eat. And the LORD God said unto the woman, What is this that thou hast done? And the woman said, The serpent beguiled me, and I did eat . . . Unto the woman he said, I will greatly multiply thy sorrow and thy conception; in sorrow thou shalt bring forth children; and thy desire shall be to thy husband, and he shall rule over thee. And unto Adam he said, Because thou hast hearkened unto the voice of thy wife, and hast eaten of the tree, of which I commanded thee, saying, Thou shalt not eat of it: cursed is the ground for thy sake; in sorrow shalt thou eat of it all the days of thy life. (Genesis 3:6-17)

26. Schimmel, Annemarie. *My Soul Is a Woman, the Feminine In Islam*. London: The Continuum Publishing Company, 1999, p. 22

27. University of Michigan Digital Library. *Holy Bible, King James Version, Leviticus 15:19-24*. University of Michigan digital library. Date accessed: March 21, 2010. http://quod.lib.umich.edu/k/kjv/browse.html

And if a woman have an issue, and her issue in her flesh be blood, she shall be put apart seven days: and whosoever toucheth her shall be unclean until the evening. And everything that she lieth upon in her separation shall be unclean: everything also that she sitteth upon shall be unclean. And whosoever toucheth her bed shall wash his clothes, and bathe himself in water, and be unclean until the evening. And whosoever toucheth any thing that she sat upon shall wash his clothes, and bathe himself in water, and be unclean until the evening. And if it be on her bed, or on anything whereon she sitteth, when he toucheth it, he shall be unclean until the evening. And if any man lie with her at all, and her flowers be upon him, he shall be unclean seven days; and all the bed whereon he lieth shall be unclean. (Leviticus 15:19-24)

28. Durrani, Zahida. *Allama Parvaiz-Lughat-ul-Quran.* Toronto: Tulu-e-Islam Trust. 2007, p. 561, last paragraph under hay.wow.ray

29. Ibid., p. 561 first paragraph under hay.wow.ray

30. Ibid., pp. 819-820 under zay.wow.jeem

31. Ibid., pp. 1522-1524 under meem.say.laam

32. Ibid., p. 1551 under meem.kaaf.noon

33. Ibid., p. 1363 under qaaf.saad.ray

34. Ibid., p. 631 under khay.ya.meem

35. Ibid., pp. 1089-1090 under tuain.meem.say

36. Ibid., p. 1436 under kaaf.ain.bay

37. Ibid., pp. 376-377 under tay.ray.bay

38. Ibid., p. 1409 under kaaf, alif, seen.

39. Ibid., p. 674 under daal.hay (small).qaaf

40. Armstrong, Karen. *Muhammad, A Biography of the Prophet.* New York: Harper Collins Publishers Inc., 1992, p. 80

41. Ibid., pp. 79-80, 144-45, 157, 181, 195-96, 233-234

42. Ibid., p. 190

43 Ibid., p. 234

   Bennett, Clinton. *In Search of Muhammad.* Great Britain: Biddles Ltd. Guildford and King's Lynn, 1999, pp. 249-251

44. Durrani, Zahida. *Allama Parvaiz-Lughat-ul-Quran.* Toronto: Tulu-e-Islam Trust. 2007, pp. 1794-1796, under ya-meem-noon.

45. Ibid.

46. Gandhi, Mohandas K. "Satyagraha In South Africa". Translated from Gujrati by Valji Govindji Desai. Navajivan Publ. House;

2nd edition, (1961), 2003, p. 169. Date accessed: June 7, 2010. http://www.forget-me.net/en/Gandhi/satyagraha.pdf

Date Accessed: October 20, 2012. http://wikilivres.ca/wiki/Satyagraha_in_South_Africa

47. Durrani, Zahida. *Allama Parvaiz-Lughat-ul-Quran*. Toronto: Tulu-e-Islam Trust. 2007, p. 1399, under qaaf-wow-meem

48. Personal communication with my good friend Abdul Fauq, who has a Ph.D and works in research department of the Mayo Clinic Florida. 2007

49. Durrani, Zahida. *Allama Parvaiz-Lughat-ul-Quran*. Toronto: Tulu-e-Islam Trust. 2007, pp. 1062-1064, under dwaad-ray-bay

50. Ibid., pp. 1621-1622, under noon-sheen-zay.

51. Barlas, Asma. *Believing Women in Islam, Unreading Patriarchal Interpretations of the Qur'an*. Austin: University of Texas Press, 2002, p. 188

52. Ibid., pp. 53, 12-25

53. Armstrong, Karen. *Islam, a Short History*. London: The Orion Publishing Group, 2000, pp. xi, 4, 6

54. Khan, M. Muhsin (translation). "Translation of Sahih-Al-Bukhari". Los Angeles: Center for Muslim Jewish Engagement. University of Southern California. Volume 1, Book 6 number 301. Date accessed: April 3, 2010. http://www.usc.edu/dept/MSA/fundamentals/hadithsunnah/bukhari

Date Accessed: October 20, 2012. http://www.usc.edu/org/cmje/religious-texts/hadith/bukhari/

Volume 1, Book 6, Number 301: Narrated by Abu Said Al-Khudri:

Once Allah's Apostle went out to the Musalla (to offer the prayer) o 'Id-al-Adha or Al-Fitr prayer. Then he passed by the women and said, "O women! Give alms, as I have seen that the majority of the dwellers of Hell-fire were you (women)." They asked, "Why is it so, O Allah's Apostle ?" He replied, "You curse frequently and are ungrateful to your husbands. I have not seen anyone more deficient in intelligence and religion than you. A cautious sensible man could be led astray by some of you." The women asked, "O Allah's Apostle! What is deficient in our intelligence and religion?" He said, "Is not the evidence of two women equal to the witness of one man?" They replied in the affirmative. He said, "This is the deficiency in her intelligence. Isn't it true that a woman can neither pray nor fast during her menses?" The women replied in the affirmative. He said, "This is the deficiency in her religion".

55. Ahmed, Leila. *Women and Gender in Islam*. New Haven: Yale University Press, 1992, pp.12-15

56. Durrani, Zahida. *Allama Parvaiz-Lughat-ul-Quran*. Toronto: Tulu-e-Islam Trust. 2007, p.473 under hay-jeem-bay

57. Ibid., p. 619 under khay-meem-ray

58. Ahmed, Leila. *Women and Gender in Islam*. New Haven: Yale University Press, 1992, pp. 26-7

59. Ibid., p. 15

60. University of Michigan Digital Library. *Holy Bible, King James Version, Genesis 3:6-17.* Date accessed: March 18, 2010. http:// quod.lib.umich.edu/k/kjv/browse.html

And when the woman saw that the tree was good for food, and that it was pleasant to the eyes, and a tree to be desired to make one wise, she took of the fruit thereof, and did eat, and gave also unto her husband with her; and he did eat. And the eyes of them both were opened, and they knew that they were naked; and they sewed fig leaves together, and made themselves aprons. And they heard the voice of the LORD God walking in the garden in the cool of the day: and Adam and his wife hid themselves from the presence of the LORD God amongst the trees of the garden. And the LORD God called unto Adam, and said unto him, Where art thou? And he said, I heard thy voice in the garden, and I was afraid, because I was naked; and I hid myself. And he said, Who told thee that thou wast naked? Hast thou eaten of the tree, whereof I commanded thee that thou shouldest not eat? And the man said, The woman whom thou gavest to be with me, she gave me of the tree, and I did eat. And the LORD God said unto the woman, What is this that thou hast done? And the woman said, The serpent beguiled me, and I did eat . . . Unto the woman he said, I will greatly multiply thy sorrow and thy conception; in sorrow thou shalt bring forth children; and thy desire shall be to thy husband, and he shall rule over thee. And unto Adam he said, Because thou hast hearkened unto the voice of thy wife, and hast eaten of the tree, of which I commanded thee, saying, Thou shalt not eat of it: cursed is the ground for thy sake; in sorrow shalt thou eat of it all the days of thy life; (Genesis 3:6-17)

61. Durrani, Zahida. *Allama Parvaiz-Lughat-ul-Quran*. Toronto: Tulu-e-Islam Trust. 2007, p. 435, under jeem-laam-bay

62. Bhutto, Benazir. *Reconciliation: Islam, Democracy, and the West*. New York: Harper Collins, 2008, p. 289

63. Zahida. *Allama Parvaiz-Lughat-ul-Quran*. Toronto: Tulu-e-Islam Trust. 2007, pp. 1151-1154 under ain-ray-fay

64. Schimmel, Annemarie: *My Soul Is a Woman, the Feminine In Islam*. London: The Continuum Publishing Company, 1999, p. 93

   Zahida. *Allama Parvaiz-Lughat-ul-Quran*. Toronto: Tulu-e-Islam Trust. 2007, p. 738 under ray-hay-meem

65. Wadud, Amina. *Quran and Women, Re-reading the Sacred Text From a Woman's Perspective*. Oxford: Oxford University Press, 1999, pp. 39-40

66. University of Michigan Digital Library. *Holy Bible, King James Version, Genesis 3:6-17*. Date accessed: March 18, 2010. (see note 53). http://quod.lib.umich.edu/k/kjv/browse.html

   Azim, Sherif Abdel. *Women in Islam vs. Judaeo Christian Tradition, the Myth and the Reality*. Kingston: Queens University Kingston Ontario, 1996, pp. 6-10

67. Wadud, Amina. *Quran and Women, Re-reading the Sacred Text From a Woman's Perspective*. Oxford: Oxford University Press, 1999, p. 39

68. Ibid., pp. 40-42

CHAPTER SEVEN

BANKING INTEREST ೞ

ISLAM AND INTEREST

It has been repeated over and over that the collection of interest in Islam is *haram* (forbidden). Consequently, so is holding money in any account that gains interest: banking loans, mortgages, investments, and everything else of this nature. This is based on various verses of the Quran which I shall further discuss in detail.

In this chapter, I have put my own research and have taken extensive help from *The Quranic concept of Ar-Riba (the Islamic Principles of Economics)* by Muhammad Shafi J. Aga. Aga's in-depth insight and detailed explanation of the "interest" concept using verses from the Quran leaves no room for denial. Since his argument was factual and had such conviction, I owe this chapter to him.

TERMINOLOGIES

First, I will outline the literal meanings of various terminologies used in the finance world and some that have been used in the Quran. They are generally accepted to mean the following:

Money:

Any circulating medium of exchange, measure of wealth, means of payment or purchasing power.

Interest:

Sum paid or charged for the use of money or for borrowing money. Such a sum is expressed as a percentage of money borrowed to be paid over a given period, usually one year.

Usury:

An exorbitant amount or rate of interest, especially in excess of the legal or reasonable rate.

Trade:

Any occupation pursued as a business or livelihood. In Arabic language, trade is usually referred to as s *tijaarat* [1] and *bai'a*; [2] any business including trade.

Below are the literal meaning of Arabic words used in finance:

Riba or *al-riba* (pronounced *"arriba"*):

An exorbitant increase or growth, or usury. Al before *riba*[3] simply means "the"—the *riba*.

Amwaal:

It is the plural of *mole* in Arabic. It means one's possessions including any tangible material goods, paper currency

217

(money), and assets. Anything a person may refer to as his or her possession. [4]

Bai'a:

any business including trading.

AL-RIBA

As we unfold the Quranic verses related to this subject, we will meet some challenges concerning the translations rendered by the exegetists. Even though it is vociferated that interest is *haram* (forbidden), it is interesting to note that the Quran in any of the related verses has not used the word "interest" (*sood)* but "usury", (the exorbitant amount charged) called "the" *riba* (generally translated as usury). The *Shariah* system has classified usury as an income that is derived only by the use of money, and the Quran classifies usury as being forbidden. I shall later offer a detailed analysis of the term "money" itself.

Before the rise of Islam, the Jewish of Madinah and many other Arabs were business people (this tradition is still evident today). As lenders, they used to charge exorbitant amounts of interest in the form of money or material goods, leaving their victims helpless and hopeless. When the Quran came, it condemned this practice and warned the Jewish and Muslims together to desist from doing such business. Previously, such lenders would justify their actions by claiming that "business is all about maximum gains". Eventually, the Quran notified everyone that those who did not stop this practice should consider themselves at "war" with God and the messenger:

Those who devour usury (al-riba) will not stand except as stand one whom the evil one by his touch hath driven to madness. That is because they say: "Trade (bai'a) is like usury (al-riba)," but Allah hath permitted trade (bai'a) and forbidden usury (al-riba). Those who after receiving direction from their Lord, desist, shall be pardoned for the past; their case is for Allah (to judge); but those who repeat (the

offense) are companions of the fire: They will abide therein (for ever).
(Quran 2:275).

Later I will present a detailed analysis of verse 2:275. Please note that the above and subsequent translations have translated *bai'a* (any business) as "trading" when in fact trading is only one type of business or *bai'a.*

"And of their taking usury (al-riba) when they were forbidden it, and of their devouring people's wealth (amwaal) by false pretenses, We have prepared for those of them who disbelieve a painful doom" (Quran 4:161).

"O ye who believe! Fear Allah, and give up what remains of your demand for usury (al-riba), if ye are indeed believers" (Quran 2:278).

"If ye do it not, then take notice of war from Allah and His Messenger" (Quran 2:279).

In the verse 30:39 below, the first in the order of revelation, it is revealed wherein we read:

"That which ye lay out min riban (as profit) *for increase (li-yr-rabu)* **through the amwaal (possession) of (other) people,** *will have no increase (yr-rabu) with Allah: but that which ye lay out for zakat, seeking the Countenance of Allah, (will increase): it is these who will get a recompense multiplied"*(Quran 30:39).

The point to observe in verse 30:39 and others related is as Aga notes, it is not *all* increases that are prohibited, but *certain* increases that one attains by taking in the *amwaal* of others. It is not one's rightful dues, just the exorbitant "increase" that is prohibited.[5] Such an increase has been termed *al-riba*, and occurs by doubling and quadrupling to usurp the *amwaal* of others (to which one is not entitled).

Any business thrives on profit. A person in business needs to charge their buyer a price that will cover costs as well as provide some income to the seller, this in the form of profit or "increase". If a seller did not add that increase to the sale and sold a product to bear the cost, the seller would not gain any income which is needed to sustain the business and the business owner's living. However, if the seller charges an exorbitant price to gain a huge amount of profit, he would be doing wrong, as he would be earning the profit at the expense of others. He would be depriving others of their rightful possessions or *amwaal*, and therefore he would not be doing an ethical or moral act.

Since this would cripple the buyer and would threaten his very survival, God does not permit this type of behaviour. Instead, It allows regular business with a reasonable profit margin: /*"Allah hath permitted business (bai'a) and forbidden usury (al-riba)"* (Quran 2:275). Verse 30:39 outlines that a huge profit which is gained by "usurping the *amwaal*" of others is not a gain at all, but in contrast giving *zakat** would be gain in the sight of God. Further to that, the Quran states: /*"O ye who believe! Devour not usury (al-riba), doubling and quadrupling. Observe your duty to Allah, that ye may be successful"* (Quran 3:130).

AMWAAL AND ITS MEANING

Please note that the Quran does not use the word "money" (*naqad*) in any of its relevant verses, and instead uses the term *amwaal* which has wider connotations than what is associated with just money. It must be God's wisdom to choose such a term instead of money. It is always us who lack the clarity and wisdom to foresee beyond our limited horizon.

As stated before, the literal meaning of money classifies it as only one medium of exchange, which provides a certain purchasing power at a given time. *Amwaal* on the other hand

---

* To nourish, to help grow, or well-being (see Chapter 5 "Rituals' under *zakat*).

has a wider meaning implying "possessions", which includes one's money. Money can be one's possession as well as a measure of value for one's possessions.[6] Thus, both *amwaal* and money cannot be separated—one has a value and the other represents that value. Hence, one can have *amwaal* in the form of money, which is its value.

Certain *amwaal* such as gold can at a given time have a certain value in terms of money. For example, when this was written in 2007, an ounce of gold was valued at ~$674 USD. Two years before, the same ounce of gold was valued at ~$450 USD.

So what does Allah mean in verse 30:39 "to increase one's wealth by devouring the *amwaal* of others", and called it *riba* and a crime? When we take more than our rightful due, and take it to exorbitantly increase our lot, this is when we commit *al-riba*. In other words, when we take more than what is due to us or charge exorbitant prices is when we are committing *al-riba*. This is exactly what Jewish and Muslims alike were doing during the time of Muhammad, justifying this behaviour by saying "business is *riba* (maximum increase)".

Let's look at this concept in the form of an example:

Imagine that two years ago I gave an ounce of gold (my *amwaal*) to a friend who said that he would return it to me after two years. But, he couldn't return me my *amwaal* in the form of gold so with my consent, he gave me its current value in the form of money. That *amwaal* of mine has in the past two years increased in value from $450 to $674. If today he gave me back only $450 instead of $674, I would be wronged and he would be committing *al-riba*: if I take $450 to the market today to purchase an ounce of gold (my rightful *amwaal*), I wouldn't be able to—I would have to add another $224 in order to receive the original *amwaal* that was given to my friend. The Quran states that:/ *"one shall have their capital amwaal back"* (Quran 2:279).

Also, if I had demanded from my friend that he pay back $800 instead of $674, then I would be committing *al-riba* and he would be wronged. This is because if I take $800 to the market today to purchase an ounce of gold (my rightful *amwaal*), I would be able to purchase it plus I would have $126 extra in my pocket to buy something else. In this instance I would not only be receiving my own original *amwaal* back (one ounce of gold or its equivalent), but I would be usurping my friend's *amwaal* by the amount of $126.

This is just one example of how one's *amwaal* can be devoured. Aga has used the example of lending a brand new car, as its value depreciates with time and use—if the borrower returns the same car after certain lapse of time, then the lender is wronged just the same as in the above example.[7]

On a broader spectrum, the word *amwaal* has wider connotations than just "possessions". As Aga pointed out, when we steal hours of work but get paid in full at the end of the month, this is also usurping the *amwaal* of our employer.[8] Similarly if one commits insurance fraud, or misuses or abuses other people's things or even food that is also usurping the *amwaal* of others (upon which we don't have any rights). Hence, from that stance we are committing *al-riba*.

It may be argued that many in government services are underpaid, and that is the reason people may not have much incentive to work hard or sincerely. Some may similarly say that insurance companies take a lot of money from us but never give us what we need when we are in need. All of these justifications is understandable, but I see no astuteness in these kinds of arguments: why overcome fraud with fraud? If we call ourselves better than those who cheat, shouldn't there be some difference? And if we are to take matters into our hands, then what is the point of having a government or for that matter God at all?

From an *al-riba* point of view, the government that is corrupt or underpays is usurping the rightful *amwaal* (a just wage) of its employees, and hence is committing *al-riba*.

So is the insurance company when it does not provide the monetary support at a time of need when one has been paying a premium. To these, God has already declared a "war" against them (Quran 2:279). For example, we have witnessed many mega-companies that have collapsed despite the fact that they were over-flowing with money. If we all take the law into our hands and decide what is right and what is wrong, then there need not to be any law in the first place. When we believe in one God who will provide justice for us, there is no need to commit fraud to overcome fraud.

INTEREST VERSUS PROFIT AND LOSS SHARING

In Islam, it has been adhered to and is unequivocally accepted that taking interest *(sood)* or giving interest is *haraam* (forbidden). Only profit and loss sharing is allowed. But how can we define profit as well as loss? And, when is a profit still a profit without becoming the *riba*?

Before going into depth about these issues, I would first like to touch on the history of money, on business *bai 'a*, and on profit and loss sharing. Later, as an example, I will compare some so-called Islamic banks with conventional banks to show how they operate in terms of providing mortgages.

MONEY AND ITS HISTORY

Money is a medium of exchange. Before this medium existed in the form of paper currency and coins, it existed in the form of corn and similar seeds. Even before that, in order to receive a good, people would barter their goods in exchange. This became very tiring and complicated due to the lack of transferability and divisibility.[9] Someone who wishes to get beans but has apples will have to find someone who needs apples and who has beans to give away in return. It would become more complicated if the goods were completely different, such as trying to barter a cow for corn—how many ears of corn must one give for the weight of a whole cow? Hence, money was created, and it represents the actual measure for our possessions or *amwaal* that we have. If the banks are using money today, it is because it measures the value of anything at a given time. Since societies have become more complex, money has helped in substituting the complicated barter system for a more efficient system.

Money therefore cannot be defined as something separate from our *amwaal* as many Quranic exegetes and *Shariah* have claimed. Based on this claim, the interest taken by a bank is *haram* (forbidden) because it is not a possession but a currency that measures value. It does not make any sense today when we see many Muslims holding possessions (*amwaal*) in the form of money. If what the *Shariah* dictates is correct, then we should all revert to the barter system.

BUSINESS (*BAI'A*) AND INTEREST

Any business (whether trading or service) needs to generate some kind of revenue. This is the total sum of one's own labour and of others (if applicable), the cost of material goods (if applicable), a portion for tax, and a reasonable amount of profit. Without this revenue, one cannot continue one's business.

When the Quran states that /*"Allah hath permitted bai'a and forbidden usury (al-riba)"* (2:275), it does not mean that one can keep doing business without having any gains. However, it is the "outrageous" gain that usurps someone's livelihood, or one's own possessions gained in this fashion that is forbidden.

> *That which ye lay out min riban* (as profit) *for increase (li-yr-rabu)* **through the possession (amwaal) of (other) people,** *will have no increase (yr-rabu) with Allah.* (Quran 30:39).

> *O ye who believe! Devour not usury (al-riba),* **doubling and quadrupling.** (Quran 3:130).

Many Muslim banks have generously used this one sentence of verse (2:275) to explain that they do not take or give interest, but work instead on a "profit or loss" system:/ *"Allah hath permitted bai'a and forbidden usury (al-riba)"*. They call this "the *halaal* way" (permitted way). Does this mean that even if the profit is so high that it cripples others and rips them off, it is not *riba* and is still *halaal* / permitted (as it does not fit into the definition of "interest")?

When the bank provides loans to people to carry out their business or buy something, it charges a certain amount of interest. If the interest amount is reasonable, it can be termed as their fee or service charge for the use of the bank's *amwaal*. That amount is the bank's livelihood and their revenue—without these charges, the bank cannot survive. In today's market, banks play a vital role without which an entire country's economy would come to a grinding halt.

If the bank simply gave out loans in the form of money (it's *amwaal*) at a certain value without adding any charges, and after certain lapse of time gets the same amount back, then the bank would be wronged. This is because the amount that it had initially loaned has lost purchasing power since its lending. Returning the same amount after a lapse in time is a loss of one's rightful *amwaal*. The Quran is very specific when it says that you shall have your *amwaal* back: /*"But if ye turn back, **ye shall have your capital (ra-oosu amwaal-e-kum)**: Deal not unjustly, and ye shall not be dealt with unjustly"* (Quran 2:279).

If, on the other hand, the bank had invested that loan amount, it would have been able to gain some profit out of it. The interest charge is therefore the same as gaining some profit, as well as covering the cost of maintaining the lending institution. Only when the bank charges an exorbitant amount of interest does it become riba, and the bank would then be unjust and doing wrong to others.

PROFIT AND LOSS

In a similar manner, profit that is considered *halaal* (permitted) can come under the *riba* if one is attaining said profit by doubling or quadrupling the price of one's goods and services that it cripples others by devouring their rightful *amwaal*. Hence, to say that profit and loss sharing is allowed is to open all doors for attaining a criminal rate of profit. The only difference is that it is not classified as "interest".

Moreover, the idea of "profit and loss" is a concept that is never mentioned in the Quran. It was created by the *Shariah* as something which is legal and allowed. The Quran only states business as being permitted whether it be trade or any other, and in business one must obtain a gain. But, the Quran speaks against the exorbitant amount of gain that hurts others: / *"Allah hath permitted business (bai'a) [with reasonable gain] and forbidden usury (al-riba) [outrageous gain]"* (Quran 2:275). (square brackets are mine)

As for loss, the Quran states *"If the debtor is in a difficulty, grant him time till it is easy for him to repay. But if ye remit it by way of charity (sadaqa), that is best for you if ye only knew"* (Quran 2:280). If the loss were to share as the profit, as per the concept of profit and loss sharing in *Shariah*, then this verse is wrong—it shouldn't have been in the Quran at all.

This verse advises the loan provider to either grant reasonable time for repayment considering the unique situation of the debtor, or on compassionate ground, forego the loan completely. It does not state that the loss must be shared by parties. What verse 2;280 says is exactly what the banks nowadays do: they either ease the repayment schedule or in certain instances, lessen or waive the whole amount (if the debtor claims bankruptcy).

When I was a student, I requested a student loan from the bank so that I could complete my studies. I am very grateful that I was provided the loan, without which I would not have been able to study further and get a degree. When the repayment time came after I had finished my studies, at some point it was difficult for me to pay the $250 per month that the bank had amortized. I asked that the bank ease my payment as I was in difficulty. They did, and provided me a new amortization schedule. They asked me how much I was able to comfortably pay every month. I said $50, and they accommodated my unique situation. In this instance, the bank followed exactly what the Quran instructed to do: /*"If the debtor is in a difficulty, grant him time till it is easy for him to repay"* (Quran 2:280).

It may be argued that the banks would agree to such a lengthening of loan terms because the amount of interest I would be paying them would be increased. I see this as their business and profit: they provided me with what I needed, and in return they want their wage. I have no problem agreeing to such a term as long as it is a "reasonable" charge and does not usurp my rightful *amwaal*.

Here, I am only advocating their system. How they practice and whether they are also conducting *riba* is another story, and covering that topic is not the intention of this book.

LENDING INSTITUTIONS AND MORTGAGES

Before I go into a comparison of a conventional and an Islamic bank, I would like to describe briefly the mortgage procedure and how the purchase of a home typically happens here in North America using a conventional bank.

Conventional Banks

Based on one's income, the bank will provide a pre-approval for a mortgage. This amount may take into account the down payment if there is any [typically it is from 0 to 5 percent, (or sometimes more) of the purchase price]. Once the pre-approval is obtained, the buyer starts to look for a house within the amount they can borrow from the mortgagee (the bank). After finding a home and going through an offer negotiation, the mortgager that is the borrower goes through the completion process and finally acquires the home. After the acquisition of the home, the mortgager then starts paying off the loan with interest (which is by law compounded semi annually and not in advance) on a monthly basis with a certain amortization period (typically 25 to 35 years), or until the loan is completely paid off.

According to historical data, overall property value increases 5 percent to 7 percent per year, which includes inflation of ~3 percent per year. In the long run, usually the property value does not depreciate, especially because the land is limited. In a conventional mortgage therefore, the borrower who pays off the loan enjoys the appreciated value of his or her home, and the bank has no share in it.

If there is a loss (in terms of the borrower being defaulted for any reason or circumstance), by law the banks are required to provide adequate time for the borrower to repay the loan. If the borrower is still not able to repay the loan, the house is eventually foreclosed, and from this the bank receives its part of the loan amount and the rest (if any) goes to the borrower.

Islamic Banks (Profit and Loss Sharing Concept)

In an Islamic banking concept, both the bank and the customer are partner/tenant and do business based on the "profit and loss" concept. In Arabic, partnership is called *musharakah* (which means to share) and tenancy or renting/ leasing out is called *ijarah*. These two terms *musharakah* and *ijarah* have been used widely in conjunction with Islamic banking businesses* especially for home financing. Since the bank and the customer are partner and tenant, they share in the profit as well as the loss from the house when the borrowed amount is paid off, or if the house is sold.

In the case of Islamic banks, I have chosen three examples: in the United States, Ameen Housing Co-operative (AHC) in California[10]; In England, HSBC's Amanah Bank[11], and the Islamic Bank of Britain (Halaal Home Financing).[12] All three of these institutions provide loans using the "profit and loss" concept.

- Islamic Bank of Britain—*Halaal* Home financing

The process of the Islamic Bank of Britain is more or less the same as the system explained above. Basically, the bank takes rent with a partner/tenant relationship. I see no difference between calling the same money rent or interest. They write in their official website:

How does it work?

Islamic Bank of Britain's Sharia'a compliant home finance is based on the accepted and widely used Islamic financing principles of *Ijara* (leasing) and *Musharaka* (partnership). We believe that using these two methods of Islamic finance offers the best solution for Sharia'a compliant home finance in the UK today. Described simply, both you and the Bank (Bristol & West plc) will each contribute towards the purchase of the home.

For example, the Bank may contribute 90 percent and you 10 percent of the purchase price. Over a period of up to 25 years, you will make monthly purchase installments through which the Bank will sell its share (90 percent) of the home to you. With each instalment

---

* Islamic banks use simple Arabic words for banking terminologies. It is an exploitation of common Muslim psyche, because for them the use of Arabic words immediately make every banking system truly "Islamic", completely "halaal" and endorsed by "Allah". Hence majority of the common Muslims fall prey to these deceptions.

paid, the Bank's share in the property diminishes while your share correspondingly increases.

While the purchase instalments are being made, the Bank will charge you a rent for the use of its share of the property, the rent being calculated according to the respective shares owned. Many see this as little different to a conventional mortgage, because under both methods monthly payments are made which may be similar in amount. However, unlike a conventional mortgage, where money is lent to help with the purchase of a property, the Bank makes its profit through the property's physical use via your occupation as a tenant. This is one of the fundamentals of Islamic finance whereby you can charge for the use of something physical, like a property, but you cannot charge for the use of money, because this is interest.[13]

The last few sentences hardly make any sense at all. I also do not see any advocacy from the Quran for the preposterous statement written above. I have added a comparison chart below which shows the calculations and what amount is actually paid at the end of the day.

- HSBC's "Amanah bank" England, UK

Here also the same methods and practices are in place, but HSBC Amanah bank goes a little further by fixing the rate at which the "rent" will be charged (using the benchmark interest rate that conventional banks are using).[14] They mention in their informational statement form for cost calculation that for every pound the Amanah Bank contributes, it will charge .51 pounds from the owner/tenant (as of May 12, 2010, their interest rate is 3 percent).[15] It is hard for me to observe the difference, where I see "pulling my ears from the front of my head or the back". Interest is interest, whether it is charged in the name of "rent" or *interest*.

For a detailed comparison, I will focus on the Ameen Housing Co-operative (AHC) bank in California.

- Ameen Housing Co-operative (AHC) bank in California, USA

Requirements (as of August 2007):

1. One must first become a member at the AHC. To become a member, one must pledge to purchase a minimum of 10 shares/calendar year at $100/ share for a total of $1000/year.[16] This is similar to the management fee that conventional financial institutions would charge for mutual funds.

2. The bank and the borrower are part owner with each owning a certain number of shares depending on the down payment (share purchase) by the borrower.[17]

3. A 25 percent to 40 percent share purchase is required (down payment), depending on the amount of share or the purchase price of the home.[18] If it is a $300,000 house, then there has to be minimum 40/60 percent share ratio.[19]

4. The customer who becomes part-owner according to his or her share amount pays rent to the AHC and thus becomes an owner/tenant with AHC. He/she will pay rent based on the fair market rental value for that home at its certain location.[20] From that rent, 40 percent will go towards the purchase of more shares from the AHC and 60 percent will go as rent to the AHC for the use of AHC's share in the property. After a year the rent will be reviewed and adjusted accordingly based on the share one has accumulated.[21]

5. If the borrower wishes to sell the house or pay off the AHC, the AHC shares in the portion of the amount with which the house value has appreciated or depreciated.[22] As per Humayun Sohail (Vice president of AHC), their formula is: if one initially contributed 50 percent of the purchase price, then at the end of the term, the bank would ask for an extra 20 percent share to reflect the appreciated value of the house, this on top of the repayment amount. If one initially contributed less than 50 percent, then at the end of

the term the bank would ask for an extra 30 percent share to reflect the appreciated value of the house, this on top of the repayment amount.[23]

6.   There is no amortization, one is released from the partner/ tenant relationship once 100 percent of the amount borrowed is paid off as well as the share in the current appreciated value of the house.

Comparison between Conventional and Islamic Bank

Please note that all calculations in the following table are done in a simplified manner in order to understand the concepts. No closing costs has been included, but are charged by both types of banks, and both a similar amount.

As per the market of 2007, the average detached house in a metropolitan area had a purchase price of $300,000. Conservatively speaking and for simplicity sake, after 25 years this house will appreciate in value by an average of 6 percent per year (bearing in mind the house price index and the inflation rate). This means it will hold a price tag of approximately $850,000 after 25 years.

For comparison purposes, I am keeping the amount of down payment/contribution the same as the minimum requirement of the AHC bank, which is 40 percent of the purchase price. As stated above, the customer who becomes the part owner according to his/her share amount pays rent to the AHC and hence becomes an owner/tenant with the AHC. He/she will pay rent based on the fair market rental value for that home. From that rent, 40 percent will go to the purchase of more shares from the AHC and 60 percent will go as rent to the AHC for the use of AHC's share in the property. Which means, after each year, unless one wishes to pay an extra amount, the amount of rent will remain the same (but in my example below, for simplicity sake, we will keep the rent constant with no extra payment). However, the percent of rent going into the purchase of more shares and the percent going into paying the AHC for the use of their share will vary.

To see how long it will take to finish the loan with the AHC, the values and the formulas were plugged into a spread sheet. The amortization came up to be 13 years approximately. This schedule had been used below in the table for both the banking system. In 13 years a house with a value of $300,000 will appreciate to nearly $600,000 if the average rate for property value consistently appreciates at 6 percent per annum:

COMPARISON TABLE (*purchase price $300,000*)[*]

	AMEEN HOUSING CO-OPERATIVE (AHC)	CONVENTIONAL BANK
Down payment/ or AHC contribution—40%	$120,000	$120,000
Share amount to be paid to partly own the home	$180,000	not applicable
Mortgage amount to be paid to own the home	not applicable	$180,000
Interest payment	not applicable	6%* (*average percent in 2004)
Monthly rent payment (includes rent + share purchase)	$2000 [a]	not applicable
Monthly mortgage payment (interest + principal)	not applicable	$1664.5
Amortization/ 100% payoff	13 years [b]	13 years
One time Investment fee	$5000 [c]	not applicable
membership share of $1000/year	$13,000 (in 13 years)	not applicable
Additional payment to buy out after 13 years. Based on the appreciated amount of the house	$91,097.68 [d]	not applicable

---

[*]   To view the spreadsheet calculation, please contact the author.

Grand total cost to the borrower and or owner/tenant	$541,097.68 [e]	$379,662 [f]

a) Average rent in a metropolitan area for a house with the value of $300,000.

b) based on the amount of rental money accumulating towards the purchase of a home as per AHC banking system: At $2000/month with rent going towards a 40% share: for example the first year, $800 will go towards the purchase of more shares from the AHC, and the rest ($1,200) towards the payment of rent for the use of AHC's share in the home. This percent varies with each year as the share of the borrower increases and the share of the AHC decreases.

c) paid by the owner/tenant at the time of application.

d) 30% profit sharing by AHC on the appreciated value of the house after 13 years, which is $303,658.94 (the house appreciated to $603, 658.94 after 13 years.

e) Grand total after 13 yrs (total rent paid $312,000+ total membership fee $13000+ down payment $120000+application fee $5000+ 30% AHC profit share payment in the amount of $91,097.68)

f) Grand total after 13 years (total mortgage payment: interest and principle ($259,662), + down payment ($120,000).

Conclusion of the Above Comparison:

From the above detailed calculation, we observe that using a conventional bank costs much less than using an Islamic bank (there is a difference of approximately $162,000, even though the conventional banks are charging "interest"). It therefore raises the question that if the Islamic banks are conducting business in a fair manner under the "profit and loss concept", why do they appear to be charging more than a conventional bank? Is not the amount of profit that the Islamic bank is making a criminal amount and hence the *riba*?

Even after 25 or 13 years of rent payment at an Islamic bank, if an owner/ tenant wish to finally own the home equity 100 percent, he/she still cannot own it until an extra amount has been paid to the bank on the basis of the appreciated value of the home. The bank would say it is sharing the profit, but to me it is a loss to the owner, and the owner is being ripped off of his or her rightful *amwaal* when they had been paying rent for 12-25 long years.

I converted the extra amount that the Islamic bank is charging to find out what it would equal if it were charged as interest, it turned out to be an astonishing 10 percent!* This is compared to the conventional bank's average of 6 percent in 2004 (the rate as of August 2010, is 3 percent-4 percent). In addition, if the borrower had paid $2,000 as the mortgage amount per month instead of $1664.50, the borrower would have finished payment in 10 ½ years instead of 13 years, which would have further lessened the amount of interest paid by the borrower in a conventional system.

How can we then justify such an unjust "profit and loss sharing" concept, where only one is profiting and the other is losing? In theory, yes the concept appears very just, but in practice it is otherwise. It is no wonder that the Quran never supported it. This situation is a result of our whims and manipulation to suit our needs, and our desire to be better writers of the Quran.

---

* [($541097.68-$120,000) / $180000 -1] / 13

NOTES:

1. Durrani, Zahida. *Allama Parvaiz-Lughat-ul-Quran.* Toronto: Tulu-e-Islam Trust. 2007, pp. 374-376, under tay.jeem.ray

2. Ibid., pp. 363-367 under bay-yeah-aain

3. Ibid., pp. 719-722 under ray-bay-wow

4. Ibid., pp. 1571 under meem-wow-laam

5. Aga, Muhammad Shafi J. *The Quranic concept of Ar-Riba (the Islamic Principles of Economics).* Third edition. Malvani, H. Colony, Mumbai: M.J. Aga. December 2000, p.3

6. Ibid., p. 6, under 1.7.3

7. Ibid., p. 6-7, under 1.7.5-1.7.10

8. Ibid., p. 5, under 1.5.4

9. Campbell, R. McConnell, Stanley L. Brue and Thomas P. Barbiero. *Macro Economics, Canada in the Global Economy.* 7th Canadian edition. Whitby: McGraw Hill Ryerson Limited, 1996, pp. 50-51, 278-79

10. Ameen Housing Co-operative, 2084 Walsh Ave, Suite B1, Santa Clara, CA 95050. www.ameenhousing.com. Tel: (408)986-9786. Date accessed: April 9, 2010. Archived at www.archive.org http://web.archive.org/web/20070206221645/http://www. ameenhousing.com/coop/why_halal.html

    Date accessed: October 20, 2012. http://www.ameenhousing. com/

11. HSBC Amanah Islamic Home Finance, 26 College Green, 2nd floor, Bristol, B515TB, United Kingdom Tel: 0800-5877-786. Date accessed: May 12, 2010. http://www.hsbcamanah.co.uk/1/2/ personal/travel-international/hsbc-amanah/amanah-home-finance;jsessionid=0000Q0zXtZt7l-JRmMg7sqUbb_C:12ntf2618

12. Islamic Bank of Britian, plc, Edgbaston House, 3 Duchess Place, Hagley Road Birmingham, B16 8NH. www.islamic-bank. com. Tel: 0845 6060 786. Date accessed: April 9, 2010.

Archived at www.archive.org http://web.archive.org/web/20070320155212/http:/www.islamic-bank.com/islamicbanklive/HomeFinance/1/Home/1/Home.jsp

13. Islamic Bank of Britian, plc, Edgbaston House, 3 Duchess Place, Hagley Road Birmingham, B16 8NH. www.islamic-bank.com. Tel: 0845 6060 786. Date retrieved April 12, 2010. Archived at www.archive.org http://web.archive.org/web/20070320155212/http:/www.islamic-bank.com/islamicbanklive/HomeFinance/1/Home/1/Home.jsp

14. HSBC Amanah Islamic Home Finance, 26 College Green, 2nd floor, Bristol, B515TB, United Kingdom Tel: 0800-5877-786. Under section D of FAQ: "Islamic Transactions: Is it permissible to use LIBOR (London Inter-Bank Offer Rate) as a benchmark?" Date accessed: May 12, 2010. http://www.hsbcamanah.com/amanah/about-amanah/faq.html#12

15. HSBC Amanah Islamic Home Finance, 26 College Green, 2nd floor, Bristol, B515TB, United Kingdom Tel: 0800-5877-786. Amanah Home finance monthly cost calculation page. Fill in information, and plug in a 35% down payment the minimum), and a 30 year term. Date accessed: May 12, 2010. http://www.hsbcamanah.co.uk/1/2/personal/travel-international/hsbc-amanah/amanah-calculator;jsessionid=0000Q0zXtZt7l-JRmMg7sqUbb_C:12ntf2618#keyfacts

16. Ameen Housing Co-operative, 2084 Walsh Ave, Suite B1, Santa Clara, CA 95050. www.ameenhousing.com. Tel: (408)986-9786. Date retrieved April 9, 2010. Archived at www.archive.org http://web.archive.org/web/20070207092834/www.ameenhousing.com/membership/index.html

http://web.archive.org/web/20070206221825/www.ameenhousing.com/forms/MemFormSec.pdf

17. Ibid., comparison table http://web.archive.org/web/20070206221859/www.ameenhousing.com/homefinance/buying_home.html

18. Ibid., under RFAL Requirements http://web.archive.org/web/20070206221859/www.ameenhousing.com/homefinance/buying_home.html

19. As per my personal telephone conversation with Humayun Sohel (Vice president), August 27, 2007.

20. Ameen Housing Co-operative, 2084 Walsh Ave, Suite B1, Santa Clara, CA 95050. www.ameenhousing.com. Tel: (408)986-9786. Date accessed: April 12, 2010. Archived at www.archive.org See comparison table http://web.archive.org/web/20070206221804/www.ameenhousing.com/coop/index.html.

21. Ibid., paragraph five http://web.archive.org/web/20070206221804/www.ameenhousing.com/coop/index.html. Also, personal telephone conversation with Humayun Sohel (Vice president) August 27, 2007.

22. Ameen Housing Co-operative, 2084 Walsh Ave, Suite B1, Santa Clara, CA 95050. www.ameenhousing.com. Tel: (408)986-9786. Date accessed: April 12, 2010. Archived at www.archive.org See comparison table http://web.archive.org/web/20070206221804/www.ameenhousing.com/coop/index.html

23. As per my personal telephone conversation with Humayun Sohel (Vice president) August 27, 2007. I requested the procedure in writing but it was not provided, despite my being assured by Humayun Sohail that it would be provided. I reminded them via email but there was no response.

AFTERWORDS

Sometimes, I wonder why Quranic verses have multiple meanings which result in such variant renditions. If God had so willed, It could have put just one meaning, making the Quran much easier to comprehend. But then the Quran would become static and rigid and would lose the universal appeal to its message. Quran offers messages which have applicability in every time and era. Indeed, God may have known that many deviate readings would be taken out of Its words, but, to keep the Quran alive for all time, this casualty had to be absorbed. Therefore, only the proper hermeneutics of the verses can measure the credibility of each individual's interpretation.

Throughout the book, my attempt has not been to portray Islam as an ideal religion but to portray Quran as yet another divine discourse, which, with its few incomprehension, still, as a whole appeals to my senses, to my reasons and natural laws. I would rather believe in a God then to become a God myself.

I also believe that whether we are considering the Quran or any other religious book, each is only a reference point and provide us a vessel to carry on with our lives and be content with only what we can perceive. Otherwise, the phenomenon of God or the Creator is so complex that if we try to learn and perfect it, we may get lost and never find our way. All we may try to do is find the meaning of our existence and see where and at what point we fit in. For this, we may create ways of life *deens* that help us contain ourselves and be at peace with our chaotic being.

We all must therefore ask a question: what is the single purpose of our being in this world? I cannot say it as articulately as Albert Einstein:

"From the point of view of daily life, without going deeper, we exist for our fellow men.... When we survey our lives and endeavours we soon observe that almost the whole of our actions and desires are bound up with the existence of other human beings. We see that our whole nature resembles that of the social animals. We eat food that others have grown, wear clothes that others have made, live in houses that others have built. The greater part of our knowledge and beliefs has been communicated to us by other people through the medium of a language which others have created".[*]

On a basic level, our lives' needs are so intertwined with our fellow humans that we are absolutely nothing but beasts without the others. Even the Quran questions: /*what aileth you that you help not one another? (37:25)*

Personally, I have come to my contentment by following moderation in every aspect of life, including *deen,* and doing what is right and good to everyone regardless of what others believe. I do follow the Quranic Islam, but I also know that I have questions that are still unanswered. Nothing is perfect except the Creator. I have made my *deen* very simple: to believe in a God and do what is right to everyone—*amle-*

---

[*]   Einstein Albert. The World As I see it. Citadel Press, Kensington Publishing Corp. May 2006, pp.3,10

swaleh—righteous deeds. We only have one earth to live in and if we want our race to survive and grow, then it becomes a duty incumbent upon us to do *amle-swaleh.*

I desire mutual benefit and happiness while I exist, and I am searching for my Creator at the 'Turning Point' on my road of life, and hoping that I will find that God by the end of the road . . .

Humera T. Ahsanullah

humerat@gmail.com

*"Lo! those who believe, and those who are Jewish,
and Sabaeans, and Christians—Whosoever believeth in
God and the Last Day and doeth right—there shall
no fear come upon them neither
shall they grieve"*
(Quran 5:69)

*"O mankind! Lo! We have created you male and female,
and have made you nations and tribes that
ye may know one another. Lo! the noblest of you,
in the sight of Allah, is the best in conduct.
Lo! Allah is Knower, Aware"*
(Quran 49:13).

GLOSSARY OF
SELECTIVE ARABIC WORDS &

Aimaanuhum, aimaan: from faith or belief to toward the right side or right hand. From strength or strong to solemn oath or solid contract. Generally translated as slave women with whom one can have sex.

Alaq: something that clings or hangs

Amle-swaleh: righteous deeds, right guidance

Amwaal: one's possessions including any tangible material goods, paper currency (money), and assets. Anything a person may refer to as his or her possession. (sing. *mole*)

Asnaad: chain of narrators (sing. **sanad**)

Asr: late afternoon prayer

Awlia: guardians (sing. **wali**)

Autad: anchor

Ayat: a verse of the Quran, signs, miracles

Bai'a: any business

Baini: conjunction, betwixt

Bait-ul—mall: house of wealth. It was a welfare system that Umar the second Caliph after the demise of Muhammad had enacted

Basher: living beings

Batn-butoonay-he: bellies, stomach

Da-ab-batin: moving creatures, living beings

Daraba: from the root darab—to beat, strike, to counsel or to prevent, travel, leave, set up, or to take away

Deen—a way of life—Quran has referred Islam not as a religion but a deen

Dukhan: gaseous mass

Eid: Muslim celebration after the hajj pilgrimage and after the fasting period of the month of Ramadan

Ehlal-kitaab: people of the book—referred to the Christians and the Jewish people in the Quran

Ehson: that which is best, see also husn

Fajr: dawn prayer

Farraqu, farraq: separate, sects, division, divide

Fataq: exploded

Feqoon: to spend, to give, or to keep it open from all sides (from the root **infaaq**)

Hadith: sayings, statements (pl-ahadith)

Hajj: pilgrimage to the house of God in Mecca.

Halaal: that which is allowed

Hama: gooey, foul smelling muck

Haraam: that which is forbidden

Hijab: a cover, partition, barrier, and/or a curtain or drape.

Hoor: extreme whiteness. (**ahwar**—masculine and **haura**—feminine)

Husn: beautiful, best, rightful

Ibaadat: an effort with benefits. In literal sense, it is a type of a flower that has many benefits but is obtained with hardship. Generally translated as worshipping or servant but the correct word for worship is *pooja*. **Aabid**—the one who makes an effort

Injeel: Gospel—holy book revealed to Jesus

Ins, insaan: human, human beings

Ijarah: tenancy or renting/leasing out. Banking terminology.

Isha: night time prayer

Izzama: bones (flesh into bones). Related to the verses in conjunction with the growth of the foetus

Jahiliyah: ignorance, illiterate, **jaheloon**—ignorant, illiterate

Janabah: sexual impurity

Jehad: struggle, to make an effort—toward righteous deeds—see amle-swaleh

Jizya: root word **jiza'a** which means to compensate. It was a tax imposed on disbelievers in order to provide protection to them. They were exempt from zakat payment—see zakat

Khalaq: created, create

Khimar : a piece of cloth, usually worn over the head as a cover

Lahm: intact flesh

Maa: water

Ma'aruf: known or accepted as correct, back to back, one after the other, or similar or a mid-point

Madga: chewed lump of flesh

Maghrib: evening prayer

Mahfooz: protected, safe

Mard (marz): disease, illness, unwell

Masnoon: rotted

Matn: the substance, the body of something, the main meaning

Mazhab: religion

Miskeen: poor, un-enriched, as the Arabs consider those who are non Arabs

Musharakah: partnership, to share

Muss-han: to rub, cleanse or lightly massage/heal

Muta: temporary marriage. A marriage that only fulfills a temporary sexual pleasure and then dissolves automatically without divorce. Shiah sect generally observes *muta* marriages believing it is endorsed by Quran.

Nazm: coherence

Noor: light

Nushuz: ill conduct, dis-obey

Nutfa: to dribble or to trickle (semen)

Nuzool: time of revelation, to bestow

Pooja: worship

Qada salaat: salaat that is gone, disconnected, missed, dead. Generally some Muslims would pray those missed prayers in order to complete their 5 ritualistic prayers.

Qawwamun 'ala: those who provide a means of support or livelihood, to keep a balance, fairness and also to fulfill needs. Generally, it is referred to men as being strong and powerful than women.

Ramadan: the hottest day, extreme heat or heat of the day. It is the month when Quran was revealed to Muhammad and it is when Muslims fast the whole month

Rataq: solid mass

Riba (al-riba (pronounced *arriba*): exorbitant increase or growth, or usury. Al before riba simply means the—the riba.

Sadaqa: charity

Sahih: canonical, authentic, original

Salaat: from **sallu**—to follow, to bend, nourish, or adhere to the laws, or to advise *salah*. It further means to honour, encourage and appreciate, to exercise resilience and to remove faults. From ritualistic point it means to pray **musalleen**—the one who prays. Generally Muslims do 5 ritualistic prayers.

Salsaalay or tayn: sticky mud

Sama-a—sky, surrounding or space

Saqfa: roof

Sawab: credits, rewards received when one does righteous deeds

sha-ar: month (pl. **ash-harun**)

Shariah: combination of divine and human disclosure

Shiah: sect, schism split, division, a sect in Islam—partisan of Ali (one of the Caliphs of Islam)

Siraaj: torch

Sood: Interest in terms of money

Sunni: follower of a practices, a sect in Islam (follower of Muhammad's practices)

Surah: a chapter of the Quran

Tasbih: from **sabha**—to swim, other meanings construed: to struggle, toil, to make effort, to revolve, to complete a revolution, or tightly woven, strong etc.

Taqwa: conduct, duty to care

Tijaarat: trading business

Torayt: Torah—holy book revealed to Moses

Ulema, alim: knowledgeable, educated person. Or a person knowledgeable in a specific field

Wahaaj: lamp

Zaboor: Psalms—holy book revealed to David

Zakat: to nourish, to help grow, and well-being

Zawj: has a wider definition including everything in pairs. It literally means pair or together. Generally, it is translated as wife.

Zohor: mid-day prayer

Zulm: torture, harm, hurt

APPENDICES

APPENDIX A ☙

REVELATION ORDER OF THE QURAN ACCORDING TO THE *NUZOOL* (Revelation time)*

Nuzool Order	Tradi-tional Order	Chapter *(surah)* Name	Chapter *(surah)* Name in English	Total Verses	Revela-tion Place †
1	96	Alaq	Clinging Substance	19	Mecca
2	68	Qalam	The Pen	52	Mecca
3	73	Muzammil	The Enshrouded One	20	Mecca
4	74	Mudathir	The Cloaked One	56	Mecca
5	1	Fatehah	The Opening	7	Mecca
6	111	Masad	The Palm Fibre	5	Mecca
7	81	Takwir	The Overthrowing	29	Mecca
8	87	A'la	The Most High	19	Mecca
9	92	Leyl	The Night	21	Mecca
10	89	Fajr	The Dawn	30	Mecca
11	93	Duha	The Morning Hours	11	Mecca
12	94	Inshira	The Solace	8	Mecca
13	103	Asr	The Declining Day	3	Mecca
14	100	Aadiyat	The Coursers	11	Mecca
15	108	Kauthar	The Abundance	3	Mecca
16	102	Takatur	The Rivalry In Worldly Increase	8	Mecca
17	107	Alma'un	The Small Kindness	7	Mecca
18	109	Kafirun	The Disbelievers	6	Mecca

19	105	Fil	The Elephant	5	Mecca
20	113	Falaq	The Daybreak	5	Mecca
21	114	Nas	The Humankind	6	Mecca
22	112	Iklas	The Unity	4	Mecca
23	53	Najm	The Stars	62	Mecca
24	80	Abasa	He Frowned	42	Mecca
25	97	Qadr	The Power	5	Mecca
26	91	Shams	The Sun	15	Mecca
27	85	Buruj	The Mansions Of The Stars	22	Mecca
28	95	T'in	The Fig	8	Mecca
29	106	Qureysh	The Quresh	4	Mecca
30	101	Qariah	The Calamity	11	Mecca
31	75	Qiyamah	The Rising Of The Dead	40	Mecca
32	104	Humazah	The Traducer	9	Mecca
33	77	Mursalat	The Emissaries	50	Mecca
34	50	Q'af	Letter Qaf	45	Mecca
35	90	Balad	The City	20	Mecca
36	86	Tariq	The Morning Star	17	Mecca
37	54	Qamr	The Moon	55	Mecca
38	38	Sad	Letter Suad	88	Mecca
39	7	A'Raf	The Heights	206	Mecca
40	72	Jinn	The Jinni	28	Mecca
41	36	Ya'sin	Ya Sin	83	Mecca
42	25	Furqan	The Criterion	77	Mecca
43	35	Fatir	The Angels	45	Mecca
44	19	Maryam	Mary	98	Mecca
45	20	Ta Ha	Ta Ha	135	Mecca
46	56	Waqiah	The Event	96	Mecca
47	26	Shuara	The Poets	227	Mecca
48	27	Naml	The Ants	93	Mecca

49	28	Qasas	The Story	88	Mecca
50	17	Bani Israil	The Children Of Israel	111	Mecca
51	10	Yunus	Jonah	109	Mecca
52	11	Hud	Hud	123	Mecca
53	12	Yousuf	Joseph	111	Mecca
54	15	Hijr	The Rock	99	Mecca
55	6	Anam	The Cattle	165	Mecca
56	37	Saffat	The Ranks	182	Mecca
57	31	Luqman	Luqman	34	Mecca
58	34	Saba	The Saba	54	Mecca
59	39	Zumar	The Troops	75	Mecca
60	40	Mumin	The Believers	85	Mecca
61	41	Fusilaat	The Expounded	54	Mecca
62	42	Shura	The Counsel	53	Mecca
63	43	Zukhruf	The Ornaments Of Gold	89	Mecca
64	44	Dukhan	The Smoke	59	Mecca
65	45	Jathiyah	The Crouching	37	Mecca
66	46	Ahqaf	The Wind Curved Sandhills	35	Mecca
67	51	Dhariyat	The Winnowing Winds	60	Mecca
68	88	Ghashiya	The Overwhelming	26	Mecca
69	18	Kahf	The Cave	110	Mecca
70	16	Nahl	The Bee	128	Mecca
71	71	Nooh	Noah	28	Mecca
72	14	Ibrahim	Abraham	52	Mecca
73	21	Anbiya	The Prophets	112	Mecca
74	23	Muminun	The Believers	118	Mecca
75	32	Sajdah	Prostration	30	Mecca
76	52	Tur	The Mount	49	Mecca

77	67	Mulk	The Sovereignty	30	Mecca
78	69	Haqqah	The Reality	52	Mecca
79	70	Ma'arij	The Ascending Stairways	44	Mecca
80	78	Naba	The Tidings	40	Mecca
81	79	Naziat	Those Who Drag Forth	46	Mecca
82	82	Infitar	The Cleaving	19	Mecca
83	84	Inshiqaq	The Sundering	25	Mecca
84	30	Rum	The Romans	60	Mecca
85	29	Ankabut	The Spider	85	Mecca
86	83	Tatfif	The Defrauding	36	Mecca
87	2	Baqarah	The Cow	286	Medina
88	8	Anfal	The Spoils Of The War	75	Medina
89	3	Aal-e-Imran	The Family Of Imran	200	Medina
90	33	Ahzab	The Clans	73	Medina
91	60	Mumtahana	She That Is To Be Examined	13	Medina
92	4	Nisa	Women	176	Medina
93	99	Zilzal	The Earthquake	8	Mecca
94	57	Hadid	The Iron	29	Medina
95	47	Muhammad	Muhammad	38	Medina
96	13	Ra'd	Thunder	43	Mecca
97	55	Rahman	The Beneficent	78	Mecca
98	76	Dahr	The Time	31	Mecca
99	65	Talaq	Divorce	12	Medina
100	98	Beyinnah	The Clear Proof	8	Medina
101	59	Hashr	The Exile	24	Medina
102	24	Nur	The Light	64	Medina
103	22	Hajj	The Pilgrimage	78	Medina
104	63	Munafiqun	The Hypocrites	11	Medina

105	58	Mujadila	She That Disputeth	22	Medina
106	49	Hujurat	The Private Apartments	18	Medina
107	66	Tahrim	The Banning	12	Mecca
108	64	Taghabun	The Mutual Disillusion	18	Mecca
109	61	Saff	The Ranks	14	Medina
110	62	Jumah	The Congregation	11	Medina
111	48	Fath	The Victory	29	Medina
112	5	Maidah	Table Spread	120	Medina
113	9	Taubah	The Repentance	129	Medina
114	110	Nasr	The Succour	3	Medina

*Sources:

Pickthall Marmaduke Mohammed. *Holy Quran: English Translation.* The government of H.E.H. Mir Osman Ali Khan, Haydrabad—Deccan, 1930.

http://www.missionislam.com/quran/revealationorder.htm
Date accessed: November 14, 2012

†Please note that the revelation location for some *surahs* (chapter) is debatable (especially, surah 99, 13, 55,76, 66, 64), I have therefore only relied on the location of the revelations as per Marmaduke Pickthall, which may not necessarily be completely correct.

APPENDIX B ❧

MAIN BATTLES OF MUHAMMAD

How long did they last?

Battle of Badar—(624 AD March 13, Ramadaan 17). Commenced in the morning and finished before noon the same day. It therefore lasted only a few hours say 6 to 8 hours.

Battle of Auhud—(625 AD March 22, Shawwaal 6). The battle lasted one day.

Battle of Trench—(627 AD March 31, Shawwaal 5). It was a siege that lasted for 27 days.

Battle of Hunain—(630 AD Jan 27, Shawwaal 6). The battle started early in the morning and lasted for one day but Muslims besieged the city for a month until Hunain broke down.

Muhammad's Islamic life equals 25 years, which is 9125 days, out of which, nearly 60 days went on battles that is less than 1percent.

Notes:

Armstrong, Karen. *Muhammad, A Biography of the Prophet.* New York: Harper Collins Publishers Inc., 1992, pp.172-176, 187-189, 203-206, 245-246

http://en.wikipedia.org/wiki/Battle_of_Badr

http://en.wikipedia.org/wiki/Battle_of_Uhud

http://en.wikipedia.org/wiki/Battle_of_the_Trench

http://en.wikipedia.org/wiki/Battle_of_Hunayn

APPENDIX C &

VERSES RELATED TO THE *SALAAT* TIMMINGS

24:58—*sallat ul fajr* and *salaat ul isha. Salaat* is used in a singular *'salaat' (fajr, isha*—early morning and late night prayers)

2:238—*salawaat* plural is used in the beginning then: *us-salaate wusta* that is mid day prayers (*zohur, asr)*

11:114—uses *us-salaata* word and asks to observe it at the 'two ends of the day': *Taraf-un-nahaar* 'at the approach': *wa zulufan*, 'of night': *min al layl (maghrib*—evening*) (fajr, isha, maghrib)*

17:78—uses *ussalaata* word to establish *salaat* at the decline of the sun *duluk-u-shams* till darkness at night *ghasik-al-layl*

4:103—*salaat* mention as prescribed in fixed times

OTHER WORKS REFERENCED ❧

1. Ali Yusuf Abdullah. *The Meaning of the Holy Quran.* Amana Publications, Maryland USA, 2004, 11th edition.

2. Pickthall Marmaduke Mohammed. *Holy Quran: English Translation.* The government of H.E.H. Mir Osman Ali Khan, Haydrabad—Deccan, 1930.

3. Khalifa Rashad. Quran: The Final Scripture Islamic Productions, Tucson, Arizona USA, 1981.

4. Thanwi Ali Ashraf Mohammad. *Anwarul quloob Quran Shareef.* H.M.saeed Company, Educational Press Karachi, n.d.

SUGGESTION FOR FURTHER READING ❧

1. Armstrong, Karen. *A History of God: the 4000-Year Quest of Judaism, Christianity, and Islam*. New York: Alfred A Knopf Inc., 1993.

2. Armstrong, Karen. *Islam, A Short History*. London: The Orion Publishing Group, 2000.

3. Armstrong, Karen. *Muhammad, A Biography of the Prophet*. New York: Harper Collins Publishers Inc., 1992.

4. Afkhami, Mahnaz (et al). *Faith and Freedom*. Syracuse, NY: Syracuse University Press, 1995.

5. Ahmed, Leila. *Women and Gender in Islam*. New Haven: Yale University Press, 1992.

6. Aga, Muhammad Shafi J. *The Quranic concept of Ar-Riba (the Islamic Principles of Economics)*. Third edition. Malvani, H. Colony, Mumbai: M.J. Aga. December 2000.

7. A.C. Bhaktivedanta Swami Prabhupada. *Sri Isopanisad.* The Bhaktivedanta Book Trust, 1969, printed in theUSA, 3rd edition.

8. Adams Fred, Laughlin Greg. *The five Ages of The Universe: Inside the Physics of Eternity.* The Free Press, Simno and Schuster Inc., 1999.

9. Barlas, Asma. *Believing Women in Islam: Unreading Patriarchal Interpretations of the Qur'an.* Austin: University of Texas Press, 2002.

10. Bucaille, Maurice. *The Bible, The Quran, and Science: The Holy Scriptures Examined in the Light of Modern Knowledge.* New York: Tahrike Tarsile Quran, Inc., 2003.

11. Brown, Daniel. *Rethinking Tradition in Modern Islamic Thought.* Cambridge Middle East Study (For Students). Cambridge: Cambridge University Press, 1996.

12. Bhutto, Benazir. *Reconciliation: Islam, Democracy, and the West.* New York: Harper Collins, 2008.

13. Collins, Francis S. *The Language of God.* Toronto: A Division of Simon and Schuster, Inc., 2006.

14. Campbell, R. McConnell, Stanley L. Brue and Thomas P. Barbiero. *Macro Economics, Canada in the Global Economy.* 7th Canadian edition. Whitby: McGraw Hill Ryerson Limited, 1996.

15. Durrani, Zahida. *Allama Parvaiz-Lughat-ul-Quran.* Tulu-e -Islam Trust. 2007. http://www.quran-gateofislam.com/quran_dictionary. asp

16. Darwin, Charles. *The Descent of Man*, 1871. London: John Murray, Albemarle Street. Bank of Wisdom eBook edition. http://www.gutenberg.org/cache/epub/2300/pg2300. epub

17. Einstein Albert. *The World As I see it.* Citadel Press, Kensington Publishing Corp. May 2006.

18. Feiler Bruce. *Abraham: A Journey to the Heart of Three Faiths.* HarperCollins publishers Inc. New York, 2002.

19. Grun Bernard. *The Time Table of History.* Third edition, 1991. New York: Simon and Schuster / Touchstone.

20. Gandhi, Mohandas K. "Satyagraha In South Africa". Translated from Gujrati by Valji Govindji Desai. 2003. http://www.forget-me.net/en/Gandhi/satyagraha.pdf

21. Hawking, Stephen. *A Brief History of Time.* Bantam Press, Ealing: Transworld Publishers Limited, 1988.

22. Hanna. E. Kasis, The Concordance of the Quran (Foreword by Fazlur Rahman) University of California Press Berkley, Los Angeles, London, n.d.

23. Hawking, Stephen W. *The Theory of Everything: The Origin and Fate of the Universe.* New Millennium Press 2003.

24. Hasan, Professor Ahmed (translation). "Introduction to Partial Translation of Sunan Abu Dawud". Los Angeles: Center for Muslim Jewish Engagement. University of Southern California. http://www.usc.edu/schools/college/crcc/engagement/resources/texts/muslim/hadith/abudawud/

25. Hidayatullah M., Hidayatullah Arshad. *Mulla's Principles of Mohamedan Law.* 19th edition. N.M Tripathi Private Limited, India, 1990.

26. Irshad, Manji. *The Trouble With Islam: A Wake Up Call For Honesty and Change.* Toronto: Random House Canada, 2003.

27. Keith L. Moore, T.V.N. Persaud. *Before We Are Born (Human Development): Essentials of Embryology and Birth Defects.*

Saunders, an imprint of Elsvier Inc. Philadelphia, 7th edition, 2008.

28. Khan, M. Muhsin (translation). "Translation of Sahih-Al-Bukhari". Los Angeles: Center for Muslim Jewish Engagement, University of Southern California. http://www.usc.edu/dept/MSA/fundamentals/hadithsunnah/bukhari

29. Knight Christopher, Lomas Robert. *The Second Messiah.* Arrow Books, Random House Group Limited 1998.

30. Lane William Edward. *Arabic—English Lexicon.* Williams and Norgate 1863. Libraire Du Liban 1968.

31. Monastersky, Richard and Mozzatenta, O. Louis. "What kind of place was Primordial Earth; Earth—History, Evolution". *The National Geographic Journal*, Vol 193, No. 3 (1998).

32. Muhammad, Fakhanda Noor. *Islamiat for Students*, Rawalpindi, Karachi, Pakistan: Ferozsons td. Lahore, 1992.

33. Nasr Seyyed Hossein. *The Heart of Islam: Enduring Values for Humanity.* Harper Collins books, San Francisco, 2002.

34. Philip G Chambers, Temple Grandin (compilers). "Guidelines for humane handling, transport and slaughter of livestock" (Chapter 7, Slaughter of Livestock, Stunning methods, Electrical stunning). "Malpractice in immobilization of livestock". *FAO (food and Agriculture Organization of the United Nations), HSI (Humane Society International)*, 2001. FAO corporate document Repository. http://www.fao.org/DOCREP/003/X6909E/x6909e09.htm

35. Rahim, Sir Abdur. *Principles of Mohammadan Jurisprudence.* Karachi Pakistan: Mansoor Book House, 1911.

36. Schimmel, Annemarie. *My Soul is a Woman: The Feminine Islam.* New York: The Continuum Publishing Company, 1999.

37. Shabbir, Ahmed. "When is the Messiah Coming?" Our Beacon. PDF from http://www.ourbeacon.com/wp-content/uploads/admin2/2007/08/messiah.pdf

38. Sykes, Bryan. *The Seven Daughters of Eve.* New York: Norton and Company Inc., 2001.

39. Sherif Abdel Azim. *Women in Islam vs. Judaeo Christian Tradition, the Myth and the Reality.* Queens University Kingston Ontario, 1996.

40. University of Michigan Digital Library. *Holy Bible, King James Version,* http://quod.lib.umich.edu/k/kjv/browse.html

41. Wadud, Amina. *Qur'an and Women, Rereading the Sacred Text from a Woman's Perspective.* Oxford: Oxford University Press, 1999.